VOLUME 1

2017 – 2018

Printed by Lulu Press, Inc., in the United States of America.

First printing, 2018.

www.jolttx.com

<u>Masthead</u>

Journal of Law and Technology at Texas

Forward

The Journal of Law and Technology at Texas has been a labor of love and a labor of will. From its beginnings as a meeting at a local bar between half a dozen people, to the current network of practitioners and business people who have personally invested in the success of this project, a lot has transpired over the past three years.

Our first year was a flurry of activity to gain traction, from presenting on self-driving cars and the law at SXSW, to hosting speakers from the Electronic Frontier Foundation, we did everything we could to become buzzworthy. Our second year included securing authors, hosting our own panels, presenting student research on cybersecurity for law firms, fundraising, and competing in the Cyber 9/12 policy competition in Washington DC. Coming in just beneath the Naval War College in the final round was a turning point for JOLTT. Our third year included hosting our first ever symposium, launching JOLTTx.com, stepping up our involvement in the community, and now publishing this first edition of the journal.

With much accomplished and much to look forward to, there are many people to thank, from professors to practitioners, mentors and friends, with special thanks to Ed Cavazos, Kay Firth-Butterfield, Derek Jinks, Bobby Chesney, EFF-Austin, Casey Baker, and the many others who have helped along the way.

Sincerely,

Alex Shahrestani
Founder
The Journal of Law and Technology at Texas

Table of Contents

A Study of the Non-Interventionist Model for Regulating Automated Vehicles: A Case Study of Texas Technology

Wendy Wagner and Lisa Loftus-Otway [*]

[*] Copyright permission obtained from Kara Kockelman. This article was submitted spring of 2017.

TABLE OF CONTENTS

I. INTRODUCTION

State regulators face new promises and perils with the emerging technology of self-driving vehicles. The technology offers the possibility of fewer accidents, less congestion, and more transportation options. But it also raises new safety and security concerns, complicates questions of liability, and challenges current logistics, like licensing requirements and road regulations.

Equally vexing for state regulators is the range of options for how, when, and whether to develop formal legal frameworks to anticipate this new technology. Should state legislators attempt to craft a single law to address these challenges in advance? Or should lawmakers operate incrementally, adjusting and creating exceptions for the new technology only when potential conflicts emerge? And of course, between these two extremes are other middle-of-the-road paths that take on the biggest risks and challenges in initial legislation and then address the remainder as they arise.

A few states have embarked on the first path and attempt to develop holistic governing legislation to oversee the new technology before the "genie is out of the bottle." These states have passed elaborate legislation that generally limits the use of the new technology to carefully regulated "pilot" or restricted areas. This legislation further imposes reporting, bonding, and other requirements.

Yet it is the non-interventionist, incremental approach that currently predominates the majority of states, perhaps because it adheres largely to the status quo.[1] Despite its prevalence, this non-interventionist approach has received much less critical attention by analysts. This oversight is regrettable, particularly given the possibility that this approach will ultimately become the preferred.

This article seeks to remedy this gap in the literature by extracting – from existing practice – a descriptive account of a typical state, non-interventionist approach for integrating autonomous and connected vehicles on state roadways. To provide a detailed, applied vantage point, we examine one state in particular – Texas. Texas is actively engaged in experimentation with automated technologies

---

[1] This approach predominates primarily because the majority of states have not passed legislation to address automated vehicles. See, e.g., http://www.ncsl.org/research/transportation/autonomous-vehicles-self-driving-vehicles-enacted-legislation.aspx But even in some states that have passed legislation, like Texas and a few other states like Florida, the legislatures adopt a non-interventionalist and inherently incremental approach to regulated automated vehicles.

without comprehensive, anticipatory regulation. Indeed, Texas recently codified its nonintervention position as a legislative matter in a law that allows the deployment of automated vehicles on Texas roadways with few restrictions.[2] Texas legislators also demonstrated their willingness to address problems as they arise – the first being a legislative modification to a particularly inflexible legal impediment that impeded truck platooning.[3] Texas thus provides a particularly informative perspective for exploring how a state actively encouraging automated vehicles also manages to integrate them into its existing legal and transportation system with minimal legislation and regulatory oversight.

This in-depth study of the incremental model in Texas, where testing and deployment of automated vehicles (AVs) is already underway, helps illuminate some of the remaining questions that lie ahead. We originally conducted this study at the behest of the Texas Department of Transportation, but we reproduce that research here since we believe that the findings have general applicability to many other states as well.[4] Texas' example thus provides a blueprint of sorts for what other states are likely to confront if they proceed in a similar vein. Our in-depth study of Texas also highlights a few legal requirements that may conflict with AVs and cannot be adapted incrementally; these legal requirements may ultimately require more triage-like, formal legislation.

We are quick to add that although we offer a descriptive account of the non-interventionist approach in Texas, we do not mean

---

[2] *See*, S.B. 2205 Leg., 85th Sess. (Tx. 2017). Section 545.454(a) provides, for example, that "[a]n automated motor vehicle may operate in this state with the automated driving system engaged, regardless of whether a human operator is physically present in the vehicle."

[3] *See*, H.B. 1791 Leg., 85th Sess. (TX. 2017).

[4] *Bringing Smart Transport to Texans: Ensuring the Benefits of a Connected and Autonomous Transport System in Texas – A Final Report*, THE UNIVERSITY OF TEXAS AT AUSTIN CENTER FOR TRANSPORTATION RESEARCH, https://library.ctr.utexas.edu/ctr-publications/0-6838-2.pdf.

to endorse this approach as necessarily the preferred option. Indeed, our investigation remains skeptical. But precisely because the evidence is lacking to understand both the benefits and risks incremental approaches have, any attempt to identify an "ideal approach" in the abstract is currently divorced from practice. Only by examining the non-interventionist approach in detail can states and analysts create more robust frameworks for how we should approach such important and potentially transformative technological changes as a regulatory matter. A descriptive account of Texas's non-interventionist approach also provides states with a template that better prepares them for the twists and turns that lie ahead.

This article begins with background on the current legal landscape governing automated vehicles, both domestically and internationally, with particular focus on the role of the states in regulating important features of the new technology. In this discussion, we consider a range of automated technologies – "driverless" and "operator-assisted" vehicles as well as autonomous (satellite-based) and connected (infrastructure-dependent) vehicles. Next, the article considers the primary legal challenges these emerging technologies present. The final part of the article offers a preliminary analysis of legal models Texas might adopt in light of these emerging technologies, ranging from reactive adjustments to anticipatory adjustments.

Our examination of the non-interventionist approach is incomplete in several respects, however. For example, issues concerning security and vehicle design standards, both of which are generally left to federal regulators. We also do not investigate issues arising in land use, transportation planning, and interstate and intercountry transit in order to ensure some focus and simplicity for our study of state regulation.

II. FACTUAL ASSUMPTIONS THAT SERVE AS THE BACKDROP FOR THE LEGAL ANALYSIS

Before delving into a legal analysis, we first set down our operating assumptions regarding the capabilities and development of automated vehicle technologies. We draw here from two well-regarded reports that offer predictions of the future technological changes; one is a report authored by the Organization for Economic Co-operation and Development (OECD)[5] and the other is a RAND report, authored by Anderson et al.[6] These reports provide accessible predictions for what to expect from automated vehicles in our near-term transportation futures. The predictions are portrayed graphically in the figure below.[7]

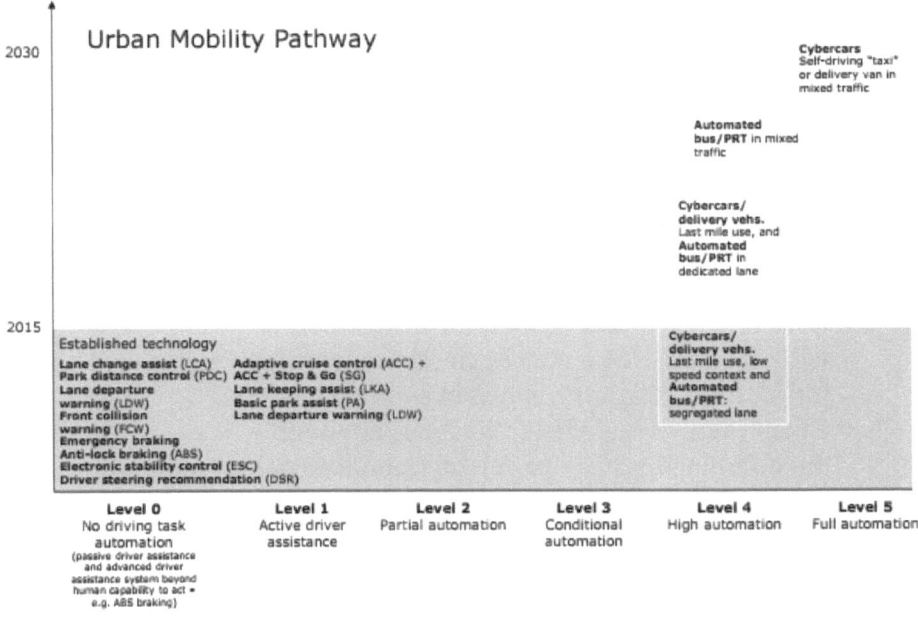

---

[5] OECD International Transport Forum, *Automated and Autonomous Driving: Regulation Under Uncertainty,* CORPORATE PARTNERSHIP BOARD, (2015), http://www.internationaltransportforum.org/pub/pdf/15CPB_AutonomousDriving.pdf.

[6] James Anderson, Nidhi Kalra, Karlyn Stanley, Paul Sorensen, Constantine Samaras, & and Oluwatobi Oluwatola, *AUTONOMOU VEHICLE TECHNOLOGY: A GUIDE FOR POLICYMAKERS* (2014). For an additional, elaborate description of the distinctive features of purely driverless technologies for autonomous and connected vehicles, see Dorothy Glancy, *Sharing the Road: Smart Transportation Infrastructure*, 41 FORDHAM URB. L. J. 1617, 1647 (2014).

[7] OECD International Transport Forum, *Automated and Autonomous Driving: Regulation Under Uncertainty,* CORPORATE PARTNERSHIP BOARD, 15 (2015), http://www.internationaltransportforum.org/pub/pdf/15CPB_AutonomousDriving.pdf.

For the near term (by 2020), these analysts predict:

- Low levels of automation will be incorporated into a growing number of new vehicles. This will involve handoff technology; for example, while in automated mode, an automated vehicle may encounter some recognized emergency (e.g., a police flagman or temporary barrier) that will default the vehicle into manual control. We anticipate that some of this automation will occur through retrofit of personal devices to augment driving activities, although it is not anticipated that such retrofits will have large market penetration of progress towards AVs.
- Testing of AVs on public roads, including connected, driverless cars with an operator in the front seat will occur.
- Infrastructure required for connected vehicles (CV) (vehicle–to–vehicle [V2V] and vehicle-to-infrastructure [V2I] capabilities) will include roadside devices transferring signals in local jurisdictions that may invest in such technology.
- Crash rates may begin to decline, although it is anticipated that the combined reality of mixed vehicles (partial automation and nonautomation) with an inevitable trial-and-error phase in perfecting handoffs and gauging operator automation preferences in automated cars will, in the short term, counteract some longer-term safety benefits of AVs.
- Individual vehicles will collect some private information on driver preferences and habits that will be transmitted to original equipment manufacturers (OEMs) and possibly other businesses.

In the longer term (2025 to 2030) analysts predict:

- Automation will become common on the roadways, handoffs will perform better in minimizing user error, and reliance on automation will be standard for highway driving, traffic jams, and parking assistance.
- Driverless cars without operators will be used in low-speed geo-fenced areas (e.g., government or college campuses) or on designated lanes, (for example truck platoons on a designated highway lane).
- Vehicle-to-infrastructure (V2I) developments may impact the types of infrastructure needed in transportation systems. The nature of the infrastructure will depend on whether V2I technologies are an important facet of AV transportation. Given

the costs, there is some skepticism about the use of elaborate connected infrastructures in the future.

- AV crashes will occur primarily as result of user errors during handoffs, users taking control and crashing, vehicle updates (either lack of or not authorized), and maintenance issues.
- AVs have the potential to generate substantial amount of information on operators and occupants. This information will be collected by OEMs but its use by enforcement personnel or other commercial or private entities is likely to be restricted for public policy reasons.

a. The Legal Landscape in General

Legal oversight of AV technologies within the U.S. has been primarily initiated at the state level. Twenty-one states have enacted legislation governing AVs as of February 2018.[8] Over thirty states have legislation moving through their legislatures as of April 2017.

Before considering individual state legislation, however, it is important to highlight the emergence of national recommendations calling for unified state oversight of AVs. In both its 2013 Statement and 2016 Policy, the National Highway, Traffic, and Safety Administration (NHTSA) had concluded that "states are well suited to address issues such as licensing, driver training, and conditions for operation related to specific types of vehicles".[9] In 2013, NHTSA indicated that it "does not believe that self-driving vehicles are currently ready to be driven on public roads for purposes other than testing." NHTSA encouraged states to develop regulations governing AV testing and to limit the use of self-driving mode to conditions

---

[8] *Autonomous Vehicles: Self-Driving Vehicles Enacted Legislation,* NATIONAL CONFERENCE OF STATE LEGISLATURES, http://www.ncsl.org/research/transportation/autonomous-vehicles-self-driving-vehicles-enacted-legislation.aspx.

[9] National Highway Traffic Safety Administration, Preliminary Statement of Policy Concerning Automated Vehicles, US DEPARTMENT OF TRANSPORTATION 10 (May, 2013), http://www.nhtsa.gov/staticfiles/rulemaking/pdf/Automated_Vehicles_Policy .pdf.

conducive to safe operation on public roadways. However, the 2016 Policy showed how fast NHTSA's thinking had evolved; NHTSA provided guidance on Level 3 and highly automated vehicles (HAVs), with the expectation of ultimate deployment of fleets of these vehicles.

The Uniform Law Commission (ULC)[10] has also garnered significant momentum for a uniform state act adopted across states governing AV testing and deployment. Uniformity between states with regard to AV operation is considered vital to create a predictable market for technological innovation and would assist and promote ease of commerce between states as AVs are integrated into the transportation system.

Several states have been very active in the oversight of AVs. State regulations of AVs range from authorization to operate AVs on public roads (Nevada), to allowing testing only in-state (California), to a lack of regulation of AVs in the majority of states. While the laws vary on key details, most states that actively regulate AVs have generally imposed some type of regulatory oversight of testing and/or deployment of AVs.[11] A few states have imposed other types of restrictions, such as mandating technologies on AV vehicles sold in the states and disclosure for consumers regarding the OEM's collection of private information after sale of the vehicle.

i. Testing and Deployment of AVs on Public Roadways

At least five states explicitly allow AVs on select public roads if they meet specified criteria [12]. Several states take this a step further and require the issuance of a license or permit as a precondition to operation.[13] Not all states actively regulate testing or distinguish between operating a AV for testing versus operating a vehicle for

---

[10] Study Committee on State Regulation of Driverless Cars, Revised Report of the Subcommittee on Issues: Exhibit A, UNIFORM LAW COMMISSION SUBCOMMITTEE ON ISSUES, http://www.uniformlaws.org/Committee.aspx?title=State.

[11] Kohler, William and Alex Colbert-Taylor, *Current Law and Potential Legal Issues Pertaining to Automated, Autonomous and Connected Vehicles*, 31 SANTA CLARA HIGH TECH. L. J. 99 (2015).

[12] *Autonomous Vehicles: Self-Driving Vehicles Enacted Legislation*, NATIONAL CONFERENCE OF STATE LEGISLATURES, http://www.ncsl.org/research/transportation/autonomous-vehicles-self-driving-vehicles-enacted-legislation.aspx.

[13] CAL. CODE REGS. tit. 13 § 227.04(d); NEV. REGS. § 8.3.

regular deployment (e.g., D.C. Code § 2352). Beyond direct oversight of testing, California and Nevada also require disclosure of disengagements (where the automated system is either switched off by the driver in car or by the system) as well as logging any accidents and near-misses occurring during testing.[14]

Nevada was the first state to enact legislation on AVs in 2011. Assembly Bill (AB) 511, defined an "autonomous vehicle" and directed the state's DMV to adopt rules for license endorsement and for operation, including insurance, safety standards, and testing [15]. The regulations were adopted in 2012 and revised in 2013. They require applicants show proof of 10,000 AV operational miles as well as a summary of statistics before they will be granted a license to test on public roads.[16] In its 2013 amendment to the law, Nevada specified that some Level 1, 2, and 3 technologies are not "autonomous," noting that autonomous technology means:

> technology which is installed on a motor vehicle
> and which has the capability to drive the motor
> vehicle without the active control or monitoring of
> a human operator. The term does not include an
> active safety system or a system for driver
> assistance, including, without limitation, a system
> to provide electronic blind spot detection, crash
> avoidance, emergency braking, parking assistance,
> adaptive cruise control, lane keeping assistance,
> lane departure warning, or traffic jam and queuing
> assistance, unless any such system, alone or in
> combination with any other system, enables the
> vehicle on which the system is installed to be
> driven without the active control or monitoring of a

---

[14] Cal. Code Regs. tit. 13 §§ 227.46, 227.48; Nev. Regs. § 10.4.

[15] A.B. 511 79th Leg., (Nev. 2011).

[16] Nev. Admin. Code § 482A (2013).

human operator.[17]

Testing licenses in Nevada are mandatory as a condition to operate AVs and the testing is limited to geofenced zones, which can be enlarged.[18] General requirements that span across all AV testing in Nevada include having two persons physically in the vehicle while testing, including one person in the driver's seat who is able to take control of the vehicle.[19] After testing is successful, Nevada only allows the AV to be deployed after the manufacturer or registered sales facility issues a "certificate of compliance."[20] The certificate can only be issued if the vehicle meets requirements set forth in Nevada regulation.[21]

California legislation and regulation provides a similar structure of oversight for AV testing and deployment. However, in contrast to Nevada, testing of AVs is allowed on all roads in the state. Like Nevada, vehicle manufacturers must obtain a testing permit from the state DMV, and comply with permit requirements when testing AVs on California roads.[22] California DMV requirements for manufacturer testing include registering the AV with the DMV, completing AV testing under controlled conditions, using qualified test drivers who sit in the driver's seat with the ability to take control of the AV, and having a $5 million insurance or surety bond backed.[23] Florida adopts some of the provisions of Nevada law, but exerts considerably less control over manufacturers testing AVs on public roadways, placing no geographical restrictions on testing. "In Florida, when a testing entity presents insurance to the Department and pays the title fees, the Department will brand the vehicle title 'autonomous' and 'autonomous vehicle' will print on the registration certificate".[24]

---

[17] S.B. 313 77th Leg. (Nev. 2013).

[18] NEV. REV. STATE. § 482A.120.

[19] NEV. ADMIN. CODE § 482A (2013).

[20] NEV. REGS. § 16.

[21] Id.

[22] CAL. CODE REGS. tit. 13, §§ 227.20, .22 (2017).

[23] CAL. VEH. CODE § 38570(A)(5).

[24] Florida Highway Safety and Motor Vehicles, *Autonomous Vehicle Report*, 5 (Feb. 10, 2014) http://www.flhsmv.gov/html/HSMVAutonomousVehicleReport2014.pdf.

Although there are requirements for AVs tested or deployed in the State, including proof of insurance at $5 million and vehicle certification, "the Department does not require an application or otherwise regulate the testing entity." [25] The DMV also does not have the authority to deny requests to test AVs in the state.

Michigan initially imposed similar restrictions on AVs while encouraging their development in the state -- such as allowing AV testing only as long as the vehicle is operated by an authorized agent of the manufacturer, with an individual present in the vehicle and able to take control immediately. In the early legislation the State also specifically banned operation of AVs for non-testing purposes.[26] In December 2016, however, the State of Michigan passed SB, 995, 996, 997, and 998 which allow self-driving cars to operate on all Michigan roads, and authorize automated truck platoons and networks of self-driving taxis. The laws are still being studied and implemented, but they appear to be the first to authorize self-driving cars without requiring an operator ready to take control.

The District of Columbia enacted the Autonomous Vehicle Act of 2012, which expressly allows the operation of AVs on District roadways.[27] The District requires only that a vehicle must operate in compliance with the District regulations and traffic laws and regulations and have a manual override with a driver in the driver's seat ready to take control.[28] The DMV was promulgating rules to implement the law including procedures for registration and issuance of permits to operate AVs.[29]

---

[25] *Id.*

[26] MICH. COMP. LAWS §§ 257.663, 665.

[27] D.C. CODE §§ 50-2351 to 50-2354 (2012).

[28] D.C. CODE § 50-2351 (2012).

[29] Tyler Lopez, *Navigation Without Representation: D.C.'s DMV Prepares for Self-Driving Cars*, SLATE (Apr. 9,2014), http://www.slate.com/blogs/future_tense/2014/04/09/autonomous_vehicle_regulations_washington_d_c_s_dmv_prepares_for_self_drivi

In 2015, both Arizona[30] and Virginia announced their decision to move forward with research and development of AV operations. In Arizona, Governor Doug Ducey signed Executive Order (EO) 2015-09 in August directing various agencies to "undertake any necessary steps to support the testing and operation of self-driving vehicles on public roads within Arizona." [31] The order establishes the Self-Driving Vehicle Oversight Committee within the governor's office to develop regulations for enabling the development and operations of AV pilot programs at selected universities.[32]

Utah authorized an autonomous motor vehicle study in May 2016 with the passage of HB 280. [33] The bill authorized each agency of the state with regulatory authority over autonomous vehicle technology testing to facilitate and encourage the responsible testing and operation of that technology. [34] It also tasked the Department of Public Safety, in consultation with other state agencies, to prepare a study on best practices for AV testing and employment; the report was published at the end of 2016.[35]

Finally, Tennessee passed legislation prohibiting any political subdivision of the state from disallowing the use of AVs as long as the vehicle complies with all safety regulations of the political subdivision.[36] This legislation makes it clear that the state wishes to take control of and presumably encourage AV use. [37] To test or use an AV, one must first obtain a state certification, however; this

---

ng.html.

[30] Ariz. Office of the Governor, EXEC. ORDER 2015-09, (Aug. 25, 2015), https://azgovernor.gov/sites/default/files/2015082510002.pdf.

[31] *Id.*

[32] *Id.*

[33] UTAH DEP'T OF TRANSP., BEST PRACTICE AND REGULATION OF AUTONOMOUS VEHICLES ON UTAH HIGHWAYS (2016). https://le.utah.gov/interim/2016/pdf/00004126.pdf.

[34] *Id.*

[35] *Id.*

[36] S.B. 598, 109th Gen. Assemb., Reg. Sess. (Tenn. 2015).

[37] *Id.*

requirement was only added a year after the bill was passed. [38]

ii. Vehicle Requirements

· NHTSA and the ULC both endorse several design features in AVs used for testing or deployment. These include a device that allows for quick disengagement from automated mode, a device that indicates to others whether the vehicle is operating in automated mode, and a system to warn the operator of malfunctions.[39] Several state laws require one or all of these features for AVs to be sold in their jurisdictions. These states include California, Florida, and Nevada, as well as the District of Columbia.[40]

Individual states have imposed other requirements. Nevada has required that Electronic Data Recorders (EDRs) capture data 30 seconds before a collision in AVs and preserve the data for 3 years.[41] California also requires a crash data recorder for AVs sold to the public and imposes detailed requirements governing the capabilities of   these   recorders.[42]

iii. Operator Requirements

NHTSA recommends that an endorsement or separate driver's license should be issued for AV operators, certifying that the operator has passed a test concerning safe operation of the AV or completed a certain number of hours operating the vehicle. [43]

---

[38] *Id.*

[39] Study Comm. on State Regulations of Driverless Cars, UNIF. LAW COMM'N, REVISED REPORT OF THE SUBCOMMITTEE ON ISSUES: EXHIBIT A, 9 (2014).

[40] *Id.* at 9.

[41] NEV. ADMIN. CODE § 482A.190 (2014).

[42] CAL. VEH. CODE § 38750(c)(1)(G) (West 2017).

[43] NAT'L HIGHWAY TRAFFIC SAFETY ADMIN., PRELIMINARY STATEMENT OF POLICY CONCERNING AUTOMATED VEHICLES 11 (2013).

Consistent with NHTSA's recommendations, both Michigan and Nevada testing regulations for AVs require a special driver's license certification and license plates.[44] Neevada, the first state to enact AV legislation, has only briefly addressed private individuals as operators as AVs, stating "[w]hen autonomous vehicles are eventually made available for public use, motorists will be required to obtain a special driver license endorsement and the DMV will issue green license plates for the vehicles."[45]

California lays out detailed requirements for a AV driver test: the manufacturer must identify the operator in writing to the DMV; the operator must have been licensed to drive a motor vehicle for at least 3 years immediately preceding application, and that during that time that the operator did not have more than one violation of specific sections of the vehicle code.[46] The operator must also have completed the manufacturer's AV training program, which includes instructions on AV technology and defensive driver training.[47]

II. ANALYSIS OF TEXAS' INCREMENTAL APPROACH TO AVS

The operation of AVs on Texas roadways is likely to intersect with existing Texas law in a number of overlapping ways.[48] We consider legal issues governing the actual operation of automated vehicles first. The recent legislation passed in 2017 clarifies a number of uncertainties governing the legal operation of these vehicles, although a few important details still remain unresolved. We then consider potential issues regarding tort liability and privacy and security in the wake of AV transportation. Neither topic has been addressed legislatively to date, but each area raises some important

---

[44] NEV. ADMIN. CODE §§ 482A.040, .050, .110 (2014).

[45] *See* NEV. DEP'T OF MOTOR VEHICLES, AUTONOMOUS VEHICLES, http://www.dmvnv.com/autonomous.htm (last visited June 29, 2017).

[46] CAL. CODE REGS. tit. 13, §§ 227.18, .20 (2017).

[47] CAL. CODE REGS. tit. 13, §§ 227.20, .22 (2017).

[48] As noted earlier, the technologies themselves are not so clearly distinct that the differences between Autonomous Vehicle and Connected Vehicle have legal relevance. Rather than an artificial parsing of CV vs. AV – which simply can't be done at present in most areas of the analysis – we take a broad view of the technologies to ensure a more comprehensive assessment of the emerging law/policy. Where there are meaningful distinctions to be drawn with regard to the law and CVs vs. AVs.

legal questions.

a. Operation of Motor Vehicles in Texas

The general structure of the Texas Motor Vehicle Code places primary responsibility on "operators" of vehicles to comply with Code requirements, rules of the road, and other laws.[49] The 2017 amendments to the Motor Vehicle Code substantially clarified the meaning of this key term as it applies to automated vehicles.

Prior to the 2017 legislation, the Texas Motor Vehicle Code considered vehicles to be driven by operators; an "operator," not surprisingly, was defined as a "person" "who drives or has physical control of a vehicle."[50] While the definition of "person" explicitly includes corporations,[51] in order to legally operate a vehicle, the "person" also has to obtain a driver license.[52] However, driver license requirements include mandatory thumbprints, photos, signatures, residences, and other information that can only be satisfied by humans.[53] Thus, prior to the 2017 legislation, the operator of a vehicle had to be a human. (Note it might still be possible for a vehicle to drive itself without any operator, but we do not address that hypothetical here).

Although this licensed "operator" had to be human, Texas law did not explicitly require the operator to be actively driving the vehicle. Instead, the most plausible interpretation of the Motor Vehicle Code requires only that the "operator" be present in the vehicle in a manner that allowed the operator to control its movement.[54]

---

[49] TEX. TRANSP. CODE ANN. § 541.001(a).

[50] *Id.*

[51] TEX. TRANSP. CODE ANN. tit. 7C § 541.001(4) (West 1995).

[52] Tex. TRANSP. CODE ANN. § 521.021.

[53] *Id.* Moreover, if there is no identifiable "operator" present in a vehicle (authorized or unauthorized per the criminal code), the vehicle could be confiscated. See Texas Transportation Code § 545.305.

Prior to 2017, any violations of the Code generally also fell on this licensed "operator".[55] Although the violations could be imposed jointly on other operators as well, initially it was the operator that would bear primary responsibility for accidents and violations.[56] The legal landscape in Texas prior to 2017 thus could be read to allow the use of AVs even without legislation. But, at the same time, but there were several ambiguities that complicated the legal use of AVs:

1) Although Texas law did not speak directly to the legality of driverless vehicles (without occupants), certain secondary prohibitions, like those against "unattended vehicles" [57] or detailed requirements for "rendering aid,[58] could be read to prohibit the use of vehicles moving without human drivers or passengers.

2) Texas law was unclear on the appropriate role of the operator in controlling the vehicle. Yet restrictions on limiting the visibility of the operator, as one example, could be read to imply that the operator needed, to some extent, be attentive.[59]

3) In cases where automated vehicles caused violations or accidents, the law's emphasis on responsibility by an operator might be complicated or at least require a decision about when an operator has relinquished control sufficient to relieve them of legal responsibility.[60]

---

[54] *See Denton v. State*, 911 S.W.2d 388, 389 (Tex. Crim. App. 1995) (finding that starting the ignition and revving the accelerator was sufficient to find that defendant "operated" the vehicle as an element in "Unauthorized Use" charge required) but *see Texas Dept. of Public Safety v. Allocca*, 301 S.W.3d 364 (Tex. App.—Austin) (sleeping defendant in driver's seat parked legally on private property does not provide "probable cause" to believe that the vehicle had been previously operated).

[55] See, e.g., Texas Transportation Code § 547.004— "a person commits an offense that is a misdemeanor if the person operates or moves or, as an owner, knowingly permits another to operate or move, a vehicle that: 1) is unsafe so as to endanger a person."

[56] See, e.g., id. at § 542.302

[57] *Id.* § 545.404

[58] *See, e.g.,* TEX. TRANS. CODE ANN. § 550.021 (operator requirements in emergencies); *id.* § 550.023 (duty to render aid), and *id.* § 550.024 (duty on striking unattended vehicle to find and notify the vehicle's operator or leave note.

[59] *Id.* § 545.417 TEX. TRANSP. CODE ANN. §§ 544.010(c), 545.417 (1996).

In part in response to these and other legal uncertainties, Texas passed S.B. 2205 to allow the unrestricted use of AVs on Texas roads, including driverless vehicles. Specifically, S.B. 2205 provides several clarifications that resolve past ambiguities:

1) The law defines the term "operator" to include the vehicle itself when functioning in operated mode (the law states that "the automated driving system is considered to be licensed to operate the vehicle").[61] Prior legal questions about the types and nature of legal operators are largely put to rest as a result of this legal amendment.

2) The law makes it clear that AVs *can* operate without human passengers or operators. Driving "unattended", in other words, is perfectly acceptable if the vehicle is an AV with its automated driving system engaged.[62]

3) The amended law places responsibility on the "owners" of an AV if the vehicle violates traffic or vehicle laws "regardless of whether the person is physically present in the vehicle while the vehicle is operating."[63] The provision also implies, that vehicle manufacturers, suppliers, and software developers are absolved of legal responsibility, again even in cases where the violations or accidents were caused by their negligence or other wrongdoing.

Despite the advances made by the legislation in integrating automated vehicles into the Motor Vehicle Code, some legal questions still remain. The nature of parties who are responsible for violations, for example, will likely require further legal fine-tuning. The new S.B. 2205 places responsibility on owners of the vehicles for

---

60 TX. TRANSP. CODE ANN. §542.302 (West 1996).

61 *Id.* at § 545.453(a)(2).

62 *Id.* at § 545.454(a).

63 *Id.* at § 545.453(a)(1).

violations of the vehicle while operating in automated mode; yet this implies that any human operator present in the vehicle might be resolved of responsibility, even if an accident was the result of their action. Alternatively, perhaps the intent is to place joint liability on owners and operators, since a separate, existing Texas provision holds the licensed operator as primarily responsible.[64] Additionally, the ability of manufacturers and others to escape responsibility under S.B. 2205, given this reading, might be viewed by the public as unduly limiting when the source of a violation is the automated system. Again, further adjustments or at least clarifications may be needed.

b. Rules of the Road and Related Requirements

The rules of the road may also raise several legal uncertainties, as AVs are deployed on Texas roads. We consider a few of these uncertainties in this section. Conveniently, one potentially significant ambiguity present in many of the state codes is avoided in Texas. Most state codes direct the rules of the road requirements to "drivers" and "operators," which could be interpreted to technically exempt self-driving vehicles since there is no "operator" or "driver" onboard. Texas has foresightedly required "vehicles" rather than "operators" to comply with rules of the road.[65] It is thus the "vehicle" and not the "operator" who must maintain speed limits and follow traffic signals; this step avoids the biggest source of uncertainties with regard to how rules of the road might apply to cars driven without operators. Nevertheless, there are a few remaining legal questions that seem likely to arise in the future.

i. Rules of the Road

A few rules of the road may restrict the operation of AVs, although the AV technology may ultimately be capable of meeting these requirements. For example, special requirements apply to operators in the presence of "emergency vehicles"[66] and when

---

[64] *E.g.*, TX. TRANSP. CODE ANN. § 547.004 states that "a person commits an offense that is a misdemeanor if the person operates or moves or, as an owner, knowingly permits another to operate or move, a vehicle that: 1) is unsafe so as to endanger a person."

[65] TX. TRANSP. CODE ANN. § 545.002 states that "a reference to an operator includes a reference to the vehicle operated by the operator if the reference imposes a duty or provides a limitation on the movement or other operation of that vehicle."

[66] TX. TRANSP. CODE ANN. § 545.156(a).

following "school buses" that stop.[67] The safety signals to stop or pass can include auditory and hand signals.[68] Moreover, the appropriate operator response—e.g., yielding or pulling over to the side of the road until the vehicle has passed—may require some operator control. AVs will need to ensure compliance with these rules of the road to avoid violations and accidents, either through handoffs (i.e., the quick transition from autonomous to human control) or other automated capabilities.

Texas law permits the use of auditory signals, temporary speed signs, and temporary traffic signals in several settings (e.g., for worker zones).[69] AVs will need to be equipped to hand off control in settings with temporary or auditory signals or be prepared to navigate in automated mode despite these alternate signals.

Texas law also assigns considerable discretion to drivers at right-of-way intersections.[70] AVs will require careful programming to ensure not only that the right-of-way is gauged correctly given the rules of the road, but also to act/perform defensively given the likely driver errors that may arise with vehicles that are not automated (e.g., miscalculating one's proper place in a queue).

ii. Safety Inspections Required for Registration

While other issues may arise during inspection and registration, at least one issue stands out as potentially needing modification to adapt to the deployment of AVs in the long-term. Texas law requires that steering systems be inspected in all vehicles. The Texas Department of Public Safety requires that a motor

---

[67] TX. TRANSP. CODE ANN. § 545.066.

[68] *Id.*

[69] *See, e.g.,* Texas Driver Handbook, 38 (Sept. 2014), (governing temporary signals), 35 (governing railroad crossings).

[70] *Id.*, p.22.

vehicle's wheel must be able to be turned by the inspectors in order for the vehicle to pass inspection.[71] As long as AVs operate with steering wheels, this requirement will not be an impediment. However, the Code requirements may need to be amended to permit vehicles without traditional steering wheels.

iii. Legal Operation of Truck Platoons

A truck platoon consists of two or more trucks that operate in close proximity through connected infrastructure so that the subsequent vehicles in the caravan can stop much more quickly than human drivers. The close proximity of the trucks is beneficial because it reduces aerodynamic drag improving fuel efficiency.

The major legal impediment to the operation of platoons – a mandated following distance between vehicles [72] – has been eliminated through recent Texas legislation that exempts vehicles with connected braking systems.[73] However, even with the adjustment of following distance, several other legal ambiguities and impediments may remain that need to be addressed:

- *Trucks (often) prohibited in passing lane.*
  Under Texas rules of the road, trucks are generally not allowed in the passing lanes. This prohibition would thus need to be amended to allow for a third, restricted lane for platoons.[74] Restrictions imposed by localities (e.g., prohibiting towing trucks from driving in passing lanes) may also need to be amended.

- *Merging.*
  Any existing restrictions on merging by towing vehicles or other oversized trucks may also need to be revisited to allow for truck platoons, although we were not able to locate any specific restrictions in place at the statewide level.

---

[71] TEX. DEP'T OF PUB. SAFETY. RULES AND REGULATIONS MANUAL FOR OPERATION OF OFFICIAL VEHICLE INSPECTION STATIONS, Austin, 4-24 (2000).

[72] TX. TRANSP. CODE ANN. § 545.062.

[73] *See*, H.B. 1791 Leg., 85th Sess. (Tx. 2017).

[74] Tom Benning, *More North Texas Highways Slated to Feature Ban on Trucks in Left Lane*, DALLAS MORNING NEWS: TRANSPORTATION BLOG (June 3, 2013), http://transportationblog.dallasnews.com/2013/06/more-north-texas-highways-slated-to-feature-ban-on-trucks-in-the-left-lane.html/.

- *Engineering Considerations regarding Weight and Length Restrictions.*
Texas imposes legally prescribed weight and length restrictions on individual vehicles.[75] When multiple trucks operate in close proximity, these restrictions may need to be revisited to ensure that the platoons are safe for bridges and other roadway situations.

c. Tort Liability

There is a general consensus that the common law liability rules developed through tort law are well-suited to assimilate AV technology in apportioning liability for crashes.[76] After providing a brief orientation to liability law in Texas, we discuss a few potential complications and ambiguities that might impact TxDOT and other litigants as AVs are assimilated onto Texas highways.

i. Background on Liability Rules

Legal responsibility for crashes in Texas is governed largely by tort law—a body of judge-made case law that determines liability according to relatively simple principles of fault. Although there have been some shifts in features of these liability rules concerning vehicular crashes, for the most part the rules governing crashes have proven to be both consistent and adaptable to changes in technology. Adjusting general liability rules to new technologies, particularly in transportation, is common.

Under the tort law of Texas and other states, operators of vehicles must behave "reasonably" while driving. When drivers fail to

---

[75] *See, generally,* TX TRANSP. CODE ANN. § 621.

[76] James Anderson et al., RAND, *Autonomous Vehicle Technology: A Guide for Policymakers 94* (2014); John Villasenor, Brookings Inst., *Products Liability and Driverless Cars: Issues and Guiding Principles for Legislation*, (Apr. 24, 2014), http://www.brookings.edu/research/papers/2014/04/products-liability-driverless-cars-villasenor; Nidhi Kalra et. al., *Cal. Partners for Advanced Transit & Highways, Liability and Regulation of Autonomous Vehicle Technologies*, 31 (2009).

act reasonably and their negligent act causes harm, they can be held liable for the damages they cause. Private victims, working through the tort system, provide incentives for operators to be "reasonable" and hold drivers accountable when their deviations cause harm. In the court's assessment of reasonableness, the actor's conduct is compared to that of a reasonable driver, with no special allowances for age, mental ability, or intoxication.

Somewhat similarly, when issues arise regarding the safe design of a vehicle, manufacturers are similarly held to "reasonable" standards of design. Manufacturers must ensure that the benefits of their design choices outweigh the risks and other social costs, particularly when compared against alternative design options. These product liability standards incorporate a flexible, "reasonableness" expectation into design choices and hold manufacturers financially liable for crashes only when the risks of a design outweigh its value. The flexible test of "reasonableness" built into the common law liability system thus provides a versatile standard for assessing manufacturer liability when crashes occur. Nevertheless, there are several ways that the well-settled common law liability system may need to change to accommodate AVs, perhaps ultimately through targeted legislation.

ii. More Complicated Crash Litigation

When operating a traditional vehicle in ways that violate rules of the road, or are otherwise unreasonable, the operator is generally the exclusive liable party. Litigation identifying the "liable" party in these kinds of crashes is relatively simple. Complicated disputes, such as those over whether a party actually operated a car in an unreasonable way, or whether the plaintiff's claimed damages resulted from the crash may arise. But, the operator is typically the primary and exclusive defendant.

Determining the liable party is not always so simple. Car crash litigation can include complicated product liability claims. For example, in crashes that result from vehicle design defects, the plaintiff can sue and recover from the manufacturer of the defectively designed vehicle. The plaintiff can also bring suit against the vehicle operator if the operator was also negligent.[77]

In the new world of AVs, product liability claims against

---

[77] See, e.g., General Motors Corp. v. Grizzle, 642 S.W.2d 837 (Tx. Ct. App. 1982).

manufacturers will become the rule rather than the exception. If an AV, operating in automated mode, is a cause of a crash, the manufacturer will likely be joined as a defendant in the litigation. Accordingly, these are likely to be complex product liability causes of action.[78]

The lower crash rate associated with AVs may eventually offset costs associated with this increased complexity. However, in the near-term, it is possible that litigation costs will increase with the use of AVs in traffic systems populated with non-automated vehicles. Indeed, some posit that the increased accidents that are likely to occur as a result of mixed human-vehicle interactions may either chill development of automated technology or lead innovators to skip the mixed human-vehicle stage and prepare vehicles that operate in fully automated mode.[79]

To avoid costly product liability claims, victims in car crashes may allege that the manufacturer of an AV operating in autonomous mode violated Section 547.004(a) of the Texas Transportation Code.[80] A successful negligence per se claim filed under tort law could help circumvent some of the complexities of product liability evidence by flipping the burden of proof to the manufacturer. Only actual experimentation will reveal whether this statutory violation will streamline litigation involving AV manufacturers.

---

[78] For example, the identification of a defect in an AV (e.g., proving an erroneous algorithm or other error in the vehicle software), the assignment of potential driver error in heeding a warning, evidence required to establish a defect will complicate discovery and raise the costs of suit for the plaintiff (including TXDOT) and/or the insurer bringing the claim.

[79] Nidhi Kalra, James M. Anderson, and Martin Wachs, *Liability and Regulation of Autonomous Vehicle Technologies,* CALIFORNIA PATH RESEARCH REPORT, at 17 (2009).

[80] This section holds that "A person commits an offense that is a misdemeanor if the person operates or moves or, as an owner, knowingly permits another to operate or move, a vehicle that: (1) is unsafe so as to endanger a person."

Additional Challenges in Determining Fault or Defect in Crashes Involving AVs

Under Texas tort law, AVs must be designed "reasonably," with "reasonable" warnings, and in ways in which the "risks outweigh the benefits."[81] Applying this test will entail considerable fact-intensive assessments, generally made by juries in case-specific crashes. As a result, manufacturers will face uncertainty with regard to how their design choices will fare in practice and with how juries will assess those choices in hindsight, often years after an accident occurred. In the next two sections we discuss the two areas where AV-related liability is likely to be most unpredictable with respect its reception in the tort system.

Handoffs for Mid-levels of Automation and Connectivity

The AV "handoff" is expected to an area where liability will operate without much precedential guidance and will hence be quite unpredictable in tort litigation.[82] In the short term, because consumers will be unfamiliar with these handoff features (e.g., a car vibrating when it crosses a highway line), manufacturers could even have a duty to safely instruct consumers on how to use the vehicles. This duty could conceivably be discharged by having users read an instruction manual, undergo a tutorial in the vehicle or at the dealership, or be certified in some way.[83]

Courts and juries will need to determine what constitutes an adequate warning for the purposes of a handoff.[84] Courts will also

---

[81] *See, e.g., Genie Indus., Inc. v. Matak*, 462 S.W.3d 1 (Tex. 2015) (utilizing both a risk-utility and a reasonable design test to resolve a product liability claim).

[82] Nidhi Kalra, James M. Anderson, and Martin Wachs, *Liability and Regulation of Autonomous Vehicle Technologies*, CALIFORNIA PATH RESEARCH REPORT, at 17 (2009). Fact-intensive questions will arise with respect to both the manufacturers and the operators: How alert and attentive should drivers be in various situations? What is expected of "reasonable drivers"? Should vehicle designers foresee the possibility that some owners will fall asleep or be slow to take over operation? What types of alert systems are needed to lead owners to use the automation, and thus prevent accidents? If operators turn off the automated feature to avoid annoying vibrations or noises, could manufacturers be liable in part for the foreseeable use of their technology?

[83] Jeffrey Gurney, *Sue My Car, Not Me: Products Liability and Accidents Involving Autonomous Vehicles*, U. ILL. JL TECH. & POL'Y, 247, 264-665 (2013).

[84] *See, e.g., DaimlerChrysler Corp. v. Hillhouse*, 161 S.W.3d 541, 550 (Tex. App. San Antonio, 2004) (imposing liability for a confusing warning).

need to decide whether and how to allow comparisons between automated and non-automated vehicles. If a handoff is designed in a way that presents some foreseeable risks of driver error, there is an argument that the AV may be compared to cars that have no automation at all regarding that feature (e.g., staying in a lane). On the other hand, the manufacturer will likely argue that vehicles should only be compared against vehicles with similar levels of automation or an even narrower class in terms of similar automation, price, and functionality.[85]

Proof of Defects in AVs

Crashes that involve some apparent failure of automated technology in AVs will inevitably raise product liability claims. Plaintiffs—whether third parties or occupants—will need to pinpoint a defect as part of their case. Collecting evidence and determining why an automated car failed in a given setting may be challenging. For example, plaintiffs must determine whether the problem was with the software, a mechanical feature, a unique trait of the roadway that had not been factored into the AV design, etc.

Because of these difficulties, it has been suggested that plaintiffs will focus initially on locating tangible design defects, such as an AV being designed with one laser sensor on the front of the vehicle instead of two.[86] Plaintiffs will still need to establish that other vehicles used two sensors and that the utility of double-sensors outweighed the risks,[87] but in cases involving improvements, these

---

[85] Gary Marchant & Rachel Lindor, *The Coming Collision Between Autonomous Vehicles and the Liability* System, 52 SANTA CLARA LAW REVIEW, 1425, 1435 (2012).

[86] Jeffrey Gurney, *Sue My Car, Not Me: Products Liability and Accidents Involving Autonomous Vehicles*, U. ILL. JL TECH. & POL'Y, 247, 264-65 (2013).

[87] *See, e.g., Genie Indus., Inc. v. Matak*, 42 S.W.3d, 3, 9-12 (Tex. 2015) (applying the risk utility factors even with a safer alternative design); *Timpte Indus. v. Gish*, 286 S.W.3d 306, 311 (Tex. 2009); Tex. Civ. Prac. & Rem. Code Ann. § 82.005(a) (1) - (2) (West 2015).

showings may not be difficult. If this type of litigation is successful, it could encourage defensive manufacturing practices (a sort of "arms race" in adding sensors, etc.) to ensure that vehicles maximize the use of obvious features on the vehicle but also minimize the risks of errors or crashes.

Plaintiffs will also encounter significant difficulties bringing claims against manufacturers in cases of inexplicable crashes involving automation (e.g., AVs careening into poles) since there may be no theory or explanation for the product failure. To date, Texas has not adopted the malfunction test in products liability, which would allow for lightened burdens for injured plaintiffs.[88] The malfunction test (adopted in several other states) operates much like the "res ipsa" doctrine in negligence.[89] When a vehicle or other good explodes spontaneously or otherwise malfunctions in ways that harms the uses, the test only requires that the plaintiff introduce evidence of the event. The burden to disprove liability then falls on the defendant-manufacturer.

The parallel negligence claim of *res ipsa loquitur*—which provides the plaintiff with an inference of negligence if the accident itself suggests negligence—may provide a lightened burden,[90] but in a product liability case, the "exclusive control" and no fault of plaintiff elements may be difficult for a driver to establish. Professor David Vladeck has suggested that courts apply strict liability principles to these cases.[91] Professors Sophia Duffy and Jamie Patrick Hopkins have also suggested that, in these cases, owners of AVs and CVs be held strictly liable and forced to maintain larger insurance policies.[92] They suggest that given the potentially low rate of accidents involving these vehicles and the low rate of inexplicable accidents in general, greater insurance requirements will neither deter AV and CV implementation by manufacturers nor their use by consumers.[93]

---

[88] *Ford Motor Co. v. Ridgway*, 135. S.W.3d 598, 601-02 (Tex. 2004).

[89] Restatement (Third) of Torts: Product Liability §3 (Am. Law Inst. 1998).

[90] *Porterfield v. Brinegar*, 719 S.W.2d 558, 559 (Tex. 1986).

[91] David Vladeck, *Machines Without Principles: Liability Rules and Artificial Intelligence*, 89 WASH. L. REV. 117, 117 (2014).

[92] Sophia Duffy & Jamie Patrick Hopkins, *Sit, Stay, Drive: The Future of Autonomous Car Liability*, 16 SMU SCI. & TECH L. REV 101, 118-122 (2013).

Conversely, such crashes may be rare enough that common law adjustments to defects law or *res ipsa* can accommodate difficult cases.

Litigants and courts may also struggle with identifying the appropriate comparators for different levels of automation or technological capabilities in product liability claims. In the abstract, courts typically consider risks and utilities of a product in relation to competitors. Yet all Level 3 automation in V2V consumer vehicles may not necessarily be similar; different AV vehicles may have significant functional differences within the same level of automation.[94] As AV technologies improve and prices drop, moreover, CVs that are older and have lower levels of automation may begin to be compared to price-equivalent but much more capable, newer vehicles. Rapid changes in the safety and price over time could make the identification of comparison products even more difficult and may lead to a de facto incentive for rapid turnover and high market demand for new vehicles.

Software Errors

Crashes from software errors or malfunctions may also complicate determining and allocating liability. Courts across the country have generally refused to subject software defects to strict liability in products liability law.[95] Since it is nearly impossible to design software without errors, plaintiffs are likely to face considerable difficulty in proving that software was negligently coded.[96] Alternatively, software could also be viewed as a component

---

[93] *Id.*

[94] Nidhi Kalra et. al., *Liability and Regulation of Autonomous Vehicle Technologies,* California PATH Research Report (2009) at 2, 31.

[95] David Polin, *Proof of Manufacturer's' Liability for Defective Software*, 68 AM. JUR. PROOF OF FACTS, 3d § 333 (West 2015).

[96] *Id.*

part of the product, which would not affect the product liability analysis. In that case, updates to the software initially integrated into the vehicle, would be considered part of the finished product. While the latter view will likely prevail, the role of software in vehicle design and in preventing crashes may raise new questions in the product liability analysis.

Further issues could arise if software updates are not automatic. For example, at least one current company, Nissan, offers its software on a subscription basis. It is plausible that other manufacturers will do the same, especially in the short term.[97] If any software update reveals defects in the original software, even if it is not automatic, plaintiffs can argue that new features in the update meet Texas's "substantial degree of control" requirement such that these manufacturers would have a continuing obligation to warn of product defects and issues in the software. Additionally, because offering updates to consumers is similar to the defendant's blade replacement program in *Bell Helicopter Co. v. Bradshaw*,[98] offering software updates would also likely constitute a manufacturer's voluntary assumption of a post-sale duty to warn. Manufacturers could potentially discharge this duty by alerting the driver via the car that an update is necessary or though more traditional means, such as, the use of regular mail or telephone. Several commentators predict, however, that these types of post-sale duty cases will raise important and complicated liability questions as a result of the rapid pace of technological innovation.[99]

Federal Safety Standards

Currently, federal safety standards do not cover AVs. Once they are promulgated, federal standards will likely exert a substantial influence on Texas liability law. Section 82.008 of the Texas Civil Practice and Remedies Code allows a defendant in a products liability action to establish a rebuttable presumption that they are not liable if

---

[97] Francesca Svarcas, *Turning a new LEAF: A Privacy Analysis of CARWINGS Electric Vehicle Data Collection and Transmission*, 29 SANTA CLARA HIGH TECHNOLOGY LAW JOURNAL 165, 165 (2012).

[98] *Bell Helicopter Co. v. Bradshaw*, 594 S.W.2nd 519 (Tex. App. Corpus Christi, 1979).

[99] *See, e.g.*, Bryant Walker-Smith, *Proximity-Driven Liability*, 102 GEORGETOWN L. J. 1777 (2014).

their product conforms to mandatory safety standards or regulations or to pre-market licensing requirements promulgated by the federal government or a federal agency.[100] NHTSA standards that satisfy this provision thus offer manufacturers added protection from tort liability in Texas. This presumption can be rebutted by a showing that the standards, regulations, or pre-market licensing requirements were inadequate to protect the public from unreasonable risks or damage or by a showing that the defendant withheld material information from the federal government or agencies.[101] However, plaintiffs would have difficulty making these showings.

Depending on the nature of federal involvement, federal standards may expressly or implicitly preempt state common law claims, including claims of inadequate warning. While this preemption is disfavored and appears to be precluded under current law (49 U.S.C. § 30103(e)), it remains a future possibility if the U.S. Congress passes legislation with express preemptive effect.

Evidence

Electronic Data Recorder (EDR) use in a vehicle ensures that information about the vehicle and occupant are available shortly before the crash. Although the use of EDRs predates and is separate from AV technology, the two do overlap. Indeed, some states require EDRs in all AVs.

Although privacy concerns of EDR data is being addressed at the federal level, such data is well-positioned to be central to tort litigation. Texas law does allow retrieval of data from EDRs by "court order".[102] Presumably in cases where EDR data would prove probative in determining the cause of an accident, the court will acquiesce. In crashes in which both or all cars involved in the accident

---

[100] Tex. Civ. Prac. & Rem. Code Ann. § 82.008 (West 2015).

[101] *Id.*

[102] TEX. TRANSP. CODE § 547.615(c)(1).

have an EDR and/or other additional data recording devices, this added evidence should prove invaluable in sorting out responsibility.

Due to the vital role EDRs are likely to play as evidence in tort litigation, however, it will also be important to ensure that their data cannot be manipulated. Until the integrity of EDRs and other recording devices can be protected, such data may need to play a more qualified role in AV litigation in the State.

Modifications to AVs by Third Parties

Several states and NHTSA have shown interest in the liability issues that arise when owners retrofit a conventional or even partially automated car with additional AV technology.[103] The aftermarket modification of conventional vehicles by consumers has historically been a concern in some states.[104] Yet safety risks associated with aftermarket modifications involving automated technologies are likely to be even more substantial. Indeed, the ULC Subcommittee identified this issue as one that might be worthy of legislative attention, while recommending that state legislators otherwise leave tort liability alone.

Under Texas common law, manufacturers are already well-positioned to defeat claims arising from third party modifications to AVs since the plaintiff has the burden of proving that a defect introduced by the manufacturer was a "producing cause of plaintiff's injuries".[105] The Texas Supreme Court has also refused to adopt and apply the 3rd Restatement of Torts (§ 3), which provides plaintiff with an inference that harm was caused by defect and that it existed at time of sale/distribution (when certain conditions are met), even when the product is not new/nearly new and has been previously modified or repaired.[106] Additionally, § 82.002 of the Texas Civil Practice and Remedies Code does not require manufacturers to indemnify sellers (which appears to include any commercial entity performing the modification) in cases where the harm was the result of the seller

---

[103] Uniform Law Commission Subcommittee on Issues, Study Committee on State Regulation of Driverless Cars, *Revised Report of the Subcommittee on Issues: Exhibit A* (Oct. 30, 2015) http://www.uniformlaws.org/Committee.aspx?title=State.

[104] *See, e.g.*, Uniform Vehicle Code §§ 3.121 and 3.122.

[105] *Ford Motor* Co. *v. Ridgway*, 135 S.W.3d 598, 600 (Tex. 2004)

[106] *Id.*

"negligently modifying or altering the product for which the seller is independently liable." While this latter provision does not immunize the manufacturer from liability, it suggests that primary liability will not necessarily lie with the manufacturer in cases of their party modifications.

iii. New Issues Affecting Governmental Liability

Texas agencies, including TxDOT, the DMV, and municipalities, generally enjoy immunity for planning and governmental functions. This includes road design and also the dissemination of information. The integration of AVs onto Texas highways is not expected to dramatically alter the government's liability, even with the heightened technological complexity of connected infrastructure. Nevertheless, there are several features of the future AV world that do create ambiguities with regard to governmental liability.

Malfunctioning Road and Traffic Signals and Related Equipment

In Texas, the installation and operation of traffic-control devices, signs, warnings, and other signals installed by governmental entities (both State and municipal) are partially protected by governmental immunity.[107] Roadside equipment (RSE) and related infrastructure needed to provide connected roadways also appears to fall within the terms of this partial immunity for road and traffic signals. (It is assumed in this analysis that connected infrastructure will fit neatly within the general concept of traffic and road control devices of § 101.060; if this is not the case, however, then additional analyses must be undertaken as to whether they are personal or real property under the Act).

While the decision to place a sign or control device is discretionary,[108] once that signal is in place, the government can be

---

[107] Tex. Civ. Prac. & Rem. Code § 101.060, see also *id.* § 101.0215(a)(21) and (31).

[108] *Id.* § 101.060(a)(1); *City of Grapevine v. Sipes*, 195 S.W.3d 689, 693 (Tex. 2006).

liable for malfunctions, stolen or missing signals, or defects in these devices, with some exceptions.[109] This liability is imposed, however, only if the government received notice and did not make repairs within a reasonable time.[110]

With respect to malfunctions of digital or "connected" signals, it is not clear how "notice" under subsection (a)(2) will be triggered for purposes of the Act. Connected roadway devices will presumably involve real time communications not only between the device and vehicles, but also between the device and the government operating the signal. In theory, then, the government may receive instantaneous "data" revealing a problem with a signal; this immediate message is not available for non-digital signs and signals.[111] The courts could thus determine that notice occurs immediately—when the malfunctioning signal is sent. Alternatively, notice could be triggered once an employee has reason to discover the defect from the incoming data. Legislative clarification of the notice requirement would be beneficial because the government may be discouraged from utilizing connected or digital technologies for fear of greater liability.

It is also possible that since connected infrastructure malfunctions occur with respect to the transmittal of "data or information" the courts might exempt malfunctions in connected infrastructure from liability altogether. This exemption would occur if the digital infrastructure is categorized in this context as "data" devices rather than "personal" or "real property."[112]

---

[109] Tex. Civ. Prac. & Rem. Code § 101.060(a)(2).

[110] In the case of destruction of the signal or device by third parties, the government must receive "actual" notice; this "actual notice" includes a "subjective awareness of fault" that goes well beyond the collection of data or even the results of a safety inspection. *TxDOT v. Anderson*, WL 186868, at *4 (Tex. App. Tyler, 2008).

[111] *See, e.g., Alvarado v. Lubbock*, 685 S.W.2d 646, 649 (Tex. 1985) (several pieces of evidence from other police citations revealing that the city knew of the discrepancy between the posted speed limit, and the speed limit authorized by ordinance was enough to cause an issue of material fact), *State v. Gonzalez*, 82 S.W.3d 322, 329-330 (Tex. 2002) (city did not have actual notice that stop sign disappeared, because even though it knew the stop sign was prone to being stolen the city had just replaced the sign), *City of Midland v. Sullivan*, 33 S.W.3d 1, 12 (Tex. App. El Paso 2000), pet. Dismissed, (city had notice of defective traffic condition by way of faded pavement markings).

[112] *See* Tx. Transp. Code § 101.021; See also *Univ. of Tex. Med. Branch v. York*, 871 S.W.2d 175, 178-179 (Tex. 1994) (holding that information is an "abstract concept, lacking corporeal, physical or palpable qualities," and thus intangible); *Univ. of Tex.*

Roadway Maintenance

AVs may also present additional liability risks to TxDOT and municipalities with respect to their road maintenance responsibilities. AVs could alter the current liability landscape in many ways, including:

- *Special defects on the roadways, such as excavations and roadway obstructions.*
  These obstructions can lead to potential liability of governmental entities if these defects are not addressed in a reasonable way—e.g., with signage, fencing, etc. (§ 101.060(c)).[113] The capabilities of AVs to detect these defects may differ from non-automated vehicles, leading to a different set of required signals for AVs. TxDOT and other governmental entities responsible for these special defects may need to develop best practices for meeting their obligation of reasonable care with respect to AVs that rely on sensors.

Health Sci. Ctr. v. Dickerson, Tex. App. LEXIS 1889, *19 (Tex. App. Houston [14th Dist.] 2014,) ("[T]he use of computers, telephones or records to collect and communicate information is not a use of tangible personal property under [the Tort Claims Act,]" and "cannot provide the basis for a waiver of immunity under the [Act]."); *Dear v. City of Irving*, 902 S.W.2d 731 (Tex. App. Austin, 1995), writ denied, ("The Supreme Court has specifically held that the Tort Claims Act does not eliminate governmental immunity for injuries resulting from the misuse of information."); *Axtell v. Univ. of Tex. at Austin*, 69 S.W.3d 261, 263 (Tex. App. Austin, 2002) ("The tangible personal property exception of the Act does not encompass an injury resulting from the disclosure of confidential information, however that information is transmitted.")

[113] "A special defect" under § 101.060(c) is "an excavation or roadway obstruction [that is a] present... unexpected and unusual danger to ordinary users of roadways." *State v. Rodriguez*, 985 S.W.2d 83, 85 (Tex. 1999). *See also Morse v. State*, 905 S.W.2d 470, 475 (Tex. App. Beaumont 1995), writ denied, holding that ten-inch drop-off along shoulder that prevented car's left wheels from re-entering the roadway once they had slipped off was a special defect; *see, e.g., State Dep't of Highways v. Kitchen*, 867 S.W.2d 784, 786 (Tex. 1993) holding that ice on bridge during winter was not a special defect because it is not unexpected or unusual.

- *Differing vulnerabilities with regard to road repair.*
AVs may have the capacity to learn of and avoid certain types of road defects, such as potholes, using digital information on landforms that far exceeds the abilities of human drivers. Conversely, there are some roadway hazards that may stump AVs but are easily avoided by human operators. Blowing debris or other visual obstructions that are not real impediments could lead to considerable delays and inconveniences for AVs but not for non-automated vehicles.

Cumulatively, TxDOT may face twice the maintenance burden, or at least a more extensive maintenance challenge, in a world of mixed vehicles where hazards are perceived differently. Moreover, the standards for reasonableness may become more of a moving target, particularly for hazards that are unique to AVs.

Implications of Liability Challenges for Insurance
At least some insurance companies predict that the effects of AVs on their net payouts and profits may ultimately be a wash. Insured AV drivers may face fewer crashes, but the cost of this vehicle—when there is a crash—may offset the reduced crash rate since the vehicle's replacement/repair value is likely to be greater than the cost of an average non-automated vehicle.[114] At best, the insurance industry seems to believe that the financial gains from insuring AVs is currently uncertain.[115]

Insurance companies are also reportedly wary of the increased costs of crash litigation as AVs become more integrated on roadways. As discussed above, these increased litigation costs result from novel product liability claims against the manufacturers that may become commonplace in crashes caused in part by a AV.[116] Insurance companies may seek to circumvent these costs by altering their contractual arrangements or by devising other methods to limit the

---

[114] Swiss Re Centre for Global Dialogue, *The Autonomous Car 2015: Mapping the Road Ahead for the Re/Insurance Industry*, (Oct. 5, 2015), http://cgd.swissre.com /topics/The_autonomous_car_2015.html.

[115] Insurance Info. Inst., *Self-Driving Cars and Insurance*, http://www.iii.org/issue-update/self-driving-cars-and-insurance.

[116] *Id.*

costs of crash litigation in the future.[117]

Finally, insurance companies are likely to take advantage of the ability of AVs to store and share data.[118] "Because connected vehicles provide rich sources of information about both vehicles and drivers, automobile insurance companies have taken a [particularly] keen interest in connected vehicles and the data they generate".[119] This data will not only be central in resolving responsibility in crashes, but may also be available to insurers in setting premiums for individual drivers.

e. Privacy and Security

One of the most significant policy challenges facing AVs is ensuring the appropriate level of privacy and security for consumers. Privacy and security are relatively new social issues and there is not a coherent legal infrastructure in place to manage them. The information-intensive features of AVs raise unresolved issues: how much data will be collected and/or recorded within the vehicle, who will "own" or have access to the data, and the resulting implications for personal privacy of users.[120] The combination of technological uncertainties and legal instability presents challenges that are particularly acute for states at the cutting edge of integrating this new

---

[117] *ITS Int'l, Motor insurance for autonomous vehicles 'will shift from drivers to OEMs*, ITS INTERNATIONAL, http://www.itsinternational.com/categories/location-based-syste ms/news/motor-insurance-for-autonomous-vehicles-will-shift-from-drivers-to-oems/ (October 2015).

[118] Leslie Scism, *State Farm is there: As You Drive*. THE WALL STREET JOURNAL: MARKETS, (Aug. 4, 2013), http://www.wsj.com/articles/SB10001424127887323 420604578647950497541958; James Anderson et al., *Autonomous Vehicle Technology: A Guide for Policymakers*, RAND, 94 (2014).

[119] Dorothy Glancy, *Sharing the Road: Smart Transportation Infrastructure*, 41 FORDHAM URB. L. J. 1617, 1647 (2014).

[120] Anderson et al., *Autonomous Vehicle Technology: A Guide For Policymakers*, 94 RAND: Santa Monica (Cal. 2014).

technology.

This section provides a very brief summary of the factual backdrop and then considers how the privacy and security issues are being treated under current law in Texas and nationally.

i. Privacy Concerns

There is widespread consensus that AVs will pose threats to traditional understandings of individual privacy. While there are risks to the disclosure of personal identifying information, the bulk of concerns are related to risks posed by having personal information collected and used—generally to the consumer's detriment—by manufacturers, insurers, and others. A great deal of data on the location, movement, habits, and other features of drivers will become available in a connected system and could even be recorded and potentially accessed in AVs that are self-contained.[121] One set of authors conclude that "[e]ven if this data is scrubbed of unique individual identifying markers, for instance VIN-numbers, or IP- or MAC- addresses, data-mining techniques will almost certainly be able to reconstruct personal identifying information about particular vehicles and by extension their regulator occupants".[122]

AVs that rely on infrastructure or vehicle communications will present the greatest risk of loss of private information,[123] particularly if the user cannot turn off sharing to third parties. The operating mechanism of these vehicles is premised on sharing information with other vehicles and/infrastructure in a type of data cloud. Moreover, information on the movement and operation of vehicles, particularly in connected systems, may also need to be stored and analyzed to improve the system. "A new car may have more than 145 actuators and 75 sensors, which produce more than 25GB of data per hour. The

---

[121] Chris Woodyard and O'Donnell Jayne, *Your Car Already Collects a Lot of Data about Your Driving and May Soon Collect Much More*, USA TODAY, (March 2013); Frank Markus, *Your Car's Contribution to the Big Data Cloud*, MOTOR TREND (July 2013); Dorothy Glancy, *Privacy in Autonomous Vehicles*, 52 SANTA CLARA LAW REVIEW 1171-1238 (2012).

[122] William Kohler and Alex Colbert-Taylor, *Current Law and Potential Legal Issues Pertaining to Automated, Autonomous and Connected Vehicles*, 31 SANTA CLARA HIGH TECH. L. J. 120-121 (2015).

[123] Dorothy Glancy, *Sharing the Road: Smart Transportation Infrastructure*, 41 FORDHAM URB. L.J. 1617 (2014).

data is analyzed by more than 70 onboard computers to ensure safe and comfortable travel".[124] In one of the most rigorous analyses of privacy and security risks associated with connected systems, Prof. Glancy identifies at least five distinct features of AVs that present particular risks to privacy.[125] The figure below illustrates the various data components in V2V technology.[126]

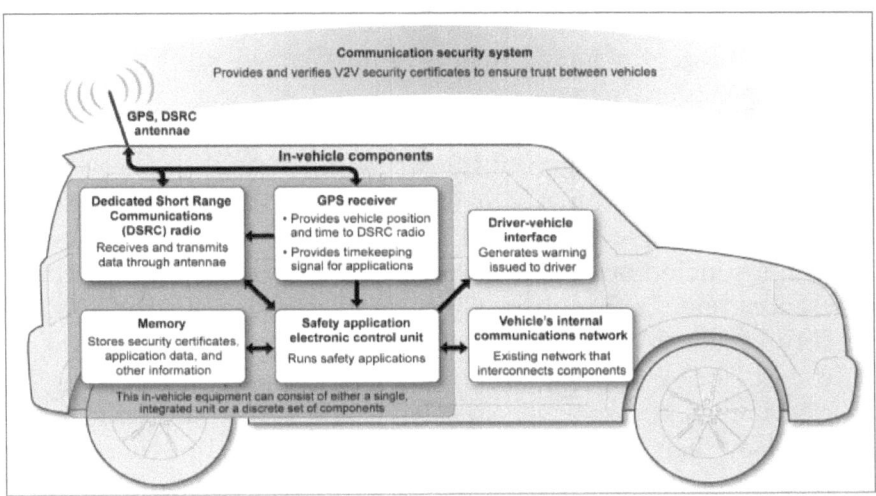

Even for self-contained AVs, privacy can be compromised in potentially significant ways. One of the most common technologies in place to record information about occupants and vehicle patterns are EDRs. EDRs, like flight recorders, are programmed to collect data on the vehicle and occupant information shortly before an impact or

---

[124] Max Glaskin, *Safe and Secure*, VISION ZERO INTERNATIONAL, 40 (June 2014).

[125] Dorothy Glancy, *Sharing the Road: Smart Transportation Infrastructure*, 41 FORDHAM URB. L.J. 1617, 1635, 2639-2640 (2014).

[126] *Intelligence Transportation Systems: Vehicle-to-Vehicle Technologies Expected to Offer Safety Benefits, but a Variety of Deployment Challenges Exist*, US GOV. ACCOUNTABILITY OFFICE, 12 (2013), https://www.gao.gov/assets/660/658709.pdf.

crash. EDRs are voluntarily installed in the majority of vehicles under production.[127]

A still greater imposition on personal privacy will likely arise from the development of various information-intensive devices built into or used by the vehicle, including entertainment systems, onboard computers, and other infrastructure.[128] Manufacturers have already obtained patents for in-car advertising, and the potential for targeted advertising of individuals using this data is generating widespread attention.[129] Route planning may also be affected this personal data. For example, third parties may be capable of rerouting individuals past specific physical locations based on a history of the owner's impulse buying and unplanned stops.

Personal data on AV drivers can be collected in a variety of ways. Some of these devices will collect information on the vehicle occupants, including their location, near misses, entertainment preferences, etc., and transfer that information to manufacturers and possibly others in real time. Other information may be stored and retrieved in the vehicle itself.

Manufacturers have signaled their intent to collect data produced by their AVs. A telematics service subscription agreement by Tesla, for example, reserves the right to obtain information about the vehicle, its operation, accidents, and the operators' use of the vehicle and services.[130] While the Tesla agreement makes clear that data will be collected, users may not fully appreciate the extent that their privacy could be compromised. The agreement allows the company to collect the following:

(x) information about the vehicle and its operation, including without limitation, vehicle identification

---

[127] To ensure the usefulness of EDRs in litigation and related matters, NHTSA requires standardized minimum features for these voluntarily installed EDRs in all vehicles built on or after Sept. 1, 2010. 49 C.F.R. § 563.

[128] Chris Woodyard and O'Donnell Jayne. *Your Car Already Collects a Lot of Data about Your Driving and May Soon Collect Much More*, USA TODAY (March 25, 2013).

[129] William Kohler and Alex Colbert-Taylor, *Current Law and Potential Legal Issues Pertaining to Automated, Autonomous and Connected Vehicles*, 31 SANTA CLARA HIGH TECH. L. J. 122 (2015).

[130] Bryant Walker-Smith, *Proximity-Driven Liability*, 102 GEORGETOWN L. J. 1777, 1788-1791 (2014).

number, location information, speed and distance information, battery use management information, battery charging history, battery deterioration information, electrical system functions, software version information, and other data to assist in identifying and analyzing the performance of your Tesla EV;

(y) information about your use of the Services; and

(z) data about accidents involving your Tesla EV.[131]

> Prof. Walker-Smith also notes that under the agreement, the customer "owns" these data but "grant[s] to Tesla a worldwide, royalty free, fully paid, transferable, assignable, sublicensable (through multiple tiers), perpetual license to collect, analyze and use" them. These data may help the company to check, maintain, analyze the performance of, and help in the maintenance of the vehicle; "research, evaluate and improve" its technology; "comply with the law and any and all legal requirements," including valid enforcement requests and orders; "protect the rights, property, or safety of" the company, the customer, or others; and "perform market research for Tesla's own purposes," a list that "is not meant to be exhaustive."[132]

Governmental entities can also collect personal information on operators driving on highways, even without a connected infrastructure and V2I communications. In the State of Texas, for example, governmental entities have collected drivers' information with Bluetooth readers and other easily available tools.[133] In the

---

[131] *Id.*, at 1789 (for example, the deployment of airbags).

[132] *Id.*, at 1790.

[133] *TxDOT Tracks Drivers to Mine Data Without their Consent*, EXAMINER (June 2, 2015). http://www.examiner.com/article/txdot-tracks-drivers-to-mine-data-without-the

future, with V2V and V2I possibilities just on the horizon, the data will not only become more readily available, but in some cases, extensive data collection will be necessary to direct traffic safely. While it is possible that the connectivity equipment could use the data only in real time, without storing it, this less intrusive option may prove inadequate for purposes of accident reports, technological capabilities, etc. Thus, TxDOT and other entities may find themselves faced with databases of consumer travel habits that contain some private information, regardless of their best efforts to avoid this scenario.

Alongside more immediate privacy concerns associated with data storage and use is the government's own routing decisions that may be viewed as "infring[ing] on the individual right to privacy, including the right to physical autonomy".[134] The government could use routing to bypass protests or provide some drivers with more rapid routes than others. The latter possibility is particularly worrisome if faster routes are reserved for drivers with a higher status or a willingness to pay for such a privilege.

The seemingly inevitable future of AV technologies is one in which expectations of privacy from private and public entities are more limited. Yet the point at which privacy and/or security interests are being violated, and the appropriate state reaction to unrestricted consumer data collection, is open to debate. The laws governing this area are still developing, offering little guidance in the interim.

ii. The Law Addressing Privacy Concerns Involving AVs

Current Texas law unevenly places restrictions on the ability of governments or private entities to collect, tabulate, sell, or even share data on individual driving habits. Meanwhile, the collection and use of remaining information that nevertheless charts the location, use, accidents, etc., of a vehicle and its operator appears largely unprotected under Texas law.

Protection of Sensitive Information

The laws in the State of Texas provide citizens with strong

---

ir-consent.

[134] William Kohler and Alex Colbert-Taylor, *Current Law and Potential Legal Issues Pertaining to Automated, Autonomous and Connected Vehicles*, 31 SANTA CLARA HIGH TECH. L. J. 99 (2015).

protection from third-party access to sensitive information and information contained in Electronic Data Recorders (EDRs). EDRs provide a particularly good reference point since much of the data collected in EDRs may not be terribly different from the types of data that can be collected through other devices installed in a AV as previously discussed. In Texas, any governmental or private access to EDR data is generally off-limits except in one of the following four narrow categories:

(1) On court order;
(2) With the consent of the owner for any purpose, including for the purpose of diagnosing, servicing, or repairing the motor vehicle;
(3) For the purpose of improving motor vehicle safety, including for medical research on the human body's reaction to motor vehicle accidents, if the identity of the owner or driver of the vehicle is not disclosed in connection with the retrieved information; or
(4) For the purpose of determining the need for or facilitating emergency medical response in the event of a motor vehicle accident.[135]

These protections of privacy in Texas are reinforced by other laws that protect other sensitive information. Under Texas Transportation Code §§ 371.001 & 371.051, license plate data collected on toll roads are not allowed to be collected or shared except for very limited, official purposes. Motor vehicle records also cannot be subject to the State's Open Records Act, thus providing some privacy protection for the release of driver's license and registration information or other personal identification information.[136] The federal Driver Privacy Protection Act reinforces Texas's law. It

---

[135] TEX. TRANSP. CODE ANN. § 547.615(c).

[136] TEX. TRANSP. CODE ANN. § 552.130(a).

prohibits state motor vehicle offices from disclosing photos, names, addresses, telephone numbers, as well as medical or disability information, with narrow exceptions.[137] Several federal statutes also protect consumer privacy in ways that would seem to at least preclude unauthorized interceptions of signals from AVs.[138]

Private businesses are also prohibited from allowing "sensitive personal information" of individuals to be accessed by third parties without consent of the owner.[139] "Sensitive personal information" for purposes of the Act includes specifically enumerated information that consists of medical information, Social Security information, drivers' license information, or credit card information. In cases of a breach or disclosure, businesses are also required to notify individuals that their sensitive personal information has been accessed illegally.[140]

Limitations in Current Laws with Respect to Privacy and AVs

While it is conceivable that data collected by manufacturers, the government, and others in a AV system would include some "sensitive" information under Texas law, personal information in the AV context likely includes a wealth of other personal information that does not fall into this "sensitive information" list but is nonetheless considered private.[141] The statute does not appear to reach this information. Accordingly, if the Original Equipment Manufacturers (OEMs), software companies, or insurers install data chips, road cameras, or other mechanisms to collect information on individual drivers outside of the EDR, there appear to be no explicit legal prohibitions, restraints, or even requirements of disclosures for these various avenues of information access under Texas law. While consumers may have claims under contract law or tort law, even these

---

[137] 18 U.S.C. § 2721. Note that the Act "prevents private actions against states." *Travis v. Reno*, 163 F.3d 1000, 1006-1007 (7th Cir. 1998); *Downing v. Globe Direct LLC*, 806 F. Supp. 2d 461 (D. Mass. 2011 *aff'd*), 682 F.3d 18 (1st Cir. 2012) ("Congress, moreover, has not abrogated the States' sovereign immunity with respect to private DPPA lawsuits.")

[138] Dorothy Glancy, *Sharing the Road: Smart Transportation Infrastructure*, 41 FORDHAM URB. L.J. 1617 (2014).

[139] TEX. TRANSP. CODE ANN. § 521.052.

[140] TEX. TRANSP. CODE ANN. § 521.053.

[141] TEX. TRANSP. CODE ANN. § 521.002(2).

prophylactic private remedies are likely to be incomplete at best.

Additionally, even with respect to "sensitive personal information," there appears to be no prohibitions for private businesses in legal possession of the data to use it for internal commercial purposes (e.g., targeted marketing strategies). The law precludes "unlawful" use and "disclosure" to third parties, but it does not appear to prohibit commercial use of data for purposes of product development, advertising, or pricing and sales.[142] Federal legislation does not fill in these gaps in state protection.[143]

Insurance companies may also be able to gain access to this non-sensitive information under current law, perhaps through sales arrangements with the OEMs or others. Through a much more fine-grained understanding of the drivers' habits (e.g., speeding, nighttime driving; handoffs; etc.), insurance companies can develop much more accurate policies to govern their clients or avoid some drivers altogether. In fact, insurance companies are currently recruiting volunteer policy-holders to use devices to track their habits, thereby reducing their premiums.[144] While this activity is voluntary, it signals the insurers' great interest and use for this personal information that falls outside of the narrower radius of "sensitive personal information."

In contrast to private parties, the Fourth Amendment does impose constraints on governmental entities' ability to collect private information on drivers.[145] It is not clear at what point at which those protections might be triggered in cases where individualized personal

---

[142] TEX. TRANSP. CODE ANN. tit. 7B, §§ 521.051-.053 (1995).

[143] GENERAL ACCOUNTING OFFICE, GAO-12-903, *Mobile Device Location Data: Additional Federal Action Could Help Protect Consumer Privacy* (2012).

[144] Dorothy Glancy, *Sharing the Road: Smart Transportation Infrastructure*, 41 FORDHAM URB. L.J. 1617 (2014). Leslie Scism, *State Farm is there: As You Drive,* THE WALL STREET JOURNAL: MARKETS (August 4, 2013).

[145] Dorothy Glancy, *Sharing the Road: Smart Transportation Infrastructure*, 41 FORDHAM URB. L.J., 1617 (2014).

data is collected or analyzed by the government beyond the infrastructure needs of V2I and V2V.[146] It seems likely that the routine management and oversight of an AV system would not trigger these constitutional protections since they do not have surveillance or the "search" of individuals as their purpose and may not provide identifying information.[147] Even in cases in which the data is used by the government in investigating the conduct of an individual driver, however, some have argued that the government may be allowed to access this data outside of the Fourth Amendment through a rigorous licensing program that provides the government with a type of implied consent to the information.[148] The scope of the government's access to the information, however, deserves considerably more analysis, which in turn will depend on a better understanding of the types of information and access that will be available in AVs in the future.[149]

In contrast, municipalities and state agencies—outside of constitutional violations—are immune from private tort claims from those whose information was shared, even in cases where sensitive information is disclosed in violation of Texas law. As discussed earlier, state agencies and municipalities may be immune from suit with respect to negligent acts that involve the disclosure of information, including presumably confidential information. Texas, in contrast to several other states, appears to have no requirements that it notify persons if or when their data has been breached, even as a result of the State's negligence.[150]

---

[146] William Kohler and Alex Colbert-Taylor, *Current Law and Potential Legal Issues Pertaining to Automated, Autonomous and Connected Vehicles*, 31 SANTA CLARA HIGH TECH. L. J. 99 (2015).

[147] Dorothy Glancy, *Sharing the Road: Smart Transportation Infrastructure*, 41 FORDHAM URB. L.J., 1617 (2014).

[148] Rachael Roseman, *When Autonomous Vehicles Take over the Road: Rethinking the Expansion of the Fourth Amendment in a Technology-driven World*, 20 RICH. L.J & TECH. 3 (2014).

[149] Dorothy Glancy, *Sharing the Road: Smart Transportation Infrastructure*, 41 FORDHAM URB. L.J., 1617 (2014), Sarah Aue Palodichuk, *Driving into the Digital Age: How SDVs Will Change the Law and Its Enforcement*, 16 MINN. J.L. SCI. & TECH. 827 (2015).

[150] Michael A. Froomkin, *Government Data Breaches*, 24 BERKELEY TECH. L.J. 1019 (2009).

Texas law not only immunizes the government but may also actively require agencies to disclose all unprotected information, even if it identifies citizens, through the Open Records Act. Protected information includes that information expressly prohibited from disclosure under § 552.130(a) and federal law; only "information considered to be confidential by law, either constitutional, statutory, or by judicial decision" is exempt from disclosure.[151] Thus, to the extent that the State collects, processes, stores, or otherwise is in possession of additional information on individual vehicles (e.g., make, model, speed, location and time), it may be required to share this information upon request.[152]

Legal Developments Outside of Texas

There is proposed legislation at the federal level that specifically addresses the risks to consumer privacy as a result of new AV technology. In July 2015, Senator Ed Markey of Massachusetts introduced the "Spy Car Act of 2015".[153] Senator Markey's bill did not make it through committee, but the bill signals Congressional interest in addressing the privacy (and hacking) issues associated with AVs (U.S. Congress 2015). The proposed law would, among other things, direct NHTSA to promulgate a rule that protects against unauthorized access to information regarding the owner, speed of the vehicle, data stored in the car, etc., and also require cars manufactured

---

[151] TEX. TRANSP. CODE ANN. tit. 7B, § 552.101 (1995).

[152] The courts impose privacy exceptions in some cases, for example, if the information sought to be disclosed is highly embarrassing and has no public value. *See, e.g., Indus. Found. of S. v. Tex. Indus. Accident Bd.*, 540 S.W.2d 668, 685 (Tex. 1976).

[153] Security and Privacy in Your Car Act of 2015 (Spy Car Act, 2015). S. 1806, 114th Cong. (2015), https://www.congress.gov/bill/114th-congress/senate-bill/1806/all-info. The bill follows President Obama's broader call for a "Consumer Privacy Bill of Rights" in 2012, which attempts to provide protections for consumer privacy across a broad range of areas; *see* William Kohler and Alex Colbert-Taylor, *Current Law and Potential Legal Issues Pertaining to Automated, Autonomous and Connected Vehicles*, 31 SANTA CLARA HIGH TECH. L. J. 99 (2015).

with accessible data to be capable of reporting and intercepting unauthorized access. The bill also directs NHTSA to conduct a rulemaking to require a "cyber dashboard" to inform consumers about the extent of protection of their privacy beyond a narrow set of sensitive data. Finally, the bill directs the FTC to conduct a rulemaking that would require that purchasers be notified of data access and collection on their activities; to provide them the option to decline this collection and retention (except for critical safety and post-accident information); and to prohibit manufacturers from using the collected information without the consent of the owner or lessee.

At the regulatory level, both NHTSA and the FTC have taken a focused interest in restricting hacking and intrusions on the privacy of consumer data in AVs.[154] The FTC, for example, already engages in some oversight of this new market through its regulation of unfair or deceptive trade practices, which could include unjustified invasions of consumer privacy.[155] The National Institute of Standards and Technology has also developed best practice standards to manage cybersecurity vulnerability which provide at least some initial protection against the worst security breaches.

Only one state appears to have passed a law to address the consumer privacy related to AVs—the State of California. California requires that a "manufacturer of the autonomous technology installed on a vehicle shall provide a written disclosure to the purchaser of an AV that describes what information is collected by an autonomous technology equipped on the vehicle."[156] Since the law is only 3 years old, it is too early to predict its implications for manufacturers of AVs sold in the State or even sold outside the state. The California law has also been criticized by consumer groups as taking too soft a stance on the ability of OEMs and others to collect private information.[157]

---

[154] Dorothy Glancy, *Sharing the Road: Smart Transportation Infrastructure*, 41 FORDHAM URB. L.J. 1617 (2014). William Kohler and Alex Colbert-Taylor, *Current Law and Potential Legal Issues Pertaining to Automated, Autonomous and Connected Vehicles*, 31 SANTA CLARA HIGH TECH. L.J. 99 (2015).

[155] Dorothy Glancy, *Sharing the Road: Smart Transportation Infrastructure*, 41 FORDHAM URB. L.J. 1617 (2014).

[156] CALIF. VEH. CODE ANN. Chapter 570, Division 16.6. § 38750(h) (2012).

[157] Danielle Lenth, *Chapter 570: Paving the Way for Autonomous Vehicles*, 44 MCGEORGE L. REV. 787 (2013).

Finally, with respect to government-related disclosures or breaches of confidential information in regards to its citizens, roughly half the States require by legislation that a governmental entity notify persons of the breach of confidentiality in cases where the government was the cause of the breach.[158] Out of these states, only a few allow suit to be brought by an individual against the state if it does not report the breach in a timely manner. In Louisiana, for example, the fine is not to exceed $5,000 for each violation, while in New Hampshire the plaintiff receives damages that "the court deems necessary and proper." Agencies in states that do not allow individuals to bring suit can still face fines or suits from the state's Attorney General or other centralized authority.

In these various laws, there appear to be two general approaches to the privacy challenges arising with respect to AVs. One approach limits or even prohibits the use of certain technological mechanisms for data collection. The second approach requires manufacturers and software developers to disclose the nature of the information they can gather on consumers in an accessible way. Despite their different institutional mechanisms of oversight, running through both approaches is the premise that without some early legal oversight of the privacy-related features of the technology, the "genie will be out of the bottle." OEMs, software developers, and perhaps even insurers that become accustomed to and develop financial plans premised on access to private data will both resist and face high costs in altering their plans if that easy data access is constrained later, down the road.

iii. Security Concerns and the Existing Law

A related but very different risk from the data-intensive operations of AVs is the potential for security breaches that endanger life, financial information, and other private information through criminal hacking of the data and infrastructure. Some of the more

---

[158] *See, generally,* Michael A. Froomkin, *Symposium: Security Breach Notification Six Years Later: Government Data Breaches*, 24 BERKELEY TECH. L.J. 1019 (2009).

frightening scenarios include a terrorist who is able to hack into a CV system and direct all cars to drive off bridges into the water or crash into one another.[159]

Those familiar with the technological systems concede that hacking risks are not trivial and that AV systems cannot be designed in ways that are completely free of hacking risks. Stop buttons may have the potential to electronically disengage vehicles, allowing some operator control over the worst types of data-hacking. Yet the ability to completely stop terrorist manipulation of transportation systems and other risks of hacking into data systems remain a concern.

Another set of scenarios involve using self-driving cars remotely as bomb-depositors or drug-traffickers. In this security breach, the larger system is not hacked;[160] rather, a single car itself or series of cars are remotely controlled for criminal purposes. Since anonymity is difficult to achieve, criminal commentators are more sanguine about the ability of the criminal system to sanction these types of uses.[161] Still, the remote use of AVs provides a new tool in the arsenal for mass attacks that will need to be factored into the larger criminal justice equation.

While not specifically tailored to the hacking of AVs, there are several federal laws that appear to penalize these attempts, including the Computer Fraud and Abuse Act, the Digital Millennium Copyright Act, the Wiretap Act, and the USA Patriot Act.[162] Texas Penal Code (Title 7, Chapter 33) also provides anticipatory deterrence against hacking. "A person commits an offense if the person knowingly accesses a computer, computer network, or computer system without the effective consent of the owner".[163] The penalty is dependent upon the aggregate amount of money involved .[164] The

---

[159] Frank Douma and Sarah Aue Palodichuk, *"But Officer, it wasn't my fault ... the car did it!"*: *Criminal Liability Issues Created by Autonomous Vehicles*, 52 SANTA CLARA L. REV. 1157, 1166 (2012).

[160] *Id.*

[161] *Id.*

[162] William Kohler and Alex Colbert-Taylor, *Current Law and Potential Legal Issues Pertaining to Automated, Autonomous and Connected Vehicles*, 31 SANTA CLARA HIGH TECH L. J. 99 (2015).

[163] TEX. PEN. CODE ANN. § 33.02(a).

[164] *Id.* at § 33.02(b-2).

aggregate amount consists of the "benefits obtained and the losses incurred because of the fraud, harm, or alteration" .[165] A violation of this statute ranges from a Class B misdemeanor to a felony of the first degree .[166] If the hacker obtains the identifying information of another, the violation is upgraded to the next level felony regardless of the amount in question.[167]

VI.   RECOMMENDATIONS ON TEXAS' INCREMENTAL APPROACH

A non-interventionist approach to integrating AVs onto state roadways takes each legal and policy challenge as it arises, resisting government action unless absolutely necessary. Through this type of hands-off approach, governmental resources and public attention are reserved for the very worst problems. There are also fewer risks of unintended consequences from governmental policies.

Nevertheless, once Texas roads are open to the unrestricted use of automated vehicles, the likelihood of future conflicts and questions between this new technology and the existing, somewhat outmoded legal system become inevitable. More important for our purposes, though, at least some of these future questions can be predicted well in advance. In this evolving legal climate, even the most devoted non-interventionist may find it beneficial to address some issues before they arise to limit disputes and avoidable accidents in the future.

Thus, for a State like Texas, what issues might benefit from this type of anticipatory legal action? Rather than answer this policy-laden question, we map out the challenges that seem likely to arise in the future, leaving it to policymakers to decide when or whether some advanced planning and legal action is beneficial. Since public support for AVs will likely be tied to the public's perception of its safety and

---

[165] *Id.* at § 33.02(c).

[166] *Id.* at § 33.02(b-2).

[167] *Id.*

trustworthiness, a successful non-interventionist will benefit from undertaking anticipatory legal moves that resolve the most significant conflicts and controversies before they occur.

In this final section, we offer a map of issues for this forward-thinking non-interventionist policymaker to consider. For Texas and other similarly-minded states, we sort out a number of various issues and challenges that lie ahead. The matrix below provides some of the most general issues. Issues of concern within each column are ordered roughly by their immediacy (bold are more immediate while italics are particularly non-urgent). Yet, regardless of the timeframe, we believe that ultimately all of the items in matrix below would seem to warrant at least some consideration as states develop regimes to facilitate the integration of AVs in the states.

Matrix on Topic Area for C/AV Policies in Texas

Safety on the Highway: Section 6.2	Liability: Section 6.4	State Responsibilities/Liability: Section 6.5	Privacy and Security: Section 6.6	Advance Broader Public Goals in C/AV Innovation: Section 6.7
Clarify Responsibility for Violations	Streamline Simple Crash Claim	**Clarify what Constitutes 'notice' for malfunction in digital traffic**	Improve Consumer Information	*Collect reports/information on C/AV*
Vehicle Registration/ Certification	Address other difficult liability issues	**Exempt license plates and other identifiable information from disclosure under the State Open Records Act**	Restrict the sharing or sale of consumer information in C/AVs to third parties	*Encourage greater innovation on wide-ranging public benefit*
Added Operator Requirements License Plate Tags or other markers		Require State Agencies to alert individuals when their privacy is breached	Criminalize hacking	
Rules for intensive uses (e.g., truck platoons)			*Encourage innovation in cyber security*	

a. Ensuring the Safety of AV Testing and Deployment on Public Highways

Although AVs promise to provide heightened safety, the newness of the technology and public concern have prompted several states to engage in the oversight of basic safety features of the emerging technology as it enters public roadways. Despite Texas's hands-off stance with regard to regulating this technology, there are several safety issues that may warrant consideration in the future.

i. Testing and Deployment of AVs on Texas Highways

Over the last ten years, the leading view has taken the position that states should regulate the use of AVs at both the testing and the full deployment stage. Specifically, the ULC Subcommittee recommends a uniform state act that "expressly prohibit[s] any use (including testing) of autonomous vehicles on public roads except as expressly permitted by the uniform act".[168] NHTSA also recommends specific assurances from persons seeking to test vehicles before allowing that testing.[169] Several states have also required agency approval for testing and deployment of AVs. Nevada requires: added insurance in order to test an AV in the state; proof that one or more of the vehicles has been driven a combined minimum of 10,000 miles in autonomous mode; a demonstration of the technology to the DMV; and a demonstration that its technology can be driven in the geographic locations designated for testing.[170] California requires identifying information to be provided to the DMV for each vehicle being tested.[171] Both Nevada and California require a license or permit for testing as well.[172]

By contrast, Texas currently has legislatively rejected this approach in passing SB 2205.[173] Under its amended law, AVs are officially legal on Texas highways. As a result, driverless vehicles with operators aboard may enter the public highways without notification to TxDOT or the Texas DMV. Yet in light of this unrestricted approach, several additional requirements may be useful or even necessary.

ii. Vehicle Registration of AVs

Under existing Texas law, AVs are treated as other vehicles provided they comply with federal standards, are equipped with data recorders (which are required by federal law), are insured, and are registered and titled.[174] Yet the DMV mandatory safety inspection for

---

[168] *STUDY COMM. ON STATE REGULATIONS OF DRIVERLESS CARS, UNIF. LAW COMM'N, REVISED REPORT OF THE SUBCOMMITTEE ON ISSUES 5 (2014).*

[169] NAT'L HIGHWAY TRAFFIC SAFETY ADMIN., PRELIMINARY STATEMENT OF POLICY CONCERNING AUTOMATED VEHICLES, 1, 11 (2013), (such as a demonstration of the technology in the past and a plan for minimizing risks during testing) https://www.nhtsa.gove/staticfiles/rulemaking/pdf/Automated_Vehicles_Poli cy.pdf.

[170] NEV. ADMIN. CODE § 482A.110(3) (2017).

[171] CAL. CODE REGS. tit. 13, § 227.16 (2017).

[172] CAL. CODE REGS. tit. 13, § 227.04 (2017); NEV. ADMIN. CODE § 482A.110(1) (2017).

[173] *See*, S.B. 2205 Leg., 85th Sess. § 1 (Tx. 2017).

vehicle registrations does not appear to take into account the possibility that a vehicle has automated features.

Yet there are several safety features that are unique to AVs that both the ULC Subcommittee and NHTSA, as well as some states, believe are essential to regulate or at least track. Moreover, since some of these elements are not required by federal law, they will not otherwise be included in the vehicle unless the manufacturer does so voluntarily:

1. Device to disengage the automated system,[175]
2. Device to indicate whether the vehicle is operating in autonomous mode, or
3. System to warn operator of failure.

For AVs, annual checks or online certifications of regular updates to the vehicle may also be valuable. Particularly in the early stages of automation, it is likely that the software and recall of vehicles may be prevalent as the technology evolves.[176] Owners will need to take responsibility for ensuring this is completed. Texas may insist on evidence that owners are fulfilling these responsibilities on an annual basis.

Regardless of the additional requirements, the State may benefit from using the vehicle registration requirement as a way to at least develop a reporting system for the number and types of AVs in use on highways. Such identification could be beneficial to law enforcement, accident tracking, highway maintenance priorities, and other areas.

---

[174] TEX. TRANSP. CODE ANN. § 545.454(b).

[175] See, *Study Committee on State Regulation of Driverless Cars, Revised Report of the Subcommittee on Issues: Exhibit A*, UNIFORM LAW COMMISSION SUBCOMMITTEE ON ISSUES, 9, for specifics on the varying requirements http://www.uniform laws.org/Committee.aspx?title=State.

[176] INT'L TRANSP. FORUM, ORG. FOR ECON. CO-OPERATION AND DEV., AUTOMATED AND AUTONOMOUS DRIVING: REGULATION UNDER UNCERTAINTY 29 (2015).

iii. Added Operator Requirements

Under Texas law, there are no additional licensing requirements imposed on operators of AVs, despite the fact that the State acknowledges that some licensed AVs may notify a human operator to take over the driving.[177] This type of "handoff," however, may benefit from added training by the operator. Indeed, some states require added endorsements or training for those wishing to operate an AV.[178] The State of California requires that the driver has undergone training by the manufacturer.[179] Since some vehicles may legally log a "request to intervene" with respect to a human operator.[180] For example, added training for this situation may be warranted to ensure that operators are able to do this novel maneuver safely.

iv. License Plate Tags or Other Indicators of AVs

Several states have enacted, and the ULC recommends, some public marker for AVs, such as a special license plate.[181] This recommendation may be particularly well-placed for the operation of truck platoons on highways. Since the requirement is imposed on owners and occurs during the licensing of the vehicle, this type of requirement would seem to have little to no negative impact on technological innovation or sales of AVs. Indeed, these demarcations could serve as a way to build public confidence and trust and may even boost the market for AVs as they become more commonplace.

v. Targeted Requirements for Intensive Uses of AVs like Truck Platoons

In its incremental H.B. 1791, Texas eliminated the legal obstacle of "following distance" from the operation of truck platoons.

---

[177] S.B. 2205 Leg., 85th Sess. § 2 (Tx. 2017).

[178] Study Committee on State Regulation of Driverless Cars, Revised Report of the Subcommittee on Issues: Exhibit A, UNIFORM LAW COMMISSION SUBCOMMITTEE ON ISSUES, 12 (2014), http://www.uniformlaws.org/Committee.aspx?title=State.

[179] CAL. CODE REGS. tit. 13, § 227.20 (2017).

[180] S.B. 2205 Leg., 85th Sess. (Tx. 2017).

[181] Study Committee on State Regulation of Driverless Cars, Revised Report of the Subcommittee on Issues: Exhibit A, UNIFORM LAW COMMISSION SUBCOMMITTEE ON ISSUES, 11 (2014), http://www.uniformlaws.org/Committee.aspx?title=State.

Without this impediment, platoons can operate freely on Texas highways. To add to this lack of restriction, SB 2205 makes it clear that localities cannot preemptively regulate AVs, including platoons. Yet legalizing platoon transportation in the State raises a series of other questions, some of which may be worth considering in advance. The following regulatory decisions have yet to be made:

- Whether to identify designated lanes and/or roadways pre-approved by TxDOT; platoons could be prohibited on other public highways in the State without advanced permission;
- Size and length requirements, presumably promulgated by TXDOT, that restrict platoon length and the maximum number of units per platoons;
- A cap on the number of platoons allowed on a public road at any given time;
- Passing requirements and restrictions; or
- Time of day rules, minimum speeds, and similar operational requirements.

The more intensive the use of highways by truck platoons, the more necessary it will be for TxDOT to revisit its pavement and bridge design standards. And, in revising these large-scale road features, there will need to be close interaction between TxDOT, the legislature, DMV, Department of Public Safety, and local jurisdictions along platoon routes. Finally, platoons will need to assemble/disassemble (or form and dissolve as directed while enroute to their destination), and the locations for this work ideally should be designated in advance, in locations that are appropriate, safe, and in keeping with the planning done by local governments.

State agencies like TxDOT are well-positioned to anticipate these and other challenges that arise from the use of truck platoons, but many of these challenges fall outside the four corners of the current legal and transportation system. TxDOT can address some of these issues reactively, yet some – engineering restrictions – may deserve more considerate, preemptive attention to stave off any problems that could alarm the public. More anticipatory and holistic attention to these issues may even pay off financially for the State. Federal funding may even be available in the future to support some of this work by TxDOT and other state agencies.[182]

b. Adjustments to Tort and Private Injury Law

The strong consensus among commentators is that tort liability laws should be left undisturbed to the extent possible to allow the flexibility of the common law to adapt to the technological changes presented by AVs.[183] Nevertheless, there are several modest adjustments that may deserve consideration to alleviate some of the most substantial concerns about the integration of AVs into existing tort liability law.

i. Streamlining Simple Crash Claims in AV Litigation

As AVs become more commonplace on highways and are implicated as the cause of crashes, what used to be "simple" crash litigation will necessarily include more complicated product liability claims against manufacturers. There are several approaches that could anticipate and alleviate some of this potential future uncertainty. The approaches could be used in all crashes or only crashes that involve a limited amount of damage (perhaps less than $75,000), since it is the smaller cases that will be most impacted by these more complicated and expensive claims.

First, in deciding cases that involve allegations that the automated features of the vehicle in part caused the crash (thereby implicating the vehicle manufacturer), the Texas courts deciding common law claims could impose a nondelegable duty on the owner/operator consistent with the insurance coverage. Non-delegable duties can be imposed under the common law by courts deciding tort cases.[184] With a non-delegable duty, the owner/operator would be the

---

[182] *See e.g.*, S. 1647, 114th Cong. (2015). (Not passed by proposing targeted funding for smart transportation.)

[183] University of Washington School of Law, Technology Law and Policy Clinic, Autonomous Vehicles Team, *Autonomous Vehicle Law Report and Recommendations to the ULC*, UNIV. OF WASH. SCHOOL OF LAW, 20, https://www.law.washington.edu/Clinics/technology/Reports/AutonomousVehicle.pdf

[184] *See Maloney v. Rath*, 445 P.2d 513, 516 (Cal. 1968) (providing examples of non-delegable duties in common law: "the duty of a condemning agent to protect a severed parcel from damage...the duty of landowners to maintain their property in a reasonably

presumptive responsible parties. While the owner/operator of the AV could engage the vehicle manufacturer and others in a third-party suit for indemnification, a case brought by an outside party could recover damages against only the owner/operator. If greater legal certainty is desired, the Texas legislature could also codify this type of legal responsibility on owners. The overriding goal of this legislative directive is to save accident victims, including TxDOT, from the expense and delay associated with unraveling responsibility among the manufacturer, driver, owner, and software developer, as well as others.

Alternatively, with respect to claims by third-party victims harmed by an AV in automated mode, or perhaps all persons - including owners - the legislature could place the burden of proof on the manufacturer of the AV to establish that the crash was not caused by a defect in the vehicle.[185] . The law could direct that crashes involving AVs be like the rules of fault and product liability in the State of Texas.[186] For example, the OEM will be considered jointly

---

safe condition…to comply with applicable safety ordinances…the duty of employers and suppliers to comply with the safety provisions of the Labor Code....”). A non-delegable duty could be placed on AV operators for the for the criminal misuse of their vehicle, for example, federal courts have placed non-delegable duties on the purchasers of guns for their criminal misuse. See, e.g., *City of Phila. v. Beretta U.S.A. Corp.*, 277 F.3d 415, 426 (3d Cir. 2002) (“Accordingly, we will dismiss plaintiffs' claims that tort liability should be assessed against gun manufacturers when their legally sold, non-defective products are criminally used to injure others.”). See *First Commercial Tr. Co. v. Lorcin Eng'g,* 900 S.W.2d 202, 205 (Ark. 1995) (holding that a firearm manufacturer is not responsible for the criminal misuse of its product); see also *Riordan v. Int'l Armament Corp.*, 477 N.E.2d 1293, 1295 (Ill. App. 1985) (“[T]he distribution of handguns by the defendants-manufacturers was intended for the general public, who presumably can recognize the dangerous consequences in the use of handguns and can assume responsibility for their actions.”)

[185] Volvo Car Group: Global Newsroom, *U.S. Urged to Establish Nationwide Federal Guidelines for Autonomous Driving,* (October 7, 2015), https://www.media.volvocars. com/global/en-gb/media/pressreleases/167975/us-urged-to-establish-nationwide-fede ral-guidelines-for-autonomous-driving, There is some indication that the OEMs themselves may already be accepting this responsibility, although it is not clear if these commitments are legally binding.

responsible with the operator unless the OEM can establish that there was no defect in the vehicle, Given the loss-spreading and low crash rate of AVs, placing this responsibility on the manufacturers may be beneficial in both streamlining liability and creating greater trust throughout the market. The implicit "guarantee" that crashes are rare will give owners an incentive to use the automation, and manufacturers will have an incentive to reduce crashes.[187] If a State licensing and certification program is in place, the placement of responsibility on manufacturers should also require that the AV was properly licensed and legally permitted at the time of the accident.

Although it is much more far-reaching, the State could adopt a no-fault approach to liability for all cars or for AVs exclusively. It could also require alternative dispute resolution or other transaction-cost saving mechanisms for resolving crash responsibility disputes that include at least one AV operating in autonomous mode. For more information on the pros and cons of these more systematic changes to the Texas liability rules, readers are referred to Anderson et al. (2014) and Funkhouser (2013).

The goal of these streamlining devices is to counteract the increased costs of litigation, particularly with respect to smaller scale crashes, associated with AVs. Without some type of anticipatory legislation, crash litigation will become more expensive, particularly for the victims harmed by AVs.

ii. Difficult Liability Issues May Benefit from Legislative Attention

The ULC Subcommittee suggests that states may need legislation to address issues associated with consumer-imposed modifications to vehicles after-market.[188] Several states have already legislated immunity for manufacturers in cases where a third party modifies a AV and those changes, rather than a defect initially present in the vehicle, cause harm.[189] The preliminary analysis in Section 2.4

---

[186] Strict liability on AVs manufacturers, as suggested by some commentators is another option, *see,* David Vladeck, *"Machines Without Principles: Liability Rules and Artificial Intelligence"* 89 WASH. L. REV. 117 (2014).

[187] Dorothy Glancy, *Sharing the Road: Smart Transportation Infrastructure*, 41 FORDHAM URB. L.J. 1617 (2014).

[188] STUDY COMM. ON STATE REGULATIONS OF DRIVERLESS CARS, UNIF. LAW COMM'N, REVISED REPORT OF THE SUBCOMMITTEE ON ISSUES 5 (2014).

suggests that these liability risks may be less significant in Texas; however, legislative codification of common law on this issue would provide added predictability for both manufacturers and those engaged in the modifications.

There are also difficult issues associated with post-market notifications and improvements.[190] The ease of software and electronic updates can create a "proximity" between manufacturer and consumer that leads to higher levels of tort responsibilities by OEMs for recalls, updates, and repairs.

Both issues, and likely others in the future, may ultimately benefit from legislative guidance. The integration of AVs onto the roadways will also create uncertainties with respect to the responsibilities and liabilities of certain State agencies, particularly TxDOT. Relatively minor legislative clarifications would enable TxDOT to better address this emerging technology.

iii. Clarify What Constitutes "Notice" for Digital Infrastructure

As discussed, if TxDOT does not make repairs to roadways, traffic signals, and similar devices and infrastructure in a reasonable time period after "notice" of the defect, the agency may be exposed to tort liability.[191] Yet, with connected infrastructure, an argument could be made that this notice occurs immediately since TxDOT or the municipality will theoretically have immediate notification of the malfunction through the digital technology.[192]

Courts will likely interpret "notice" in keeping with the

---

[189] NEV. REV. STAT. § 482.090; FLA. STAT. § 316.86(2); D.C. CODE § 50-2353; MICH. COMP. LAWS § 257.817

[190] Bryant Walker-Smith, *Automated Vehicles are Probably Legal in the United States*, 1 TEX, A&M L. 411 (2014).

[191] TEX. CIV. PRAC. & REM. CODE § 101.060 (1985).

[192] Note that the "actual notice" required under Section (a)(3) for destruction of traffic control devices by third parties requires a "subjective awareness of fault," which goes well beyond passive data collection.

"reasonable" expectations for agency action and provide TxDOT with additional time to process the data as part of its reasonable response time. Nevertheless, the legislature could be cautious and add interpretive words to "notice" in Section 101.060(a)(2) to signal that TxDOT is allowed time to reasonably process digital data of malfunctions after the data is received. An amendment that adds "actual" to modify "notice" in both Sections (a) (2) and (a) (3) would be the most straightforward approach. Alternatively, "notice" in Section (a)(2) could be modified to accommodate digital infrastructure by adding a parenthetical "notice" (or in the case of digital and connected infrastructure, notice must include a reasonable data processing time). Finally, the legislature could simply clarify that connected infrastructure is simply not "real or personal property" for purposes of the Federal Tort Claims Act. Instead, it could clarify that "absence, condition, or malfunction" occurs with respect to the transmittal of data or other information.

While these options each constitute relatively small changes, some type of clarification will be helpful in providing predictability to TxDOT and municipalities in allocating their scarce resources. Such a clarification might encourage even more rapid integration and use of digital RSE since the liability risks will be reduced for the government entities operating them.

iv. Create an Exception for Identifiable Travel Information under the State Open Records Act

Under current law, the privacy of individuals in the State is protected strongly for a narrow set of sensitive information and is effectively unprotected for most information, including travel information that contains identifiable information. Indeed, agencies may be required to share the latter more general information with requestors under the State Open Records Act.

To produce better protection of privacy, the legislature could limit the private information on citizens that must be disclosed through the Open Records Act. For example, the legislature could create a new exception to the Open Records Act that extends the information protected under Texas Transportation Code §§ 371.001 & 371.051 to all highways in the State. This extension would only prohibit the disclosure of the registration, licensing, and other identifying information under the Open Records Act (without restricting agency use of the information).

v. Require State Agencies to Alert Individuals that Their Privacy Has Been Breached

In situations where consumer confidentiality is breached in violation of State or federal law, the State agency responsible for the breach could be legislatively required to provide a notification to the individual. Similar requirements are in effect in more than half of the States.[193] Such a requirement need not be enforceable with private damages. But, it would provide Texas citizens with added assurance that, they will be alerted if breaches of sensitive information occur so that they can take preventative action.

c. Privacy and Security Recommendations

Data privacy and hacking concerns are largely unaddressed by current laws and yet appear to rank among the most significant concerns regarding the use of the technology in the future. There are legitimate reasons for a "wait and see" approach with respect to gauging the need for state interventions given the interest in these issues by Congress and NHTSA and the potential overlap of AVs with other technological innovations, such as drones, which present similar risks to privacy and security.[194]

On the other hand, there are a few relatively modest steps the State of Texas could take to increase privacy and security without affecting the development of the technology itself. Both immediate and longer-term recommendations are offered here.

i. Privacy

Consistent with the strong recommendations of NHTSA and the ULC Subcommittee, legislative prescriptions on privacy standards

---

[193] Michael Froomkin, *Government Data Breaches*, 24 BERKELEY TECH. L. J. 1019 (2009).

[194] Dorothy Glancy, *Sharing the Road: Smart Transportation Infrastructure*, 41 FORDHAM URB. L.J. 1617, 1647 (2014).

for AV technologies seem premature.[195] Yet, the contrast between the protection of sensitive data in Texas and the unrestricted nature of all other identifying information, such as license and registration information, suggests the need for some realignment of privacy protections within Texas law. Beyond amending the Open Records Act, as previously discussed, there are several other ways that consumer privacy might be better protected in the State as AVs are assimilated onto Texas highways.

ii. Improve Consumer Information on Collection and Use of Data by OEMs, Software Companies, and Others

The legislature could provide greater assurance for consumer privacy in the current, unregulated market of AVs in several ways.

Accessible Contracts

First, the legislature could supplement contract law by requiring that citizens at least be alerted to the types of information that will be collected about them as a result of the purchase of a AV from the OEM and others. California has passed such a law.[196] The legislature may determine that complicated contracts of adhesion, like Tesla's, may be insufficient to meet the legislative demands for clear disclosures. Contracts instead would need to be clear and accessible. With respect to potential intrusions on consumer privacy, a separate boldfaced explanation may be needed. The State legislature might also encourage OEMs, software developers, and others to provide consumers with "opt-out" provisions with respect to some of the data collection that is not essential to operation through a privacy rating system or other incentives. Finally, the State itself could request standardized information on the autonomy and privacy features of each new model marketed in the State (all vehicles; not simply AV) and collate the information for Texas citizens to inform their purchasing choices.

Rewarding Privacy Protection

Second, the Texas legislature could reward or encourage the

---

[195] STUDY COMM. ON STATE REGULATIONS OF DRIVERLESS CARS, UNIF. LAW COMM'N, REVISED REPORT OF THE SUBCOMMITTEE ON ISSUES 5 (2014).

[196] *See, e.g.*, Calif., Chapter 570, DIVISION 16.6. § 38750(h).

development of vehicles that offer added privacy protection for operators and occupants. For example, the State could provide a ranking system for AV privacy protections. For example, an optional dashboard that identifies when added information is being collected on a CV and provides opportunities to block that data gathering, could earn 3 stars in a 3-star system. A consumer's ability to readily block targeted advertisements that can be loaded into the computer systems could receive one star. However, the reward system is accomplished, Texas could serve as a leader in encouraging OEMs to make consumer privacy a high priority by rewarding privacy innovation in the Texas marketplace.

Reporting Data

Finally, the State could require all OEMS of new models of all vehicles sold in the State to provide a state agency like TxDOT with an annual report on the data collection enabled by various models and vehicles. The report could be structured so as to allow easy comparison among vehicles and reports. This information could then be used to inform future legislative activity.

Restrict the Sale or Sharing of Private Consumer Data by Businesses

The State could also expand its current prohibition against businesses from sharing or selling "sensitive" consumer information with third parties without their consent, codified in Section 521.052, to a broader range of consumer information that includes information about driving habits, entertainment preferences, or perhaps all information collected through AV technologies. Such a legislative amendment would preclude OEMs and software developers from selling or sharing all (not just sensitive) consumer data collected through AV technology to advertisers, insurers, etc.

Moreover, in cases where consumers may unwittingly consent to third-party sharing in complicated contract clauses, the legislature could require that the contracts meet standardized plain language requirements. This could include a bold, underlined passage that signals that the consumer, for example, *understands they are allowing the manufacturer to collect personal information and share it with third parties, including insurers and advertisers."*

iv. Security

Federal leadership is underway on cybersecurity concerns. Thus, at present it does not appear there is a significant role for states to play in revising or adjusting their existing criminal law to deter these activities.

Criminalization of Hacking

The need for anti-hacking laws in the context of AVs has generated national attention. Given the prominence of this issue at the national level, coupled with the existence of both federal and state laws that penalize this type of tampering, the criminalization of hacking may be an issue that does not require short-term legislative attention.

Encouraging Innovation in Cybersecurity

There are important federal developments regarding the cybersecurity of AVs that, even though not complete, signal a national interest in addressing at least some of these challenges. NHTSA and the USDOT, along with industry, are focused on addressing the security risks associated with AVs.[197] NHTSA publicly announced its intent to set minimal standards governing cybersecurity protections for vehicles by 2017.[198] The Spy Car Act of 2015 is an indication of congressional attempts to mandate the promulgation of cybersecurity standards for all AVs sold in the United States. While the bill is unlikely to pass in this session, it provides a starting point for ongoing legislative discussions about cybersecurity.

Encouraging Technological Innovation in AV Development

The State's leadership in AV testing allows it to play a leading role in influencing the development of the technology. These final recommendations position the State as a national leader in using the

---

[197] William Kohler & Alex Colbert-Taylor, *Current Law and Potential Legal Issues Pertaining to Automated, Autonomous and Connected Vehicles*, 31 SANTA CLARA HIGH TECH. L. J. 99 (2015).

[198] NATIONAL HIGHWAY TRAFFIC SAFETY ADMINISTRATION, National Motor Vehicle Crash Causation Survey: Report No. DOT HS 811 059, (2013).

market to encourage even smarter technological innovation.

Collating Information about the Use of AVs in the State through Reporting

There are multiple social benefits to AVs. The State could require annual reporting of basic features of AVs used in the State to ensure they are understood and to educate citizens and guide future policies. Several simple reporting requirements seem particularly fruitful in light of the large amount of information and data that OEMS of AVs are likely to obtain from each vehicle sold. Indeed, without a reporting requirement, this valuable information on social benefits may not be available to the State even though it is possessed by the manufacturers. The mandated reports could include, among other things, a report of all accidents that occur and general statistics, such as accident/miles traveled; emissions/miles traveled; ratio of urban/highway miles traveled; and other related information.

Incentivizing Still Greater Innovation in the AV Market

The legislature could also create stronger incentives for technological innovation in AVs by spurring greater demand in the consumer market for vehicles that include other socially beneficial features. For example, the legislature could subsidize the consumer purchase of AVs with added sensors for safety, extra low emissions, etc., through tax subsidies. The legislature could also require State agencies to purchase certain types of AVs (e.g., low emission) with additional, socially beneficial features.

Mandated or even voluntary reporting by OEMs on the extent to which models meet "add-on" social goals could also be collected and collated by the State to enable more informed purchases by citizens.[199] These disclosures, in turn, could spur positive research and development on related attributes of AVs by OEMs if add-on values

---

[199] Validation of the reports will be necessary, which could entail some costs through random audits; expert committee oversight; etc. But these costs may be more than offset by the gains to the market and to rewarding innovation in AVs for values that go beyond safety and convenience to the owner or operator.

increase market power. Several "add-on" social benefits that could be calculated and disclosed by OEMs to facilitate a more informed consumer market in Texas include:

- Emissions reductions that are lower than comparable vehicles in non-automated categories;
- Reduced transaction costs in tort litigation when OEMs contractually agree to bear all tort liability on behalf of a driver in a crash where the vehicle is in automated model and causes an accident;
- Quantification of lower transit costs for certain types of functions (shuttles) to make transportation more affordable for a wider group of citizens;
- Installation of sensors that avoid workers/pedestrians/cyclists (and/or development of helmets, etc. that provide easy recognition for these groups); and,
- The provision of added privacy protections for consumers that go beyond what is required by law.

IV. CONCLUSION

Widespread adoption of automated vehicles would remedy many of conventional automobile transportation's flaws. These vehicles, if used properly, can be more safe, efficient, and convenient than manually-operated cars. However, the opportunities presented by this technology are accompanied by a litany of legal ambiguities. As automated vehicle technology matures, so too must our understanding of transportation law. Some of the issues automated vehicles present will be traditional, from tort liability to insurance requirements. Others will involve areas of the law that did not exist when the first automobile was developed, like regulation of cybersecurity and digital privacy.

This article has outlined some of the challenges facing lawmakers, manufacturers, and users when dealing with automated vehicles, as well as offered potential solutions. Although it is impossible to predict with certainty what the future will hold for automated vehicles, this technology has the potential to fundamentally reshape the way we use and regulate transportation.

Law Firm Cybersecurity:
Commensurate with Capital

Benjamin Bolin [*]

[*]   University of Missouri Kansas City Law School, candidate for JD, 2018, learn more at benjaminbolin.com. The author wishes to thank Professor Paul Callister, Director of the Leon E Bloch Law Library and Professor of Law at the University of Missouri Kansas City Law School.

TABLE OF CONTENTS

In an age of digital crime, law firms are looking for solutions to protect their clients' data. However, traditional conversations on law firm cybersecurity have failed to recognize the solutions necessary are commensurate with a law firm's size. Current standards for attorney client privilege explain lawyers must take reasonable measures determined by the amount of resources available. Neglecting to recognize the relationship between resources and solutions can lead to liability and inefficient spending. This comment discusses a full picture of the cybersecurity landscape for law firms, explicitly acknowledging the expectations, requirements, and threats to law firm cybersecurity. Then, the piece concludes by dividing new and old cybersecurity solutions by the size of a law firm. This comment projects to establish a new standard in cybersecurity discussions.

I. INTRODUCTION

Ironically, in the first story to coin the term "cyberspace," the author imagined a world of cyber attackers. In 1981, when the internet was still in its infancy, William Gibson recognized the silent struggle between companies seeking to protect their data, and hackers motivated by money.[200] In *Burning Chrome*, Gibson introduced the first and last line of defense to hackers, Intrusion Countermeasure Electronics (ICE). ICE is the science fiction equivalent to modern day cybersecurity. Today, his stories come to life as industries struggle to keep their data secure from foreign threats. Attacks can come from governments, companies, or even individuals like Gibson romanticized. As former Secretary of Defense Leon Panetta warned in October of 2012, everyone's data is set for an impending "cyber Pearl Harbor."[201] As awareness of this threat grows in industries across the globe, intruders are looking elsewhere.

Today, law firms are becoming the new target for theft of intellectual property, business secrets, and confidential information. Cyber attackers realize law firms can house significant stores of sensitive client information. These same attackers have also

---

[200] William Gibson, fiction writer, essayist, Phillip K. Dick Award recipient.

[201] Secretary Panetta on Cybersecurity to the Business Executives for National Security, Leon Panetta, Sec'y of Def., U.S. Dep't of Def., New York, NY (Oct. 11, 2012), http://archive.defense.gov/transcripts/transcript.aspx?transcriptid=5136.

discovered the legal community generally has weak cybersecurity. These threats pose significant challenges for law firms, as they seek to keep client information confidential, but accessible. The basic challenge to law firms includes compliance with "reasonable measures" of security as demanded by statute. However, no one solution fits every law firm. Resources vary depending on a law firm's size, and reasonable security measures vary depending on their total risk. Discussions of solutions for law firms need to keep this essential fact in mind. The problem is, no discussion of law firm cybersecurity discusses both the full picture of cybersecurity and solutions departmentalized by the size of the firm.[202]

In an attempt to fill this void, this piece will present and intersect four sets of knowledge: first, what the current standards are for law firms including their professional responsibility requirements and statutory obligations; second, who attacks law firms and why they are attacked; third, the liability law firms face; and fourth, solutions for law firms. The first three sections present the full picture of cybersecurity from hacker to statute. The conclusion, the fourth section of this piece, presents a breakdown of cybersecurity solutions for small, medium, and large law firms, using current standards, hacker motivations, attorney liability, and resources available as a guide for digital protection.

---

[204] *See* Alan W. Ezekiel, *Hackers, Spies, and Stolen Secrets: Protecting Law Firms from Data*, 26, Harv. J. L. & Tech 649 (2013) (discussing the growing pains of cybersecurity in law firms but advocating law changes and general increase of security); Erin F. MacLean and Deborah M. Micu, *Protecting Yourself from Cyber Threats, Internal Office Practices can Make or Break Law Firm's Cybersecurity*, 41, Mont. Law. 16 (2015) (making various comparisons to other fields and only one solution); Timothy J. Toohey, *Beyond Technophobia*, 21, Rich. J.L. & Tech. 9 (2015) (discussing the ethics, risks, and obligations of various technologies but not discussing causes nor identifying threats); *but Cf.* Carrie A. Goldberg, *Practicing Law in the Age of Surveillance and Hackers*, 38 Am. J. Trial Advoc. 519 (2015) (recognizing small firms face different criminals than large firms and even advocating solutions tailored to small firms but failing to discuss the full gamut of troubles and solutions for firms of all sizes).

The current stage of cyberspace is full of hackers. By tailoring solutions for law firms, this comment may help improve the legal community's modern-day ICE.

II. Current Standards: A Summary

In general, the problem with the word "cybersecurity" is it implies a single standard or set of laws. However, data-security standards for law firms are an aggregate of many distinct but related standards.[203] In order to better understand the liability and the solutions law firms face, it is necessary to understand each set of requirements. Requirements set by professional responsibility, state law, federal law, and common law combine to govern this field. Industry certifications are optional and expensive, but also contribute to the standards set for some attorneys.

a. Professional Responsibility

Professional responsibility expects lawyers to keep client information confidential while adopting new technology. However, the requirement data be secured by "reasonable measures" leaves much to be desired.

The American Bar Association (ABA) Model Rule 1.6 requires confidentiality of information.[204] Subsection (c) requires reasonable measures to prevent unauthorized access.[205] Factors considered to be reasonable measures include the sensitivity of the data and the laws that seek to protect it.[206] A client may require even

---

[205] *See* Lorelei Laird, *Cybersecurity Laws Are a Worldwide But Evolving Patchwork*, ABA Journal (Mar. 18, 2016, 10:52 AM), http://www.abajournal.com/ news/ article/cybersecurity_laws_are_a_worldwide_but_evolving_patchwork (describing the large body of diverse law between nations and states).

[206] *See* MODEL RULES OF PROF'L CONDUCT r. 1.6 (Am. Bar. Ass'n 2015) ("A lawyer shall not reveal information relating to the representation of a client unless the client gives informed consent").

[205] *See Id.* r. 1.6 (c) (2015).

[206] *See Id.* r. 1.6 cmt. 19 (2015).

further standards or, alternatively, consent to poor security communication methods.[207] As a lawyer tries to meet these expectations, Model Rule 1.1 requires attorneys provide competent counsel to their clients.[208] This competence can extend to "the benefits and risks associated with relevant technology."[209] And, if confidential data is breached, Model Rule 1.4 mandates attorneys tell their clients.[210]

Many states have weighed in on the cybersecurity requirements set by the ABA Model Rules by various means. In North Carolina, for example, the rules have been amended to require lawyers to stay up-to-date of "the benefits and risks associated with the technology relevant to the lawyer's practice."[211] North Carolina then uses similar language to ABA Model Rules requiring attorneys make reasonable efforts to prevent unauthorized data breaches.[212] Florida, instead of making changes to its rules of professional conduct, supplements them with an advisory opinion to stress the importance of cybersecurity.[213] Many more state bar associations

---

[207] *See Id.*

[208] *See* MODEL RULES OF PROF'L CONDUCT r. 1.1 (Am. Bar Ass'n 2015) ("In determining whether a lawyer employs the requisite knowledge and skill in a particular matter, relevant factors include. . .")

[209] *Id.* r. 1.1 cmt. 8 (2015).

[212] *See* MODEL RULES OF PROF'L CONDUCT r. 1.4 (Am. Bar Ass'n 2015) (requiring attorneys keep clients reasonably informed on the status of their case).

[213] N.C. RULES OF PROF'L RESPONSIBILITY r. 1.1 cmt. 8 (2016), https://www.ncbar.gov/for-lawyers/ethics/rules-of-professional-conduct/rule-11-competence/.

[214] *See Id.* at r. 1.6(c) (2015), https://www.ncbar.gov/for-lawyers/ethics/rules-of-professional-conduct/rule-16-confidentiality-of-information/.

[215] *Compare* Fla. Bar Prof'l Ethics, ADVISORY OP. 10-2 (2010), http://www.floridabar.org/DIVEXE/RRTFBResources.nsf/Attachments/566CF30AE31 72CF385257D5B006CB4D1/$FILE/Ethics%20Opinion%2010-02.pdf *with* FlA. Bar Code Prof. Resp. D. R. 4-1.6(e) & R. 4-1.6(e) cmt. (2016) (Florida rule broadly

have issued similar comments and opinions.[214] Other states rely on progressive interpretations of the already existing language; for example, Missouri has none of the language from Model Rule 1.1.[215] It may, however, be read into the rule because it requires knowledge and skill in changes of the law and its practice.[216] Like the states above and the ABA Model Rules, the Missouri Model Rules also require reasonable precautions to ensure confidentiality.[217] Each of these rules and opinions display at least a common requirement of reasonable measures for data security.

In sum, many states and the ABA require attorneys to embrace new technology and take reasonable measures to ensure data security. The reasonable measures standard calls upon lawyers to balance the sensitivity of the client data against the laws in place to protect the information.[218] This balance can be difficult and subjective because the line between reasonable and unreasonable can be blurred. For example, an attorney has "Class A" and "Class B" security provisions for case data. Class A security is used for high-risk cases, so the data is encrypted and access by phone is prohibited. Class B security is used for low-risk cases, so the data is unencrypted and may be accessed on any device. Where do medium-risk cases go? Using Class

---

requires reasonable efforts and advisory opinion urges lawyers to keep abreast of technology that can be a threat to confidentiality).

[216] *Compare* State Bar of Ariz. Ethics, FORMAL OP. 09-04 (2009), available at http://www.azbar.org/Ethics/EthicsOpinions/ViewEthicsOpinion?id=704 (explaining attorneys must take reasonable measures to defeat unauthorized access to client data) *with* Ariz. R. of Prof'l Conduct, r. 1.6(e) & 22-23 (2016); *Also compare* N.J. Bar Ass'n Advisory Comm. on Prof'l Ethics, FORMAL OP. 701 (2006) http://njlaw.rutgers.edu/collections/ethics/acpe/acp701_1.html *with* N.J. R. of Prof'l Conduct, r. 1.6(c) 2016 (the rules state protection must be granted as "reasonably necessary" to prevent substantial economic harm, while the opinion calls for to use "reasonable care" to protect client data from cyber-attacks); *Compare* N.Y. Bar Ass'n Comm. on Prof'l Ethics, OP. 842 (2010), http://www.nysba.org/CustomTemplates/Content.aspx?id=1499 *with* N.Y. R. of Prof'l Conduct, r. 1.6(c) cmt. 17 (2016) (both requiring reasonable measures and the opinion explicitly guiding attorneys to protect sensitive client data).

[217] *Compare* MO. SUP. CT. r. 4-1.1 cmt. 6 (2007) *with* Model Rules of Prof'l Conduct r. 1.1 cmt. 8 (Am. Bar Ass'n 2013).

[216] MO. SUP. CT. R. 4-1.1 cmt. 6 (2007).

[217] MO. SUP. CT. R. 4-1.6 cmt. 16 (2007).

[218] *See* MODEL RULES OF PROF'L CONDUCT r. 1.6 cmt. 19 (Am. Bar Ass'n 2013).

A security, medium-risk measures receive more protection than they deserve; but using Class B they do not receive enough. Perhaps the ABA wants attorneys to be conservative with protection of user data. This example also displays how an attorney is forced to compare risk and make a subjective determination as to what level of security is appropriate. There are many more situations in which the line between using different security measures would be unclear.

b. State Statutes

In addition to professional responsibility requirements, some state statutes have more stringent requirements. For instance, some states require notification within short timeframes if client data is breached.[219] While a minority of states require specific data security measures, some states' requirements can include encrypting all records and training employees.[220]

Forty-seven states have statutes governing data breach notification, which apply to law firms who store client data. California enacted the first notification law in 2002, and many states followed suit.[221] California, like most other states, requires entities who hold personal information about their clients to notify them upon discovery of a data breach without unreasonable delay.[222] Although

---

[219] Gina Stevens, Cong. Research Serv., R42475, Data Security Breach Notification Laws 7 n.35 (2012).

[22] *See* CAL. CIV. CODE § 1798.81.5 (2015) (stating data security requirements to be used broadly), 201 Mass. Code Regs. 17.04 (requiring encryption of personal information), Nev. Rev. Stat. § 603A.040 (2015) (stating data security requirements to be used by business who accept payment cards), *N.J. Stat.* § 56:8-197 (2015) (stating data security requirements to be used by health insurance carriers).

[221] Gina Stevens, Cong. Research Serv., R42475, Data Security Breach Notification Laws 1 (2012).

[24] *See* CAL. CIV. CODE § 1798.82(a) (2015); *See generally* MODEL RULES OF PROF'L CONDUCT r. 1.6 cmt. 19 (Am. Bar Ass'n 2013).

most states require notification, many statutes vary widely on issues such as the timeframe in which you must notify affected persons, civil or criminal penalties, and notification of law enforcement.[223] Some states impose strict liability for failure to notify.[224] Additionally, some states set a capped penalty for failure to notify, while others use a calculation.[225] States like Missouri have created a "safe harbor" for data breach notification if the data was encrypted.[226]

A handful of states have enacted laws requiring data security standards to protect personal information.[227] These state laws protect against data breaches and require businesses to implement and maintain reasonable security measures similar to the requirements set for attorneys by the ABA model rules. For example, Massachusetts data privacy regulations are very comprehensive.[228] The statute requires every "person" or entity holding or processing Massachusetts resident's data to: develop a written policy, encrypt all records, and train employees on compliance with data security policies.[229] Rhode Island, Oregon, California, and a few others have passed similar legislation.[230] Others, like Missouri, are trying to pass only specific

---

[223] *See* CAL. CIV. § 1798.82 (premising breach notification on the "legitimate needs of law enforcement"); Mo. Rev. Stat. § 407.1500.2(8) (2015) (requiring the attorney general be notified Kan. Stat. Ann. § 50-7a01(g)(3) (2015) ("[P]ersonal information does not include publicly available information that is lawfully made available to the general public from . . . government records.")lable information that is lawfully made available to the general public from . . . government records.").

[224] Reid J. Schar & Kathleen W. Gibbons, *Complicated Compliance: State Data Breach*
Notification Laws, 12 Privacy & Security Law Report 1381, 1382 n.9 (2013) (California, Illinois, Massachusetts, and Washington).

[225] *Id.* at 1384 nn.30-31

[226] MO. REV. STAT. § 407.1500.1(9), 2(1) (2015).

[227] *See* CAL. CIV. CODE § 1798.81.5 (2015), MD. CODE ANN., COM. LAW § 14-3501 (2008), NEV. REV. STAT. § 603A.210 (2006), OR. REV. STAT § 646A.622 (2015), 11 R.I. GEN. LAWS § 11-49.2-2 (2016).

[228] *See generally* 201 MASS. CODE REGS. §§ 17.00-.04.

[229] *Id.*

[230] *See* CAL. CIV. CODE § 1798.81.5 (2015), MD. CODE ANN., COM. LAW § 14-3501 (2008), NEV. REV. STAT. § 603A.210 (2006), OR. REV. STAT § 646A.622 (2015), 11 R.I. GEN. LAWS § 11-49.2-2 (2016),

protections, such as security for student data.[231]

c. Federal Law

More than 50 federal statutes focus on various issues in cybersecurity but there is no nationwide standard for data breach notification.[232] Efforts have been made to pass a nationwide standard for data breach notification, but Congress has yet to pass anything.[233]

There are, however, several relevant statutes necessary to understand the scope of data security standards for firms. The Health Insurance Portability and Accountability Act ("HIPAA") for example, requires health care providers to maintain high security standards to protect medical data.[234] Health Information Technology for Economic and Clinical Health extended HIPAA requirements to "business associates" who handle health information, including law firms who deal with such data.[235]   There are many similar federal laws for

---

[231] *See* H.B. 1240, 98th Leg., 1st Sess. (Mo. 2015) (seeking to protect student data, currently pending); *See also* H.B. 16-1423, 70th Gen. Assemb., 2d Reg. Sess. (Co. 2016),
H.B. 331, 188th Gen. Ct. (Mass. 2013) (seeking to protect student data, currently pending).

[232] Eric A. Fischer, Cong. Research Serv. R42114, Federal Laws Relating to Cybersecurity: Overview of Major Issues, Current Laws, and Proposed Legislation (2012); *See generally* Intl. Business Publications, U.S National Cybersecurity Strategy and Programs Handbook, 173 (vol. 1 2013) (illustrating legislation along a timeline of evolving technology).

[233] *See* Taylor Armerding, *Final Attempt to Pass Cybersecurity Legislation Appears Doomed,* CSO Online (Nov. 14, 2012, 7:00 AM), http://www.csoonline.com/article/ 2132553/malware-cybercrime/final-attempt-to-pass-cybersecurity-legislation-appears-doomed.html (explaining the failed effort of the 2012 Cybersecurity Act and the subsequent executive order Obama had drafted).

[234] Health Insurance Portability and Accountability Act (HIPAA) of 1996 § 1173(d)(2), 42 USC § 1320d-2(d)(2) (2010).

[235] *See* American Recovery and Reinvestment Act of 2009, Pub. L. 111-5, § 13402(b) (2009), 42 USC § 17932(b) (2010).

banking, student data, and more.[236]

d. Federal Common Law & the FTC

The FTC and federal common law set only a few limited standards for law firms to abide by; but as litigation multiplies, attorneys cannot afford to miss the requirements set by the FTC and future common law cases.

The FTC has the authority to act as both the prosecutor and advisor when it comes to data privacy. In 2014 and 2015 the FTC has filed more than 50 general privacy lawsuits.[237] In 2014, the FTC filed a complaint against the hotel chain Wyndham Worldwide Corporation and three of its subsidiaries were sued for misrepresenting security measures and for failing to safeguard client information.[238] Wyndham lost, but it appealed on the basis the FTC does not have the authority to sue for alleged failure to protect consumer data.[239] However, that argument did not succeed, and on August 24, 2015 the United States Court of Appeals upheld the FTC's authority.[240] Failure to comply with these standards can result in litigation by the FTC and damages.

The standards set by the FTC include controlling access to data, requiring passwords and authentication, addressing vulnerabilities as they arise, and securing devices and paper.[241] Each of these standards extends to law firms. The solution section of this

---

[236] For brevity, this article does not explore the individual requirements of many federal laws. These laws typically target specific clients and provide too many exceptions and requirements to categorize solutions based on law firm size. In fact, entire papers are written discussing compliance with just one federal law.

[237] *See Privacy and Data Security Update* (2015), FTC (January 2016) https://www.ftc.gov/reports/privacy-data-security-update-2015 *and 2014 Privacy and Data Security Update,* FTC (2014), https://www.ftc.gov/system/files/ documents /reports/privacy-data-security-update-2014/privacydatasecurityupdate_2014.pdf (listing detailed information about cases).

[238] *FTC v. Wyndham Worldwide Corp.*, 10 F.Supp.3d 602, 607 (D.N.J. 2014), *aff'd* 799 F.3d 236 (3d Cir. 2015).

[239] *Wyndham,* 799 F.3d at 240

[240] *Id.* at 259 (by upholding FTC's authority, the court effectively gave the FTC "more teeth").

[241] *See generally* Richard Bergsieker, Richard Cunningham & Lindsey Young, The *Federal Trade Commission's Enforcement of Data Security Standards, 44* Colo. Law. 39 (2015) (further discussing the FTC's de facto law and standards of care).

paper reflects on these requirements.

The litigation for cybersecurity breaches is mostly imposed by the FTC because of the difficulty plaintiffs face in showing sufficient damages, which is a required element for a class action case to be litigated. Since the Supreme Court's decision in *Clapper v. Amnesty International*, courts have traditionally dismissed claims for lack of standing where victims of data breach had not alleged actual misuse of the data.[242] However, with the recent *In Re Adobe* decision, plaintiffs may find it easier to meet the damages requirement and make claims against corporations and firms.[243]

It is difficult to assess damages because of the digital medium. Many questions remain unanswered when security is breached, such as: What information was stolen? What reputation damage resulted to the victim? Who was attacked? Answering these "damages" questions is difficult for plaintiffs—resulting in little litigation against law firms and other corporations outside the FTC's crusade. But, with *In Re Adobe* as a recently set precedent, higher accountability standards for data breaches are on the rise and litigation will be available to more plaintiffs.

e.   Industry Certifications

Industry certifications set an optional and expensive set of standards. These certificates are not required by statute or common law but some firms are finding them important to stay competitive. For example, ISO/IEC 27001 certification is part of a growing family of standards created by the International Organization for

---

[242] *Clapper v. Amnesty Int'l USA*, 133 S. Ct. 1138, 185 (2013) (holding the fears were "highly speculative" and based on a "highly attenuated" chain of possibilities that did not result in "certain impending injury"); *In re Sci. Applications Int'l Corp. (SAIC) Backup Tape Data Theft Litig.*, 45 F. Supp. 3d 14 (D.D.C. 2014); *Polanco v. Omnicell, Inc.*, 988 F. Supp. 2d 451 (D.N.J. 2013) (same). Supp. 2d 451 (D.N.J. 2013) (same).

[243] *See In re Adobe Sys., Inc. Privacy Litig.*, 66 F. Supp. 3d 1197 (N.D. Cal. 2014) (stating similar claims in *Clapper* are sufficient to show damages).

Standardization.[244] The standard for security was published in 2013 to provide requirements for establishing, implementing, maintaining, and continually improving an information security management system.[245] In 2015, John Anderson, CIO at Shook, Hardy & Bacon said his IT team spent 18 months and $60,000 to reach the certification.[246] Another optional standard for businesses is NIST SP 800-53, a government publication of guidelines for executive agencies.[247]

f. Current Standards: A Conclusion

Laws governing cybersecurity for businesses and law firms vary widely. Law firms balance numerous requirements from professional responsibility rules to the common law. The resounding requirement is to take "reasonable measures" in security as determined by the state laws and model ABA rules. These measures must account for the liability of the data provided. In other words, the common requirement is a risk analysis for each set of sensitive information. Notification laws are a second layer of requirements for law firms. However, each state has different deadlines and provisions. Specific measures as set by the FTC range from encryption and passwords to particularized security software. Finally, industry certifications are an optional and expensive solution some law firms are beginning to implement.

Keep these standards and certification options in mind for the solutions section discussion. However, before getting to the solutions section and with this important background in mind, it is paramount to understand who commits cyberattacks on firms in order to draw

---

[244] *ISO/IEC 27001 - Information Security Management*, Int'l Org. for Standardization (last checked May 20, 2016), http://www.iso.org/iso/home/standards/management-standards/iso27001.htm.

[245] *ISO/IEC 27001:2013 (en)*, Int'l Org. for Standardization (last checked May 20, 2016), https://www.iso.org/obp/ui/#iso:std:iso-iec:27001:ed-2:v1:en.

[246] Susan Hansen, *Cyber Attacks Upend Attorney-Client Privilege*, Bloomberg (Mar. 19, 2015, 1:56 PM), http://www.bloomberg.com/news/articles/2015-03-19/cyber-attacks-force-law-firms-to-improve-data-security.

[247] Barry Williams, Information Security Policy Development for Compliance, IX (2013).

more defined security solutions.

III. CYBER ATTACKERS: A SUMMARY

Individuals, organizations, and state actors serve as a combined threat to a law firm's valuable data. They are typically motivated by economic gain for themselves or for their country.

"Nearly two-thirds of organizations are potential targets for nation-state cyber-attacks."[248] Cyberattacks are often thought as Hollywood espionage against foreign governments, and countries spying on one another is certainly a problem.[249] However, strong motivation for nation-states to perform industrial or corporate espionage exists as well. For example, in China, weak intellectual property enforcement is used to favor Chinese competitors.[250] Nation-state sponsored hackers are the most well-funded and difficult-to-defend-against hackers.[251] Using various methods, these state-sponsored groups break through defense contractors, newspapers, Fortune 500 companies and more.[252]

---

[248] Warwick Ashford, *Nation-state Cyber Attacks Could Target Most Organizations*, Comput. Wkly (Aug. 17, 2015 4:30 PM), http://www.computerweekly.com/news/4500251856/Nation-state-cyber-attacks-could-target-most-organisations-survey-shows (study was conducted during Black Hat USA 2015 from over 200 attendees).

[249] *See* Ellen Nakashima, *U.S. Said to Be Target of Massive Cyber-Espionage Campaign*, Wash. Post (Feb. 10, 2013), http://articles.washingtonpost.com/2013-0210/world/37026024_1_cyber-espionage-national-counterintelligence-executive-tradesecrets (Cyberattacks were once viewed "as a concern mainly by U.S. intelligence and military").

[250] Chet Nagle, *China is Stealing American Property*, Daily Caller (Sep. 24, 2015 2:40 PM), http://dailycaller.com/2015/09/24/china-is-stealing-american-property/ (2013 report cited in the former CIA agent's article states that China is the largest source of the hundreds of billions per year in international theft of American IP).

[251] *See Masters of the Cyber-Universe*, The Economist (April 6, 2013), http://www.economist.com/news/special-report/21574636-chinas-state-sponsored-hackers-are-ubiquitousand-totally-unabashed-masters (pointing to how China's government is the perpetrator to the largest attacks on US businesses).

Non-state organizations are the second largest threat and can be more dangerous because of their focus on economic gains.[253] Traditional methods include malware, viruses, and vulnerability exploits.[254] More advanced options for small organizations include advanced persistent threats (APTs). APTs take advantage of vulnerabilities in software that are known but not yet patched to infiltrate networks undetected.[255] These intrusions can be undetected for years, giving hackers a foothold into a company's network.[256]

Individuals are the last threat group, which are typically less sophisticated and have weaker motivations. Some individual hackers are called hacktivists, which are hackers seeking political or social change.[257] Hacktivists typically target other individuals, companies, and governments.[258] Script kiddies are another subset of individual hackers. Script kiddies are hackers who utilize easy to use malware, spam, ransomware, and pre-made scripts to gain access and vandalize sites.[259] Script kiddies and hacktivists typically do not spend time learning to hack in novel ways. Because this group relies on pre-made and known malware, traditional security prevention may be effective.

IV. LAW FIRM LIABILITY: A SUMMARY

---

[252] *See Id.*

[253] James Carafano Ph.D., *Fighting on the Cyber Battlefield: Weak States and Nonstate Actors Pose Threats*, Heritage (Nov. 8, 2013), http://www.heritage.org/ research/commentary/2013/11/fighting-on-the-cyber-battlefield-weak-states-and-nonstate-actors-pose-threats (describing how non-state actors are geared to accumulate wealth and seek to disrupt).

[254] Johan Sigholm, Comment, *Non-State Actors in Cyberspace Operations*, 4 J. Mil. Stud. 1, 1-15 (2013), http://ojs.tsv.fi/index.php/jms/article/view/7609/pdf_1 (listing the methods of various cyber attackers).

[255] Jill D. Rhodes, Vincent I. Polley, A.B.A. Cybersecurity Handbook 13 (2013).

[256] *Id.*

[257] Johan Sigholm, Comment, *Non-State Actors in Cyberspace Operations*, 4 J. Mil. Stud. 1, 15 (2013), http://ojs.tsv.fi/index.php/jms/article/view/7609/pdf_1 (listing the methods of various cyber attackers).

[258] *Id.* at 13.

[259] *Id.*

After identifying the standards for law firms and who cyber attackers are, the next and greatest challenge is to acknowledge the liability present in law firms. Law firms are prime targets because they tend to have the weakest security measures for very valuable and personal information. Moreover, liability for cyberattacks will only increase as insurance coverage falls.

a. Why Law Firms?

Cyber attackers target law firms because of the high volume of data and the low level of security. Law firms do not have the same level of resources that large companies have to secure client data. This means that firms are the weakest link in the information security chain, and thus low-hanging fruit for hackers. This situation is a result of the balancing act inherent to the practice: weighing security against adoption of new technology.[260]

Hackers attack law firms for their valuable information. As established in the previous sections, a hacker's main motivation is economic or political. These motivations carry over in the attack of law firms—especially given the amount and type of sensitive information in their networks.[261] A law firm inherently deals with sensitive and personal information. Attorneys are also privileged with non-public information from businesses—whether that be a lawsuit, merger, or business secret. Much of this personal information is stored digitally in a network. A firm's network may contain information about a very large number of clients. Hackers seek non-public information on mergers and acquisition deals to get an advantage on the stock market.[262] State actors seek the information to

---

[260] *See* discussion *supra* Section II a.

[261] *See Law Firms Prime Targets of Cyber Attacks*, A.B.A. (Feb. 05, 2012, 9:30 AM), http://www.americanbar.org/news/abanews/aba-news-archives/2013/08/law_firms_prime_targ.html (quoting highlights from the Standing Committee on Law and National Security).

[262] Michael Riley, Sophia Pearson, *China-Based Hackers Target law Firms to Get*

undermine America's long-term competitiveness.[263] Inherently, law firms are a digital treasure trove of valuable client information.

Unfortunately, law firms are also at a disadvantage in protecting important client information they hold. Current standards for law firms are not comprehensive; instead, they are a hodgepodge of many different standards,[264] which can lead to conflicting requirements. For example, the ABA's Model Rules of Conduct (and the modified versions adopted by many states) compel an attorney to take reasonable measures to keep client data secure—while embracing new technology systems to stay competitive and communicate effectively.[265] However, the adoption of new technologies with the expectation of maintaining security of data comes with inherent problems. Introducing new technologies without proper risk assessment can create major liabilities. For another example, the use of personally owned smartphones to perform law-related work increased to seventy percent according to the 2016 ABA Legal Technology Survey.[266] While smartphones are a convenient and efficient medium for work and communication, they are very insecure, especially when personally owned.[267] Thus, there is a conflict between adopting new technologies like smartphones, which

---

Secret Deal Data, Bloomberg (Jan. 31, 2012 3:37 PM), http://www.bloomberg.com/news/articles/2012-01-31/china-based-hackers-target-law-firms (discussing how China has worked to get secret deal data from American companies).

[263] *See Foreign Spies Stealing US Economic Secrets in Cyberspace,* Off. of Nat'l Counterintelligence Exec., 9-10 (2009-2011), http://www.ncsc.gov/publications/reports/fecie_all/Foreign_Economic_Collection_2011.pdf (describes how foreign attacks against the United States seek in part economic information to undermine the nation's prosperity).

[264] *See* discussion *supra* Section II - CURRENT STANDARDS: A SUMMARY.

[265] *See* David G. Ries, *Cybersecurity for Attorneys: Understanding the Ethical Obligations,* Law Practice Today (Mar. 2012), http://www.americanbar.org/content/dam/aba/publications/law_practice_today/cyber-security-for-attorneys-understanding-the-ethical-obligations.authcheckdam.pdf (discussing the duty to provide services across all platforms and the inherent rules of confidentiality; note the revisions discussed have since been adopted in the current A.B.A. Model Rules).

[266] Mobile Technology, www.americanbar.org/publications/techreport/2016/mobile (last visited April 5, 2017).

[267] *See generally The Cost of Insecure Mobile Devices,* Ponemon Inst. L.L.C. (2014), http://www.ponemon.org/local/upload/file/AT%26T%20Mobility%20Report%20FINAL%202.pdf (discussing the costs and threats of using mobile devices in the workplace).

offer better communication, and confidentiality, which would require conducting business through more secure means that personally owned smartphones. Hackers may recognize this conflict and are target law firms accordingly.

Law firms are further disadvantaged by their lack of available resources. Often, law firms are more vulnerable than their clients when such clients tend to be large companies with more resources to invest in securing data.[268] Law firms are the biggest liability in any company's cybersecurity strategy.[269] The law firm's identity as the weakest link may be the result of partner stalwarts with respect to making changes in technology. For example, "enhanced network passwords [require] intense partner debate and discussion rather than simple acceptance."[270] As Mary Galligan, a previous head of the FBI explained, "[a]s financial institutions in New York City and the world become stronger, a hacker can hit a law firm and it's a much, much, easier quarry."[271]

b. Recent Attacks: Examples

---

[268] *See generally* David Mandell, Karlas Schaffer, *The New Law Firm Challenge*, A.B.A. (Mar. 2012), http://www.americanbar.org/content/dam/aba/publications/ law_ practice_today/the-new-law-firm-challenge-confronting-the-rise-of-cyber-attacks-and-preventing-enhanced-liability.authcheckdam.pdf (law firms generally spend less on securing their systems than other businesses).

[269] *See* Daniel Garrie, *Attacking the Weakest Link*, Huffington Post (Sep. 10, 2013 5:40 PM), http://www.huffingtonpost.com/daniel-garrie/attacking-the-weakest-lin_b_386 2354.html (after several hypotheticals discusses how the weakest link can be pinned back to law firms' devices).

[270] *Information Security -- Are Law Firms "The Weakest Link"*, Law Risk Mgmt. Blog (Apr. 2, 2012), http://www.lawfirmrisk.com/2012/04/information-security-are-law-firms.html (highlighting Rupert Collin's report on law firm security).

[271] Michael Riley, Sophia Pearson, *China-Based Hackers Target law Firms to Get Secret Deal Data*, Bloomberg (Jan. 31, 2012 3:37 PM), http://www. bloomberg.com/news/articles/2012-01-31/china-based-hackers-target-law-firms.

A discussion about recent data breaches may help put into perspective why law firms are attacked. At least 80 percent of the top U.S. law firms have had their security breached by cyber attackers.[272] According to a 2012 report analyzing 137 events from 2009-2011, the average cost of a data breach was $3.7 million.[273] A Ponemon Institute report displayed the average cost of cybercrime for retail stores in 2014 was $8.6 million per company, which represented a double in cost from the previous year.[274]

The following true examples of cyberattacks illustrate why the liability law firms face is paramount. In 2010, the law firm Gipson Hoffman & Pancione saw their employees were receiving social engineering emails that were coming from spoofed email addresses carrying malware that could compromise the firm's security.[275] It was later discovered that the attacks emanated from China.[276] The cyberattacks methodology of using spoofed email addresses is known as "spear phishing," which is a common way to gain access to a network.[277] Spear phishing uses emails that intentionally appear to be

---

[272] Stuart Poole-Robb, *Law Firms Are a Hackers Treasure Trove*, IT Pro Portal (Mar. 3, 2015), http://www.itproportal.com/2015/03/30/law-firms-hackers-treasure-trove/#ixzz3VruQlKmI; Hannah Bender, *Do As I Say, Not As I Do*, Property Casualty 360 (Jan. 16, 2015), http://www.propertycasualty360.com/2015/01/16/do-as-i-say-not-as-i-do-most-law-firms-lack-adequa (the study was completed in 2011 from the cybersecurity firm Mandiant).

[273] *Experts Warn Law Firms to Protect Themselves Against Cyberattacks*, A.B.A. (Feb. 18, 2014 11:43 AM), http://www.americanbar.org/news/abanews/aba-news-archives/2014/02/experts_warn_lawfir.html.

[274] *See* Riley Walters, *Cyber Attacks on U.S. Companies in 2014*, Heritage (Oct. 27, 2014), http://www.heritage.org/research/reports/2014/10/cyber-attacks-on-us-companies-in-2014#_ftn2.

[275] *See* Michael Riley, *China Mafia-Style Hack Attack Drives California Firm to Brink*, Bloomberg (Nov. 27, 2012 5:01 PM), http://www.bloomberg.com/news/articles/2012-11-27/china-mafia-style-hack-attack-drives-california-firm-to-brink.

[276] *See* Ashby Jones, *China and the Law: Did Chinese Hackers Attack LA Law Firm*, Wall St. J. (Jan. 14, 2010 9:36 AM), http://blogs.wsj.com/law/2010/01/14/china-and-the-law-did-chinese-hackers-attack-la-law-firm/.

[277] *See generally* Kim Zetter, *Hacker Lexicon: What are Phishing and Spear Phishing*, Wired (April 7, 2015 6:09 PM), http://www.wired.com/2015/04/hacker-lexicon-spear-phishing/ (discussing the dangers of phishing and spear phishing).

coming from colleagues but are actually fake. Fortunately, in this case, technology-aware attorneys recognized the emails as potentially dangerous and the malware was not released.[278]

Another more recent attack was on Ziprick & Cramer. The small firm in California faced a new kind of Cryptolocker-type virus around the date of January 25, 2015.[279] Cryptolocker is a type of ransomware, where an unwanted program encrypts files on a network and then denies access to the files, unless the user pays money to restore the information.[280] As the ABA Legal Technology Guide proclaims, "[y]ou can rest assured ransomware will continue onward until law firms recognize the importance of having backups that are not connected to the network as a drive letter!"[281] Griesing Law suffered a similar attack in July of 2016 as featured in the ABA Journal.[282]

Law firms must be prepared for these attacks that they could likely face. A great majority of law firms are facing or have faced some kind of cyberattack. However, as seen in the Gipson Hoffman & Pancione case, technology-aware lawyers can thwart some of these attacks.

c. Law Firm Liability: A Conclusion

---

[278] *See* Stacy Berliner, *Hackers Are Targeting Law Firms: Are You Ready*, A.B.A. (Aug. 27, 2013), http://apps.americanbar.org/litigation/committees/womanadvocate/articles/summer2013-0813-hackers-are-targeting.html.

[279] *See* Susan Hansen, *Cyber Attacks Upend Attorney-Client Privilege,* Bloomberg (Mar. 19, 2015, 1:56 PM), http://www.bloomberg.com/news/articles/2015-03-19/cyber-attacks-force-law-firms-to-improve-data-security.

[280] *Id.*

[281] Sharon Nelson, John W. Simek, Michael Maschke, Solo and Small Firm Legal Technology Guide 333 (2015).

[282] Julie Sobowale, *Managing Cyber Risk*, ABA J., at 34 (Mar. 2017).

Law firms are liable for data breaches now more than ever. As described in previous sections, law firms are often the weakest link in a company's data security chain. Breaches can cause average money damages in the millions. For cyber attackers motivated by either economic or political gain, the vast amount of information law firms hold is the metaphorical low-hanging fruit. Cybersecurity must be taken seriously to protect clients and firms. After analyzing the standards law firms must abide by, who the cyber attackers are, and the liability law firms face, it is necessary to turn to the solutions.

V. SOLUTIONS: A NEW PERSPECTIVE

The problem with traditional papers, articles, and discussion on cybersecurity is that they fail to particularize security provisions by the size of the firm.[283] It's no secret that cost is the biggest barrier to entry for cybersecurity solutions.[284] Generally, a firm's resources reserved for security measures depends on the size of the firm. To make a loose division, firms can be divided into small (boutique), medium, and large sizes. No further definition of "large firm" versus "small firm" is provided, mostly in the interest of brevity.[285]

For small firms, they lack both the institutional knowledge to recognize how far they must go to secure their data and the financial resources to implement such solutions. Further, small firms have no guide on what cybersecurity solution meets minimum requirements. For example, if a small firm grows from 5 to 10 attorneys, how does their cybersecurity requirements change? Medium firms are the in hardest spot when it comes to cybersecurity. They may have key pieces of data on a large corporation and therefore a high level of threat. However medium firms lack the resources available to protect

---

[233] *See supra,* note 204.

[284] *See* Julie Sobowale, *Managing Cyber Risk,* ABA J., (Mar. 2017) at 36 ("Each person quoted in this article mentioned cost as a major factor for why law firms are lagging in preparing for cyberattacks").

[285] Defining small firm versus large firm is difficult and largely irrelevant to this piece. A 30-attorney firm may be a small firm in California, but in Missouri some would call it a medium firm and expect high cybersecurity. This piece also seeks to establish a new standard in cybersecurity discussions, where authors recognize their solution may not be affordable to all firms. General divisions make these discussions much more approachable. A separate piece could be written on hard-line divisions for the size of a law firm and its cybersecurity requirements using the arguments here.

the data like a large firm. Medium firms are also more likely to deal with clients who want constant access to their sensitive data. If law firms are the low hanging fruit to sensitive data, medium firms are the weakest link. Large firms may have it the easiest, despite being constantly bombarded with attacks and threats, large firms have the knowledge base and finances to secure data. Once more, large firms can more easily rest assured they are meeting the current standards for their client's data security.[286]

In the following section, solutions are articulated determinative of the size of the law firm. If a firm is capable of more provisions, however, it is encouraged that the firm adopt tools and steps outside any defined zone. For example, if Firm A is a small firm and fulfills or is fulfilling all the measures dignified here and has resources to fulfill a medium or large firm provision, all the better for Firm A. Each of the provisions described scale up to larger law firms. Thus, medium firms should fulfill everything a boutique (small) firm does and medium firm provisions. Large firms ought to complete everything in their descriptor plus medium and boutique size provisions. Therefore, the discussion begins with small firms, describing all the requirements set by the current standards section of this paper, and how to begin to meet those requirements. The discussion ends with big firms, describing large scale measures over current standards that could and ought to be completed to protect client data. Note that not included in this discussion is the obvious minimum requirements: those set by clients, but only if the client requires more than the minimum standards described herein.

VI. SMALL FIRMS: AN INTRODUCTION

---

[286] This comment could be an argument for the survival of big firms. Big firms are much more capable of handling cybersecurity threats than smaller firms because they can afford the time and resources necessary to prevent cyber intrusions. Small and medium firms may need to grow to large firm size if they want to stay competitive and offer high levels of cybersecurity. This section explains the advantage big firms have over their peers.

Small firms are in a pickle. Every day cybercriminals pump out about 250,000 novel variants of viruses and malware.[287] These threats are a major issue for big firms. Yet, small firms are exposed to the same attacks as large firms, but with limited resources available.[288] The Gipson attack may not have gone as smoothly for a firm the size of Ziprick & Cramer. However, troubles like the spear phishing attack at Gipson Hoffman & Pancione were resolved by tech savvy lawyers, not expensive technology. Often simple, cheap solutions can effectively quell modern day problems.

The proposed set of solutions for small firms keep the goal of simple, cheap solutions for firms without many resources in mind. Within each section is a short description of how the solution complies with one or many of the current standards discussed above.

Small firms should keep in mind the risk of the data they handle. Even if a firm is small, all of its cases—not just the multimillion dollar cases—deserve comprehensive security solutions. Even for small law firms, the bigger the risk a data breach poses, the more a firm should focus on its security.

a. Training

Training can prevent many cyber threats. In fact, the above discussion of the Gipson Hoffman & Pancione breach showed how training can be the last line of defense for a firm. In that situation, malware was prevented from entering the firm's system when trained lawyers identified dangerous materials. Past any or all security measures the firm may have had, well-trained lawyers stopped the threat. Trained attorneys can also help halt internal threats. During the ABA Techshow in 2014, security experts highlighted a survey that forty-one percent of IT security professionals regard "rogue" employees as a major security threat.[289] A study by Verizon found that a company's legal department is much more likely to open

---

[287] *See* Mark Ward, *Why Small Firms Struggle with Cyber Security*, BBC News (Feb. 6, 2015), http://www.bbc.com/news/technology-31039137.

[288] *See id.* (quoting Maxim Weinstein, security advisor at Sophos a security firm).

[289] *See* Mark Hansen, *4 Types of Employees Who Put Your Cybersecurity at Risk, and 10 Things You Can Do To Stop Them*, ABA Journal (Mar. 28, 2014 5:45 PM), http://www.abajournal.com/mobile/article/war_stories_of_insider_threats_posed_by_u napproved_data_services_and_device.

phishing emails than all other departments.[290] As established in the *Recent Attacks* section, these social engineering tactics are a mainstay of hackers. Ransomware is another malicious program that requires similar social engineering of employees. Despite how important training can be to the security of a law firm, in the 2016 ABA Legal Technology Survey, thirty percent of respondents believed their employers offered no technology training:[291] hardly better than the *2015* Legal Technology Survey.[292] For small firms, specifically, training is even less likely. Forty-five percent of solo practitioners and thirty-five percent of law firms with two to nine attorneys have no technology training program.[293] The solution to many threats both internal and external, is training. The *ABA Cybersecurity Handbook* asks firms to foster a culture of training.[294]

i. *Educate attorneys on the current cybersecurity threat environment.*

Trained attorneys will be on high alert for malware, spear phishing, and pesky social engineering tactics. Educate attorneys on protective measures in place to prevent attacks. Attorneys are already required to provide competent counsel, extending to benefits and risks in technology.[295] This requirement includes internal firm standards

---

[290] *See* Frank Strong, *Infographic: Cybersecurity Stats for Legal Tech*, Business of Law Blog, LexisNexis (Aug. 21, 2015), http://businessoflawblog.com/2015/08/ cyber security-legal-tech/.

[291] Technology Training, https://www.americanbar.org/publications/techreport/2016/ training.html (last visited April 5, 2017).

[292] *Id.*

[293] *Id.*

[294] Jill D. Rhodes, Vincent I. Polley, A.B.A. Cybersecurity Handbook 13, 145 (2013).

[295] *See* MODEL RULES OF PROF'L CONDUCT r. 1.1 & cmt. 8 (Am. Bar Ass'n 2015) ("In determining whether a lawyer employs the requisite knowledge and skill in a particular

not to use external USB drives, or how the security software at the firm actively prevents cybersecurity breaches. The ABA Cybersecurity Handbook believes awareness of company policy and security measures can help attorneys negotiate contracts against unreasonable data security language.[296]

ii. *Educate attorneys to use strong unique passwords.*

Attorneys should also be trained—if not required—to change their passwords to email, their computer, and their phone frequently. Having an ineffective password on devices can leave someone dangerously exposed.[297] The passwords created should use combinations of symbols and letters or even phrases.[298] If firm employees cannot remember their passwords, train them to use programs like KeyPass, Password Safe, or other password programs, some of which are free.[299] Further, passwords and authentication are a standard set by the FTC for companies handling client data. If attorneys use no form of authentication, FTC guidelines require they change or face litigation.

Educate attorneys to update their computers. Non-state and individual hackers make use of security exploits in older versions of software. Updating software and applications closes those security holes!

Education extends past attorneys to include secretaries, contractors, and anyone employed by the firm. Any weak link in the chain of cybersecurity can cause a breach of data. To ensure the awareness is comprehensive and complete, firms must require new lawyers, and established attorneys, to complete data privacy and data security training programs.[300] The American Bar Association now

---

matter, relevant factors include. . .").

[296] Jill D. Rhodes, Vincent I. Polley, A.B.A. Cybersecurity Handbook 13, 145 (2013).

[297] Brian Krebs, Spam Nation 282 (2014).

[298] *Id.* at 282.

[299] *Id.* at 283.

[300] Jill D. Rhodes, Vincent I. Polley, A.B.A. Cybersecurity Handbook 13, 134 (2013).

offers a series on cybersecurity which comes with its own certification at the end of the program.[301] Alternatively, small firms can look for free resources and videos online.[302]

b. Security Software

Security software is the biggest protection a small law firm can have. The *2015 Solo and Small Firm Technology Guide* recommends internet security suites that give much more functionality at a lower price than individual software recommendations.[303] The book does not recommend targeted protection, such as antivirus software, claiming it is not sufficient to keep systems protected.[304] Enterprise versions of security software suites can be the best protection against an individual hackers tools: spam, viruses, malware.[305] The tools in these suites can include firewall management and secure file sharing (like Workshare). Most software, like Kaspersky, even includes functions to change settings on laptops once an employee leaves with the device.[306]

Security provisions should also be implemented on mobile devices such as phones. At minimum, phones should have a

---

[301] *ABA Cybersecurity Series*, Am. Bar Ass'n (accessed Nov. 14, 2015), http://www.americanbar.org/content/ebus/events/ce/cyber-security-core-curriculum .html?sc_cid=CECSEC-A1.

[302] *See generally Stop. Think. Connect. Small Business Resources*, Homeland Security (accessed Nov. 17, 2015), http://www.dhs.gov/publication/stopthinkconnect-small-business-resources (Homeland Security offers several one page or several page documents on how to stay secure while traveling or for general reference).

[303] *See* Sharon Nelson, John W. Simek, Michael Maschke, Solo and Small Firm Legal Technology Guide 105 (2015).

[304] *Id.*

[305] *See Id.* at 106-10.

[306] *See Id.* at 109.

password, and have some means of remotely wiping the data.[307] The FTC requires devices, even cellphones, be secured.[308] Both iPhone and Android have either built in software or apps to wipe and track these devices. It is also recommended firms use more secure phones, like Android and Blackberry, which are more capable of using security software.[309]

c. Notification Laws

Small firms must also ensure their compliance with state data notification laws. Forty-seven states have laws governing data breach notification.[310] Despite state data breach notification laws, Model Rule 1.4 mandates attorneys tell their clients if data is breached.[311] The only question to a small firm therefore is, when must I notify my client? Small firms can easily research their state standard and adopt policies accordingly.

Firms could also add the notification law to their education provisions. A firm should be aware of not only the timeline in which notifications must be made, but also the level of data breach necessary in order to justify notification. If a small firm has clients across multiple jurisdictions, a firm can more easily adopt the most restrictive standards.[312]

d. Encryption

---

[307] *See* Nelson, *supra* note 305, at 185.

[308] *See* Richard Bergsieker, Richard Cunningham & Lindsey Young, The *Federal Trade Commission's Enforcement of Data Security Standards, 44* Colo. Law. 39 (2015).

[309] *Id.*

[310] *See* Gina Stevens, Cong. Research Serv., R42475, Data Security Breach Notification Laws 7 n.35 (2012).

[311] *See* Model Rules of Prof'l Conduct r. 1.4 (Am. Bar Ass'n 2015) (requiring attorneys keep clients reasonably informed on the status of their case).

[312] *See* Jon Frankel, *California Amends Data Breach Notification Laws - Other States to Follow?* Zwill Gen (Oct. 17, 2015), http://blog.zwillgen.com/2013/10/17/california-amends-data-breach-notification-law-states-follow/; *See also State Data Breach Notification Chart*, Midwest Cyber Security Alliance (Sep. 1, 2015), http://www.midwestcyber.org/wp-content/uploads/2015/09/QB-State-Data-Breach-Notification-Chart-09.01.2015.pdf.

Encryption is probably the most inexpensive and effective form of protecting client data. Encryption is a formula that transforms computer data anyone can read, into data only those with a password can read.[313] Both Windows and Mac computers with enterprise licenses have built in encryption software. Once implemented, hardware like laptops, hard drives, USB drives, and more can only be accessed by those that know the password. Encryption can also be used to protect data in motion, such as over wired or wireless networks, including the internet.[314] Firms can encrypt their phone lines too, making conversations with their clients secure and confidential. Encryption is so powerful that the FBI Director James Comey has been lobbying to gain "backdoor" access to encrypted data.[315] However, encryption is only as effective as the password used, so firms should push for training their employees on effective password management.

Encryption is also available on phones. The *2015 Solo and Small Firm Technology Guide* recommends using Android or Blackberry because their software architecture is much more conducive to encryption mechanisms.[316] Smartphones are always with us and susceptible to being lost or stolen. Encryption is one effective

---

[313] David G. Ries, John W. Simek, *Encryption Made Simple for Lawyers*, Am. Bar Ass'n (2012), http://www.americanbar.org/publications/gp_solo/2012/ november_december 2012privacyandconfidentiality/encryption_made_simple_lawyers.html (also discussing the general need for encryption, discussing data breaches were attorneys have left valuable USB drives on trains and buses).

[314] *Id.*

[315] Dina Temple-Raston, *FBI Director Says Agents Need Access to Encrypt Data to Preserve Public Safety*, National Public Radio (July 8, 2015 7:32 PM), http://www.npr.org/sections/thetwo-way/2015/07/08/421251662/fbi-director-says-agents-need-access-to-encrypted-data-to-preserve-public-safety.

[316] Sharon Nelson, John W. Simek, Michael Maschke, *Solo and Small Firm Legal Technology Guide* 185 (2015).

mechanism to protect the history of phone calls made to that client, and the search on LexisNexis for that case.

If client data is compromised, encryption provides a "safe harbor" in some states.[317] If a state has "safe harbor" laws, then so long as the data is encrypted, law firms do not have to notify their clients of the breach. However, Model Rule 1.4 requires notification regardless.

e. Bring Your Own Device Policies

For a small firm, bring your own device can be both a blessing and a risk. Bringing your own device allows attorneys to use software and services their firm does not provide for them. However, an attorney can expose a firm to a host of new malware and viruses when they bring their device within Wi-Fi signal of the firm.[318] But attorneys want and sometimes need to take their materials home or away from the office.[319]

Bring your own device policies need to be managed to account for the added risk. Current standards resoundingly ask for "reasonable measures" for a firm, accounting for the risk of the material. The risk phones pose to personal information is great, but is it enough to outweigh the benefits? The best provision would be to eliminate bring your own device provisions and present attorneys with dedicated devices for work. Such a provision would allow a firm to implement specific security measures on all devices, and ensure compliance with policy. However, this can be a major expense for small firms.

f. Written Plan & Policy

If a firm does not have a plan for security breaches, or a written policy on computer use, get one. A written policy for a small firm can provide guidance to attorneys and prevent potential problems. A written policy can be more effectively taught to other

---

[317] *Compare* Mo. Rev. Stat. § 407.1500.1 (2015); *with* 2016 Tenn. Pub. Acts 9168 (Missouri provides a safe harbor for encryption, while new law in Tennessee removes the safe harbor).

[318] Jill D. Rhodes, Vincent I. Polley, A.B.A. Cybersecurity Handbook 57, 108-109 (2013).

[319] *Id.*

attorneys in the firm. It also provides a standard to which everyone is held accountable. If one employee creates a cybersecurity threat for breaking the written policy, they may be reprimanded accordingly. A plan also requires the firm to consider potential threats proactively, bringing cybersecurity to the forefront of a firm's mind. A written plan further helps a firm comply with FTC standard of addressing security vulnerabilities.

g. Small Firms: A Conclusion

Small firms are in a tough spot when it comes to cybersecurity. They face the same threats as a large firm, but with less resources. Solutions like encryption, written plans and policies, managing bring your own device provisions, notification and training are simple, and mostly inexpensive solutions to a firm's needs. This starting point for small firms provides nearly comprehensive protection from threats and liability.

VII. MEDIUM FIRMS: AN INTRODUCTION

Medium firms are hard to present security provisions to that would not fit into either the large firm or small firm categories. Medium firms have substantially more resources than small firms to devote to cybersecurity, but not as many resources as a large firm. Medium firms must meet the standards set by small firms. Because medium firms have more resources than small firms, medium firms should implement strict bring your own device policies.

Medium firms ought to hire information technology expertise and purchase cybersecurity insurance. Combined, these provisions will offer tailored advice on how to better secure client information and protect a law firm's bottom line from liability.

a. Information Technology Expertise

Medium firms should seek out information technology

expertise. Law firms are already mining for cybersecurity lateral hires, in the wake of clients seeking better security protection.[320] Whether a firm chooses to hire, contract, or consult an information technology specialist, the expertise they can offer is incredible. More than this paper can offer, an expert in the field can make specific assessments of risks and solutions for any size firm. However, these services usually come at a high rate, and may be precluded from some medium firms.

b. Cybersecurity Insurance

Cybersecurity insurance is an effective but expensive solution for medium-size law firms. As law firms become increasingly liable for data breaches, owning cybersecurity insurance would protect against losses from the inevitable cyber incidents, including business interruption, network damage, and data breaches.[321] For now, cybersecurity insurance can be obtained--in some cases--with few requirements, perfect for a medium firm. Currently, premiums and limits are determined using traditional point-in-time risk assessments.[322] However, this method may change as insurance companies strengthen their minimum cybersecurity standards.[323]

VIII. LARGE FIRMS: AN INTRODUCTION

Large firms have many more employees and data to secure. They are expected to not only monitor the security of all of their attorneys in many departments, but also store their data effectively. No wonder the "likelihood of data breach increased to 50% among companies with more than $4 billion dollars in revenue."[324] Large

---

[320] *See* Frank Strong, *Infographic: Cybersecurity Stats for Legal Tech*, Business of Law Blog, LexisNexis (Aug. 21, 2015), http://business oflawblog.com/2015/08/ cybersecurity-legal-tech/.

[321] *See Cybersecurity Insurance*, Homeland Security (Dec. 2, 2015), http://www.dhs.gov/cybersecurity-insurance.

[322] *See* Jon Oltsik, *The State of Cyber Insurance*, Network World (Nov. 16, 2015, 8:12 AM), http://www.networkworld.com/article/3005213/security/the-state-of-cyber-insur ance.html.

[323] *Id.*

firms, however, have more resources for cybersecurity solutions. They can afford premium security suites, professional technology training, and can spend more time planning for the inevitable cyber breach. In total, law firms are spending as much as 1.9% of their gross annual revenues—seven million dollars per year—on information security.[325]

For large firms, the previous sections look very similar but with more effective means. Large firms can conduct training with professionals, video recordings, or the firm's IT specialist. Notice can be a difficult subject for large firms, as they must reach clients in multiple jurisdictions with different laws. In those cases, where jurisdiction is across multiple states or countries, large firms should follow the lead of large corporations and comply with the most stringent standards.

Large firms may go above and beyond small and medium firm provisions to keep secure their clients' data. The term "may" is used here willingly, as no amount of policy or statute can demand the provisions below. Rather, the provisions described are more ethical obligations, or good practice, than mere compliance with broad standards. However, clients may expect--or demand--the following provisions.

a. Cybersecurity Alliance

Large law firms have the new opportunity to join a cybersecurity alliance. A cybersecurity alliance is a venue for firms, banks, and other companies to share information about cyber threats and develop defenses and best practices to prevent them.[326] In fact,

---

[324] *Id.*

[325] Chase Cost Management, *AMLAW 200 Firms Spending As Much As $7 Million on Information Security*, PR Newswire (Aug. 27, 2015, 8:45 AM), http://www.prnewswire.com/news-releases/amlaw-200-firms-spending-as-much-as-7m -per-year-on-information-security-300133976.html.

[326] *See* Allison C. Shields, *Simple Steps: Guarding Against Cyber Attacks and Other*

82% of businesses with high performing security practices collaborate with other businesses to grow their cybersecurity protection.[327] Corporations in the Midwest have created their own alliance called the Midwest Cyber Security Alliance (MCSA).[328] It recently held a micro-conference in Saint Louis, Missouri, bringing in IT experts, attorneys, government agents, and more to collaborate on this tough subject.[329] There is also the National Cyber Security Alliance (NCSA), composed of many businesses from across the nation.[330] Security alliance membership is a great venue for large firms to meet, share, and learn best practices to defeat cyber threats.

Recent legislation aims to aid such alliances. The Cybersecurity Information Sharing Act (CISA), passed by the U.S. Senate in October of 2015, allows the government to share its security indicators in these discussions.[331] The legislation also allows big companies to share cyber threat data with their competitors without antitrust litigation.[332]

b. Full Reports

Large firms should explore paying information technology specialists to proactively prevent attacks. Wall Street banks already pay information technology specialists to dig into shadowy online forums to see how their brand and information is abused.[333] For

---

Security Breaches, 41 Frontline 5, 16 (Sep. 2015).

[327] *See Why You Should Adopt the NIST Cyber Security Framework*, PWC (May 2014), https://www.pwc.com/us/en/increasing-it-effectiveness/publications/assets/adopt-the-nist.pdf.

[328] *See* Jennifer L. Rathburn, *Midwest Cybersecurity Alliance Launces, Marks Cybersecurity Awareness Month*, Quarles and Brady L.L.P. (Oct. 5, 2015), http://www.quarles.com/news/%E2%80%8Bmidwest-cyber-security-alliance-launches-marks-cyber-security-awareness-month/.

[329] *Id.*

[330] *See generally* NCSA (May 21, 2016), https://www.staysafeonline.org/about-us/.

[331] S. 754, 114th Cong. (2015).

[332] *See* Shannon Young, *US Senate Passes CISA, a "Cybersecurity" Bill that Critics Say Will Expand Mass Surveilance*, Truthout (Oct. 30, 2015), http://www.truth-out.org/news/item/33460-us-senate-passes-cisa-a-cybersecurity-bill-critics-say-will-expand-mass-surveillance.

instance, banks hire companies like Black Cube that search the "deep web" for data on their client.[334] The company essentially befriends potential enemies before a cyberattack.[335] Black Cube then shares the cyber attackers' intent, information, and means with their client.[336] Sometimes, once Black Cube has enough information, they turn in the hacker to the authorities.[337] Another company, Fox-IT, was even able to get the source code to a new malware program from similar work and share it with their clients.[338] For a law firm, paying for the information available on the deep web can provide a full picture of cybersecurity and proactively prevent future attacks.

c. Standardized Certification & Frameworks

Large firms could also seek out standardized certification and frameworks. In recent years, several standardized certifications have been passed that allow a firm to stand out from its competitors. As clients continue to recognize the importance of cybersecurity at their law firm, these certifications are a great way to prove a firm is meeting a certain standard of security. However, these certifications require time, money, and expertise not usually available for small or medium firms. The below is a framework and certification to consider.

---

[333] *See* Brian Krebs, Spam Nation, X (2014), for details on how hackers cooperate, manipulate, and attack big businesses.

[334] *See generally* Black Cube, http://www.blackcube.com/cyber-intelligence/ (last visited August 7, 2016).

[335] Orr Hirschauge, *Ex-Spies Join Cybersecurity Fight*, The Wall Street Journal (Sept. 15, 2015, 2:29 PM), http://www.wsj.com/articles/ex-spies-join-cybersecurity-fight-1442341771.

[336] *Id.*

[337] *Id.*

[338] *Id.*

The National Institute of Standards and Technology for Cybersecurity Framework (NIST) is one type of standardization framework that is possible for law firms.[339] The NIST framework is great for large firms that are still making big strides to secure their information. The framework divides cybersecurity protection into four tiers. The tiers can be used to identify where a business is in terms of security, and where they can go.[340] Major provisions of the standard include assessing major threats, continuously monitoring those threats, and implementing certain provisions to correct each threat. An added benefit of the NIST framework is it highly encourages collaboration between other participants. As a result, a firm can learn from others who have attained the certification.

The International Organization for Standardization (ISO) has its own set of standards called ISO 27001 Certification. As described above, Shook, Hardy, & Bacon recently attained this certification.[341] The certification is designed to assess risks for businesses and divert assets to protect the riskiest information. Once the requirements of the certification are complete, companies are entitled to market their firm as ISO 27001 Certified.

Because the certificates above push security provisions based on risk assessment, the reasonable measures standard can likely be met by firms who attain these certifications.

d. Lobby for Standards and Laws

Large law firms should also lobby for more effective and efficient laws to combat cyber attackers and educate lawyers. The government's statutory laws need the input of law firms in order to better address cybercrimes and set a comprehensive standard for the legal community. One statutory solution to combat cyber criminals is to increase the punishment for cybercrimes. The EU in 2013 assigned harsher penalties to cybercriminals.[342] The US sought to do the same

---

[339] *See generally* Barry Williams, Information Security Policy Development for Compliance, IX (2013)..

[340] *See generally Why You Should Adopt the NIST Cyber Security Framework*, PWC 2 (May 2014), https://www.pwc.com/us/en/increasing-it-effectiveness/publications/assets/adopt-the-nist.pdf.

[341] *See* discussion *supra* Section II e. - Industry Certifications.

[342] *See* Dara Kerr, *EU Increases Penalities for Cybercriminals and Hackers*, CNET

with the Deter Cyber Theft Act of 2014.[343] However, harsher penalties for cybercrimes have done little to deter cyber criminals.[344] Large firms should instead lobby for a more effective means to discourage cyber criminals.[345] Large firms should lobby for solutions that give law enforcement more tools to find and arrest criminals, including funding to promote such programs.[346] Large firms could also educate lawmakers on the legal industry's relationship to cybersecurity, as the American Bar Association Cybersecurity Handbook recommends.[347] Being a part of the conversation on these laws can ensure that firms can take reasonable measures to secure their data.[348]

Large firms can also lobby the American Bar Association House of Delegates to pass more strict and uniform standards for attorneys. The ABA House of Delegates did attempt to make more concrete cybersecurity requirements on August 12, 2014.[349] However,

---

(Jul. 4, 2013, 3:58 PM), http://www.cnet.com/news/eu-increases-penalties-for-cyber criminals-and-hackers/.

[343] Deter Cyber Theft Act, S. 884, 113113th Cong. (2013-2014).

[344] Brian Krebs, Spam Nation, 14 (2014).

[345] *See generally* Merideth Levinson, *Why Law Enforcement Can't Stop Hackers*, CIO (Nov. 15, 2011, 7:00 AM), http://www.cio.com/article/2402264/security0/why-law-enforcement-can-t-stop-hackers.html ("The problem is that hackers rarely serve maximum sentences . . . Because the evidence against them is usually so incriminating, hackers often enter plea agreements with prosecutors... While plea bargaining has its benefits . . . it weakens the deterrent effect that prison sentences are intended to have.").

[346] *Id.* (". . . law enforcement doesn't have the resources to investigate and prosecute all of these cybercrime cases . . .")

[347] *See generally* Jill D. Rhodes, Vincent I. Polley, ABA Cybersecurity Handbook, Am. Bar Ass'n 135 (2013).

[348] *Id.*

[349] American Bar Association [ABA], House of Delegates Res. 109, at 1, ABA Doc. (Aug. 12, 2014), http://www.americanbar.org/content/dam/aba/events/ law_national_

the passed resolution is unabashedly vague. The original legislation required all law firms, big and small, to come up with cybersecurity standards that complied with national and international requirements.[350] The legislation was largely rejected by small firms.[351] However, such a requirement could do wonders for the legal industry. For small and medium firms, understanding how "reasonable measures" would apply to the data they store can be difficult. Large firms should take the lead on establishing requirements that are much clearer for firms of all sizes. Although more defined requirements for law firms may push some firms to spend more resources on security, it is a necessary evil. One firm that has ineffective security might create a bad reputation for the legal profession as a whole. For example, if a client presents very sensitive information to their attorneys, and that information is leaked due to weak cybersecurity, that client may reconsider disclosing sensitive information to any firm in the future. It is important that clients feel protected at any law firm to some extent. Therefore, the culture of attorney client privilege is a motivator for large firms to lobby these changes.

e. Large Firms: A Conclusion

Large law firms have more resources to devote to cybersecurity, but also have more responsibilities. Large firms must keep track of more employees who handle a greater quantity of precious client information. However, large law firms can implement the provisions in this section to increase their cybersecurity and raise the whole culture of law firm data security.

IX. CONCLUSION

In an attempt to improve the legal community's cybersecurity, this piece presented remedies for law firms based on their size: small,

---

security/2014annualmeeting/ABA%20%20Cyber%20Resolution%20109%20Final.aut hcheckdam.pdf (passed).

[350] Merideth Levinson, *Why Law Enforcement Can't Stop Hackers*, CIO, 333 (Nov. 15, 2011, 7:00 AM), http://www.cio.com/article/2402264/security0/why-law-enforcement-can-t-stop-hackers.html

[351] *Id.*, 334.

medium, and large firms.

Conversations on cybersecurity for law firms need to recognize that solutions are related to the size of the law firm. Discussions must recognize small, medium, and even large law firms have limits and unique cybersecurity problems. Further, conversations must recognize causes of these threats, the requirements lawyers must strive to meet, and contemplate the liability for failure to address such attackers. The full picture of the cybersecurity landscape is necessary for any size firm to truly recognize why and to what extent each solution is needed. The threats may be the same for each type of firm, but for smaller firms more simple and cheap solutions are preferred. While for large firms, simplicity may be traded for higher security.[352]

When the internet was in its infancy, William Gibson imagined hackers trying to break cybersecurity boundaries. Gibson recognized decades ago the reality of today; industry locked in a battle to protect their data. However, hackers are currently moving away from hacking the industry, and are now attacking law firms. Law firms are the metaphorical low hanging fruit for cyber criminals, due to their low security standards and abundance of sensitive information. Therefore, it is important for law firms to get a full understanding of the cybersecurity landscape. With this knowledge, firms can work efficiently and effectively to shield themselves from liability and data breaches. Unfortunately, current discussions of cybersecurity for law firms have failed to both acknowledge the full picture of cybersecurity and tailor solutions by the size of the firm. This paper displayed many avenues that bring a law firm up to the current required standards and beyond.

Like the ICE envisioned by Gibson, this piece introduced several modern-day methods to protect a client's private digital information. In total, this paper hopes to change the cybersecurity discussion, for solutions to recognize their target audience and their

---

[352] An alternative argument could be that cybersecurity solutions and requirements should be presented based on the size of the client. Some boutique firms handle larger clients that expect and demand high cybersecurity solutions. In these cases, law firms should bargain for enough resources to ensure client data is protected.

needs.

The World Still Looks To California: The CalECPA as a Model Step for Privacy Reform in the Digital Age

Abby Wolf [*]

[*] J.D., U.C. Davis, School of Law, 2016, B.A. in History, U.C. Berkeley, 2011. I would like to extend my sincerest thanks to Professor Anupam Chander for his guidance and encouragement throughout the writing of this paper. I am also very grateful to the Andrew W. Mellon Foundation for sponsoring the course in which this paper was written: Privacy, Surveillance, and "Sousveillance," a Sawyer Seminar for comparative research on the historical and cultural sources of contemporary developments. All errors are my own. Abby Wolf © 2017

TABLE OF CONTENTS

I. INTRODUCTION

"In circumstances involving dramatic technological change, the best solution to privacy concerns may be legislative… A legislative body is well situated to gauge changing public attitudes, to draw detailed lines, and to balance privacy and public safety in a comprehensive way."

- Justice Alito, in his concurrence to *United States v. Jones*[353]

"We can pioneer the new technologies that emphasize quality over quantity and we can make the tools to lift millions out of poverty and ignorance. The world still looks to California."

- Jerry Brown, Governor of California[354]

Fourth Amendment protections have lagged behind technology. Consequently, electronic data is vulnerable to surveillance and seizure by law enforcement on a mass scale, which courts have been both unwilling and unable to recognize. Traditional frameworks for Fourth Amendment analysis were developed before the advent and ubiquity of the Internet and electronic communication.[355] Thus, the law was not designed to cover the ever-increasing range of human activities that occur in intangible mediums.

Recent Supreme Court cases, such as *U.S. v. Jones*[356] and

---

[353] United States v. Jones, 132 S. Ct. 945, 964 (2012).

[354] This quotation is from California Governor Jerry Brown's State of the State Address in 1982, and it is also included in a placard below his gubernatorial portrait in the California State Capitol.

[355] For example, the landmark Supreme Court case, *Katz* v. *United States*, which created the two-part "reasonable expectation of privacy" framework, occurred in 1967. Katz v. United States, 389 U.S. 347 (1967). The first personal computer, the MITS Alstair 8800, however, was not introduced until 1975. *See* Dan Knight, *Personal Computer History: The First 25 Years*, LOW END MAC (Apr. 26, 2014), http://lowendmac.com/2014/personal-computer-history-the-first-25-years/.

Riley v. California,[357] have revealed a willingness of the Court both to take into account both how important digital content is to modern life[358] and to adopt jurisprudence that is sensitive to privacy concerns when technological improvements enable law enforcement to record and investigate far more than what individual officers could accomplish.[359] However, more must be done to create meaningful protection for electronic data. While the Fourth Amendment explicitly protects "persons, houses, papers, and effects"[360] from warrantless searches and seizures, it is less clear whether those same protections extend to information stored on a computer or electronic device.[361]

In response to this lacuna in Fourth Amendment coverage, California Senators Mark Leno, a Democrat from San Francisco, and Senator Joel Anderson, a Republican from San Diego, spearheaded a bipartisan bill to bring Constitutional protections into the modern age.[362]

---

[356]   132 S. Ct. 945 (2012).

[357]   134 S. Ct. 2473 (2014).

[358]   In *Riley*, the Court went so far to as say that "modern cell phones, which are now such a pervasive and insistent part of daily life that the proverbial visitor from Mars might conclude they were an important feature of human anatomy." Riley, 134 S. Ct. at 2484.

[359]   Justice Alito made this point in his concurrence when he commented on the power of the GPS technology used by the police to track Jones: "[t]he Court suggests that something like this might have occurred in 1791, but this would have required either a gigantic coach, a very tiny constable, or both – not to mention a constable with incredible fortitude and patience." Jones, at 958 n.3; *See also*, Harold Laidlaw, *Shouting Down the Well: Human Observation as a Necessary Condition of Privacy Breach, and Why Warrants Should Attach to Data Access, Not Data Gathering*, 70 N.Y.U. ANN. SURV. AM L.. 323, 326–8 (2015).

[360]   U.S. CONST. amend. IV.

[361]   Anupam Chander, *Can California Lead on Privacy Moving from Pen and Paper to Cloud Computing?*, AM. CONST. SOC. (BLOG) (Sept. 4, 2015), http://www.acslaw.org/ac sblog/can-california-lead-on-privacy-moving-from- pen-and-paper-to-cloud-computing.

[362]   Ca. State. Ass. Floor Analysis (Third Reading) (Aug. 28, 2015) at 4 (According to the author of the bill, law governing criminal investigations "has not been meaningfully updated to account for modern technology."); Dave Maass, *CalECPA and the Legacy of Technology: An Open Letter to Gov. Jerry Brown*, ELEC. FRONTIER FOUND. (Sept. 23, 2015), https://www.eff.org/deeplinks/2015/09/open-letter-gov-jerry-brown-calecpa-and-legacy-technology ("As our devices have shrunk, as their storage capacity has grown, as cloud services have begun hosting more of our information ... our laws have failed to reflect the privacy protections enshrined in the California Constitution: the guarantee

The bill, S.B. 178, also known as the California Electronic Communications Privacy Act ("CalECPA"), was designed to strengthen privacy protections and to prevent warrantless law enforcement access to data.[363] At a high level, the bill effects two main changes. First, it articulates clear standards for the acquisition of electronic data by state actors, notably with a warrant requirement. Second, it creates a notice requirement, so individuals will be made aware when they are being observed by law enforcement.[364]

The CalECPA received widespread support from advocacy organizations concerned with privacy and civil liberties, such as the Electronic Frontier Foundation ("EFF") and the American Civil Liberties Union ("ACLU").[365] Many of the largest tech companies, including Google, Twitter, and Facebook, also backed the bill.[366]

---

that the people be free from unreasonable searches and seizures." [hereinafter Open Letter to Gov. Brown]; Sen. Mark Leno and Sen. Joel Anderson, *Electronic Privacy Bill Protects Privacy Rights and Public Safety*, SACRAMENTO BEE (OPINION) (Sept. 9, 2015), http://www.sacbee.com/opinion/op-ed/soapbox/article34625526.html ("This bill updates California law for the modern digital age ....While technology has advanced exponentially, California's communications laws are stuck in the dark ages, leaving our personal emails, text messages, photos and smartphones increasingly vulnerable to warrantless searches.").

[363] S. B. 178 (Ca. 2015) Privacy: Electronic Communications: Search Warrant, https://leginfo.legislature.ca.gov/faces/ billNavClient.xhtml?bill_id=201520160SB178.

[364] R. Taj Moore, *So What's in the California Electronic Communications Privacy Act?*, LAWFARE (Oct. 22, 2015), https://lawfareblog.com/so-whats-california-electronic-communications-privacy-act.

[365] In fact, the ACLU of California, Electronic Frontier Foundation, and California Newspaper Publishers Association were co-sponsors of the bill.

[366] On the day the bill passed, the ACLU of Northern California noted in its press release that the following organizations had supported the bill: Adobe, Airbnb, American Library Association, Apple, Asian Americans Advancing Justice, Bay Area Council, California Chamber of Commerce Association, California Attorneys for Criminal Justice (CACJ), California Public Defenders Association, Center for Democracy and Technology, Center for Media Justice, Centro Legal de la Raza, Citizens for Criminal Justice Reform, Civil Justice Association of California, Color of

Google even emailed its subscribers directly to solicit their support for S.B. 178.[367] A poll conducted after the bill was introduced showed that eighty-two percent of Californians believed the police should need a warrant before accessing email or Internet activity.[368] Before its passage by both houses of the California legislature, even the state's most prominent law enforcement organizations removed their opposition to the bill[369] after provisions were added which allowed for

---

Change, Common Sense Kids Action, ConnectSafely, Consumer Action, Consumer Federation, Council on American-Islamic Relations (CAIR), Dropbox, Engine, Facebook, Foursquare, Google, Internet Archive, Legal Services for Prisoners with Children, LinkedIn, Media Alliance, Microsoft, Mozilla, NameCheap, National Center for Youth Law, National Center for Lesbian Rights, New America: Open Technology Institute, Privacy Rights Clearinghouse, reddit, Restore the 4th, San Diego Police Officers Association, Small Business California, TechNet, Tech Freedom, The Internet Association, and legal scholars, who "teach and write extensively about criminal procedure, information privacy law, cyber law, and related fields" from across the nation. *In Landmark Victory for Digital Privacy, Gov. Brown Signs California Electronic Communications Privacy Act into Law*, ACLU (Oct. 8, 2015), https://www.aclunc.org/news/landmark-victory-digital-privacy-gov-brown-signs-california- electronic-communications-privacy; Letter from Legal Scholars, to Sen. Mark Leno, Cal. State Sen. (Mar. 13, 2015), https://www.eff.org/document/legal-scholars-sb-178-support-letter.

[367] Alexander Reed Kelly, Google to Californians: Help Us Protect Your Electronic Privacy, TRUTHDIG (Jun. 10, 2015), http://www.truthdig.com/eartotheground/item/googl e_to_californians_help_us_protect_your_electronic_ privacy_20150610/. Amongst other things, the email said, "The California Electronic Communications Privacy Act (CalECPA) would update our privacy laws to protect all electronic communications and records from warrantless inspection by the state, regardless of format or age." The email included a fact sheet about the bill created by the EFF and ACLU. The email also had a link to support Google's efforts to pressure the legislature to pass the CalECPA.

[368] The poll further showed that 79% of Californians support a warrant requirement for tracking cell phone activity and 77% support a warrant requirement for accessing text messages. *See* Memorandum from Ben Tulchin, Corey O'Neil and Kiel Brunner, Tulchin Research, *California Statewide Survey Finds Voters Concerned about Digital Privacy and Support Requiring Police to Get a Warrant*, ACLU OF N. CAL. (Aug. 21, 2015), http://www.aclunc.org/sites/default/files/technology/20150821-polling_data_get_ a_warrant.pdf.

[369] Letter from Alan Wayne Barcelona, President of California Statewide Law Enforcement Association ("CSLEA"), to Sen. Mark Leno, California State Senate (Aug. 10, 2015), https://www.eff.org/document/california-statewide-law- enforcement-association-removes-opposition-sb-178-calecpa; Letter from Sean Hoffman, Director of Legislation, California District Attorneys Association (CDAA), to Sen. Mark Leno (Aug. 31, 2015), https://www.eff.org/ document/california-district-attorneys-association-remove-opposition-sb-178-calecpa; Letter from Aaron R. Maguire, Legislative Counsel, California State Sheriff's Association to Sen. Mark Leno (Aug. 26, 2015), https://www.eff.org/document/california-state-sheriffs-association-remove-opposition-sb-178-calecpa. The San Diego Police Officer's Association even voiced support for the

some leeway in conducting confidential or emergency investigations.[370] Because S.B. 178 proscribed limits on the use of relevant evidence, the California Constitution required the bill to receive a two-thirds vote of both the House and the Senate.[371] Governor Jerry Brown signed the bill into law on October 8, 2015,[372] and the moment was

---

bill. Letter to Sen. Mark Leno from Brian R. Marvel, President of the San Diego Police Officers Association, Inc. (Sept. 1, 2015), https://www.eff.org/document/sdpoa-support-letter-sb-178-calecpa.

[370] Open Letter to Gov. Brown, *supra* note 364.

[371] Cal. Const. art. I, § 28(2), "Right to Truth-in-Evidence. Except as provided by statute hereafter enacted by a two-thirds vote of the membership in each house of the Legislature, relevant evidence shall not be excluded in any criminal proceeding . . .."

[372] Interestingly, Governor Brown vetoed previous bills with similar provisions multiple times: S.B. 914 in 2011, S.B. 1434 in 2012, and S.B. 467 in 2013. *See* Hanni Fakhoury, *Another Year, Another Electronic Privacy Veto for California Governor Brown*, ELEC. FRONTIER FOUND. (Oct. 14, 2013), https://www.eff.org/deeplinks/2013/10/another-year-another-electronic-privacy-veto-california-governor-brown. This was also noted by the California State Assembly's Committee on Public Safety in its report on the CalECPA. *See* Ca. State. Ass. Comm. on Pub. Safety Report, Bill Quirk, S.B. 178 (Leno) as Amended July 7, 2015 (Jul. 14, 2015) at p. 12: S.B. 914 was written to overrule People v. Diaz, 51 Cal. 4th 84 (2011), a California Supreme Court decision which allowed police to search an individual's cell phone without a warrant. *See* Sen. Bill 914: Search Warrants: Portable Electronic Devices, 2011–2012 Regular Session, http://leginfo.legislature.ca.gov/faces/billNavClient.xhtml?bill_id=201120120SB914.
S.B. 1434 would have required the government to get a warrant in order to obtain location data from an electronic device. *See* Sen. Bill. 1434: Location Information: Warrants (Leno), 2011–2012 Regular Session, http://leginfo. legislature.ca.gov/faces/billNavClient.xhtml?bill_id=201120120SB143. S.B. 467 was the most similar to CalECPA. It would have required a search warrant when the government seeks to obtain the contents of a wire or electronic communication that is stored, held or maintained by a provider of electronic communication services or remote computing services. *See* Sen. Bill 467, Privacy: Electronic Communications: Warrant (Leno), 2013–2014 Regular Session, http://leginfo.legislature.ca.gov/faces/billNavClient.xhtml?bill_id=201320140SB467. Governor Brown had argued in his veto message that law already required a warrant, subpoena, or court order to access electronic communication in most cases, and the notice requirements of that bill could impede ongoing criminal investigations. Ca. State. Ass. Comm. on Appropriations Report, Jimmy Gomez, S.B. 178 (Leno) as Amended Aug. 17, 2015 (Aug. 19, 2015) at 2.

celebrated as a triumph for privacy as well as for California, a state known for being a leader in legislation that protects civil liberties.[373]

It should be noted that California is not the first, nor is it the only state, to pass legislation to protect electronic data.[374] There has been a "wave of privacy legislation" across the nation because the issue has crossed political and ideological lines.[375] However, the CalECPA is among the most comprehensive laws passed thus far.[376] Therefore, this law is poised to have a tremendous impact on the nearly thirty-nine million residents who live in the state of California.[377] This paper seeks to evaluate the effectiveness of the CalECPA in terms of how the statute will work in practice, because the bill may serve as a model for reforms by other states or even the federal government.[378] It

---

[373] Susan Freiwald, *It's Time to Look to California for Robust Privacy Reform — CalECPA*, AM. CONST. SOC. BLOG (Sept. 8, 2015), http://www.acslaw.org/acsblog/it%E 2%80%99s-time-to-look-to-california-for-robust-privacy-reform-%E2%80%94-calecpa; Dave Maass, *Victory in California! Gov. Brown Signs CalECPA, Requiring Police to Get a Warrant Before Accessing Your Data*, ELEC. FRONTIER FOUND. (Oct. 8, 2015), https://www.eff.org/deeplinks/2015/10/victory-california-gov-brown-signs-calecpa-requiring-police-get-warrant-accessing.

[374] Five states have legislation to protect digital communications, and nine states have legislated protection for GPS information. Colleen Kriel, *California Senate Says Cops Need Warrant to Search Smartphones, Tablets*, SILICONANGLE (Jun. 4, 2015), http://siliconangle.com/blog/2015/06/04/california-senate-says-cops -need-warrant-to-search-smartphones-tablets/. California, Maine, Texas, Utah and Virginia all enforce strict policies for digital records. Cassidy Fix, *Digital Privacy Enhanced by New California Law*, WESTERN SUN (Oct. 21, 2015), http://www.westernsun.us/digital-privacy-enhanced-by-new-bill/.

[375] Sagiv Galai and Tekendra Parmar, *How Edward Snowden Changed Everything*, THE NATION (Nov. 12, 2015), http://www.thenation.com/article/how-edward-snowden-changed-everything/.

[376] Hanni Fakhoury, senior staff attorney for the Electronic Frontier Foundation, stated that only Maine and Utah had similarly comprehensive laws on the books prior to California. Bree Fowler, *New California Law Extends Privacy Rights to Electronic Data*, ASSOC. PRESS (Oct. 9, 2015), http://bigstory.ap.org/article/bfd1c4d1ecad4eaba446 bcecb8935d69/new-california-law-extends-privacy-rights-electronic-data.

[377] This estimate is current as of July 1, 2014. *QuickFacts*, U.S. CENSUS BUREAU, http://www.census.gov/quickfacts/ table/PST045214/00,06.

[378] The EFF explicitly voiced this hope on the October 8 passing of the bill: "We hope that California's success will lend momentum to the federal Electronic Communications Privacy Act." Dave Maass , *Victory in California! Gov. Brown Signs CalECPA, Requiring Police to Get a Warrant Before Accessing Your Data*, ELEC. FRONTIER

argues that the CalECPA is a good first step in balancing both individual privacy rights and law enforcement needs; however, it will not be able to fully close the gap in Fourth Amendment protection, as it still leaves some important questions unanswered. Part I lays out the relevant background and Fourth Amendment framework for electronic data. Part II discusses the robust privacy safeguards the bill creates and what problems the CalECPA is able to solve. Part III describes what is not covered by the bill and highlights some areas of concern. The final section concludes.

II. BACKGROUND

The historical purpose of the Fourth Amendment was to prohibit "general warrants,"[379] a tactic the English colonial government employed in order to enforce unpopular trade and navigation acts.[380] Today, they are also referred to as "writs of assistance." [381] General warrants gave officers carte blanche to search the papers, homes, and possessions of any person,[382] and they did not give a sufficiently particularized description of the

---

FOUND. (Oct. 8, 2015), https://www.eff.org/deeplinks/2015/10/victory-california-gov-brown-signs-calecpa-requiring- police-get-warrant-accessing.

[379] The Supreme Court explicitly stated in *Riley* that "the Fourth Amendment was the founding generation's response to the reviled 'general warrants' and 'writs of assistance' of the colonial era, which allowed British officers to rummage through homes in an unrestrained search for evidence of criminal activity." Riley v. California, 134 S. Ct. 2473, 2494 (2014).

[380] *See* PHILLIP A. HUBBART, MAKING SENSE OF SEARCH AND SEIZURE LAW 23 (Carolina Academic Press, 2nd ed. 2015).

[381] *See* "assistance" Encyclopedia Britannica. 2015. http://www.britannica.com/topic/writ-of-assistance.

[382] David Snyder, *The NSA's "General Warrants: How the Founding Fathers Fought an 18th Century Version of the President's Illegal Domestic Spying,* ELEC. FRONTIER FOUND. 2, https://www.eff.org/files/filenode/att/general warrantsmemo.pdf.

person or thing to be seized or the place to be searched.[383] The English Government used general warrants to search colonists, regardless of whether they were suspected of committing a crime.[384]

Today general warrants would be considered unconstitutional because they fail to meet the Fourth Amendment's specificity requirements.[385] Though it may seem anachronistic to discuss centuries-old evidentiary procedure, general warrants were on the minds of the legislators writing the CalECPA. When California State Assemblyman Jay Obernolte (33rd Assembly, Republican) introduced the bill to the California Senate, he specifically mentioned how the "hated writs" were a catalyst of the American Revolution.[386] He also noted how the founders "enshrined the hatred of those kinds of searches into the Fourth Amendment."[387]

a. The Reasonable Expectation of Privacy in Electronic Information

The Fourth Amendment protects against unreasonable searches and seizures by the government.[388] In early interpretations, the Fourth Amendment was thought to limit only searches and seizures of tangible property within constitutionally-protected areas.[389]

---

[383] Historically, a general warrant was issued by the English Secretary of State for the arrest of an author, printer, or publisher of seditious libel, but the warrant did not name the person(s) to be arrested. WARRANT, Black's Law Dictionary (10th ed. 2014).

[384] Snyder, *supra* note 384, at 1.

[385] WARRANT, Black's Law Dictionary (10th ed. 2014).

[386] He proclaimed that the writs of assistance, "allowed any government official to search a person anytime, at any place, and for any reason, without even suspecting that person of a crime." *See* Asm. Obernolte Introduces S.B. 178☐ – Opening Remarks (video of Sept. 8, 2015), Ca. Assemb. G.O.P. Vimeo, https://vimeo.com/138779358.

[387] *Id.*

[388] U.S. Const. amend. IV.

[389] *Olmstead v. U.S.*, 277 U.S. 438 (1928), held a search required a physical trespass of property; while *Goldman v. U.S.*, 316 U.S. 129 (1942), held a search required a physical intrusion. In that case, the police held a cup against a wall to listen to the defendant, but the Court determined that only things being "searched for" were the suspects' voices, which are not tangible property. *Cf.* Professor Orin Kerr, *The Curious History of Fourth Amendment Searches.* GWU Law School Public Law Research Paper No. 2012-107 (September 30, 2012), http://ssrn.com/abstract=215461(arguing that the pre-*Katz*

However in the 1967 watershed *Katz* case, the Supreme Court expressly overruled that understanding and created the "reasonable expectation of privacy" framework to analyze whether a search was prohibited by the Fourth Amendment.[390] Justice Harlan's concurrence became the guiding directive with a two-part inquiry: 1) Did the target of the search have an actual, subjective expectation of privacy? and 2) Is the target's subjective expectation of privacy one that society is prepared to recognize as reasonable?[391]

The second, objective prong of the analysis has been the principal challenge for those wishing to protect privacy rights in digital or electronic content because of the nature of the way data is transferred and shared with various providers, websites, and platforms. The third-party doctrine and exceptions to the warrant requirement, such as exigency or consent, are also problematic for the protection of electronic content. The consent exception is especially injurious to Fourth Amendment safeguards because the government does not need probable cause, nor reasonable suspicion of criminal activity, if it has consent to perform a search.

b. The Third-Party and Public Disclosure Doctrines

The Supreme Court has ruled that there is no Fourth Amendment protection for information voluntarily disclosed to third parties.[392] The basic premise of the third-party doctrine is that a

---

"trespass test" history was an invention of the *Katz* court and tracking the real history of the Fourth Amendment by examining case law).

[390]   Katz v. U.S., 389 U.S. 347 (1967).

[391]   *Id.* at 361.

[392]   *See* Smith v. Maryland, 442 U.S. 735, 743 (1979) (saying there is no reasonable expectation of privacy in the dialed phone dialed numbers because individuals "know that they must convey numerical information to the phone company."); U.S. v. Miller, 425 US 435, 442 (1976), (finding there is no reasonable expectation of privacy in bank

person loses all reasonable expectation of privacy to information disclosed to someone else.[393] It makes no difference if a person revealed that information only for a limited time or a limited purpose.[394] The California Supreme Court has noted that for all practical purposes certain disclosures are "not entirely volitional", and it has tried to provide additional protections when necessary.[395] Features of

---

records because they were voluntarily given to the banks and their employees). However, Justice Sotomayer has expressed a desire to reexamine this doctrine:

> More fundamentally, it may be necessary to reconsider the premise that an individual has no reasonable expectation of privacy in information voluntarily disclosed to third parties. *E.g., Smith,* 442 U.S., at 742, 99 S. Ct. 2577; *United States v. Miller,* 425 U.S. 435, 443, 96 S. Ct. 1619, 48 L.Ed.2d 71 (1976). This approach is ill suited to the digital age, in which people reveal a great deal of information about themselves to third parties in the course of carrying out mundane tasks. People disclose the phone numbers that they dial or text to their cellular providers; the URLs that they visit and the e-mail addresses with which they correspond to their Internet service providers; and the books, groceries, and medications they purchase to online retailers. . . . . I would not assume that all information voluntarily disclosed to some member of the public for a limited purpose is, for that reason alone, disentitled to Fourth Amendment protection. See *Smith,* 442 U.S., at 749, 99 S. Ct. 2577 (Marshall, J., dissenting) ("Privacy is not a discrete commodity, possessed absolutely or not at all. Those who disclose certain facts to a bank or phone company for a limited business purpose need not assume that this information will be released to other persons for other purposes"); see also *Katz,* 389 U.S., at 351–352, 88 S. Ct. 507 ("[W]hat [a person] seeks to preserve as private, even in an area accessible to the public, may be constitutionally protected").

United States v. Jones, 132 S. Ct. 945, 957 (2012). With the Court's recent grant of certiorari to *Carpenter v. U.S.,* No. 16-402, there is a possibility this doctrine may change when the Court reviews the Fourth Amendment's applicability to historical cell-site data. U.S. v. Carpenter, 819 F.3d 880 (6th Cir. 2016), *cert. granted* 137 S. Ct. 2211 (2017).

[393] Monu Bedi, *The Curious Case of Cell Phone Location Data: Fourth Amendment Doctrine Mash Up,* 110 Nw. U. L. Rev. Online 61, 64 (2015), http://scholarlycommons .law.northwestern.edu/cgi/viewcontent.cgi?article= 1231&context=nulr_online.

[394] Miller, 425 U.S. at 443.

[395] Burrows v. Superior Court, 13 Cal. 3d 238, 247, (1974) ("The underlying dilemma in this and related cases is that the bank, a detached and disinterested entity, relinquished the records voluntarily. But that circumstance should not be crucial. For all practical purposes, the disclosure by individuals or business firms of their financial affairs to a bank is not entirely volitional, since it is impossible to participate in the economic life of contemporary society without maintaining a bank account. In the course of such

electronic devices, such as location data, may also implicate the "public disclosure" doctrine, which addresses a person's movements in public that can be viewed by others.[396] In *United States v. Knotts*, the Supreme Court held a person does not have a reasonable expectation of privacy in movements subject to visual surveillance,[397] including what may be observed by flying a plane overhead.[398]Additi onally, without Fourth Amendment protection of third-party records, the government is able to access an extensive amount of personal information, which is especially complicated by technology.

c. Technology-Specific Problems

How to treat electronic information has befuddled Fourth Amendment analysis since its inception. One principal reason is because there has long been a divide between content—which earns protection—and information that is not classified as content, such as metadata—which does not.[399] The Fourth Amendment is not always perceived to encompass the latter, which includes IP addresses, email to/from field information, search terms, browsing history, or location data.[400]

---

dealings, a depositor reveals many aspects of his personal affairs, opinions, habits and associations. Indeed, the totality of bank records provides a virtual current biography."); and *Id.* at 247–48, ("Development of photocopying machines, electronic computers and other sophisticated instruments have accelerated the ability of government to intrude into areas which a person normally chooses to exclude from prying eyes and inquisitive minds. Consequently judicial interpretations of the reach of the constitutional protection of individual privacy must keep pace with the perils created by these new devices.").

[396] Bedi, *supra* note 395, at 66.

[397] United States v. Knotts, 460 U.S. 276, 281–82 (1983).

[398] California v. Ciraolo, 476 U.S. 207, 212–13 (holding there was no Fourth Amendment violation because "[a]ny member of the public flying in this airspace who glanced down could have seen everything that these officers observed.").

[399] *Id.*

At the federal level, there is a split regarding bulk metadata collection of cell phone location data.[401] Some judges have held that "the indiscriminate, daily bulk collection, long-term retention, and analysis of telephony metadata almost certainly violates a person's reasonable expectation of privacy."[402] Other courts have held the opposite to be true.[403]

Internet security expert Susan Landau has argued that metadata may actually be *more* revealing than content.[404] When a person calls someone else, and who they call, may act as a proxy for content.[405] Former National Security Agency (NSA) General Counsel Stewart Baker once proclaimed: "metadata absolutely tells you everything about somebody's life. If you have enough metadata, you don't really need content." Gen. Michael Hayden, former director of the NSA and the CIA, has stated publicly: "We kill people based on metadata." [406]

---

[400] Freiwald, *supra* note 375. Quite simply, and almost tautologically, metadata is data about data. *See* "metadata." Merriam-Webster Online Dictionary. 2015. http://www.merriam-webster.com/dictionary/metadata.

[401] Monu Bedi, *The Curious Case of Cell Phone Location Data: Fourth Amendment Doctrine Mash Up*, 110 Nw. U. L. Rev. Online 61, 62 (2015)..

[402] Mem. Op. of Nov. 9, 2015, Klayman v. Obama, Civil Action No. 13-851 (D.C. Cir.), http://pdfserver.amlaw.com/nlj/NSA_klayman_20151109.pdf, at 26.

[403] Mem. & Order of Dec. 27, 2013, ACLU v. Clapper, Civil Action No. 13-3994 (S.D.N.Y.), https://www.aclu.org/files/assets/order_granting_governments_motion_to_d ismiss_and_denying_aclu_motion_for_ preliminary_injunction.pdf at 2.

[404] Mike Godwin, *Our Inboxes, Ourselves*, Slate (Sept. 15, 2015), http://www.slate.com/articles/technology/future_tense/2015/09/ecpa_reform_the_1986_ email_privacy_law_might_f inally_get_updated.html.

[405] Landau shows how one may be able to discern intimate details of a person's life by using the example of a call log where an individual receives a call from a gynecologist, then that person places a call to an oncologist, and then she makes calls to her family members. *Id.*

[406] *Id.*

Location information can be particularly sensitive. As Professor Catherine Crump explained in her TED Talk, it can reveal whether or not you see a "therapist, attend an Alcoholics Anonymous meeting, if you go to church or if you don't go to church."[408] Furthermore, the creation of some location data, like other forms of metadata, may not be entirely voluntary. For example, iPhones have the ability to track a person's "Frequent Locations." This feature records places someone has recently been, as well as when and how often they have been there.[409]

Additionally, the search of electronic devices raises additional challenges for Fourth Amendment law because of the incredible storage capacity of the devices.[410] For example, if one were to carry an eight gigabyte flash drive, that device would be able to store

---

[407] Edward Snowden, TWITTER (Nov. 2, 2015), https://twitter.com/Snowden/status/6613 05566967562240.

[408] Catherine Crump, *The Small and Surprisingly Dangerous Detail the Police Track About You*, TED (Dec. 2014), https://www.ted.com/talks/catherine_crump_the_small_an d_surprisingly_dangerous_detail_the_police_track_about_you/transcript?language=en at :50.

[409] *See* Apple Support, support.apple.com/kb/HT5594.

[410] Orin Kerr, *Executing Warrants for Digital Evidence: The Case for Use Restrictions on Nonresponsive Data,* 48 TEX. TECH. L. R. 1, 1 (Fall 2015), https://ssrn.com/abstract=2628586, [hereinafter *Executing Warrants*].

approximately 520,000 pages of Microsoft Word documents.[411] Professor Elizabeth Joh has remarked that "nearly all of the world's stored information today is digital, and we are surpassing existing mathematical terms to quantify it."[412] This technological change represents not only a difference in degree but also a difference in kind, a distinction that the judiciary must recognize.[413]

As the Supreme Court remarked in *Riley*:

> Modern cell phones, as a category, implicate privacy concerns far beyond those implicated by the search of a cigarette pack, a wallet, or a purse. A conclusion that inspecting the contents of an arrestee's pockets works no substantial additional intrusion on privacy beyond the arrest itself may make sense as applied to physical items, but any extension of that reasoning to digital data has to rest on its own bottom.[414]

Californians use technology everyday "to connect, work, and learn."[415] Today nearly two-thirds of Americans own a smartphone,[416]

---

[411]   *Id*, at 1 n.2; *See generally, How Many Pages in a Gigabyte?*, LEXISNEXIS, https://www.lexisnexis.com/applieddiscovery/lawlibrary/whitePapers/ADI_FS_PagesInAGigabyte.pdf.

[412]   Elizabeth E. Joh, *The New Surveillance Discretion: Automated Suspicion, Big Data, and Policing*, 10 HARV. L. & POL'Y REV. 15, 20 (2016).

[413]   Galai and Parmar, *supra* note 377. "Admittedly, what metadata *is* has not changed over time. As in *Smith*, the *types* of information at issue in this case are relatively limited: phone numbers dialed, date, time, and the like. But the ubiquity of phones has dramatically altered the *quantity* of the information that is now available, and *more importantly*, what that information can tell the Government about people's lives." Mem. Op. of Dec. 16, 2013, Klayman v. Obama, Civil Action No. 13-851 (D.C. Cir.), http://legaltimes.typepad.com/files/obamansa.pdf.

[414]   Riley v. California, 134 S. Ct. 2473, 2488–89 (2014).

[415]   Sen. Loni Hancock, S.B. 178 (Leno) – Privacy, Senate Committee on Public Safety Report p. 7, 2015-2016 Regular Session (Mar. 16, 2015), https://www.eff.org/document/senate-pubic-safety-committee-sb-178-analysis.

and these devices are used for much more than just calling, texting, or taking "selfies."[417] Sixty-two percent of smartphone owners have used their phone in the past year to look up information about a health condition, while fifty-seven percent have used their device to do online banking.[418] Forty-three percent have looked up information about a job, and eighteen percent have even submitted a job application using their phone. [419] Individuals with lower incomes are "especially likely" to rely on their phones for a job search.[420]

Another technology-specific question in Fourth Amendment jurisprudence is what should become of non-responsive data, data that falls outside the scope of a warrant, that is inevitably retrieved in device searches. Without some type of limit on the use of non-responsive data that is seized under a warrant, the warrant runs the risk of becoming a general warrant. There really is no physical-world equivalent to this type of problem.

---

[416] Aaron Smith, *U.S. Smartphone Use in 2015*, PEW RESEARCH CENTER (Apr. 1, 2015), http://www.pewinternet.org/2015/04/01/us-smartphone-use-in-2015/, [hereinafter *Pew Report*].

[417] It has been estimated that on average, a million "selfies" are taken each day. Marvin Heiferman, *Who's Who? The Changing Nature and Uses of Portraits*, NY TIMES (BLOG) (Nov. 16, 2015), http://lens.blogs.nytimes.com/2015/11/16/whos-who-the-changing-nature-and-uses-of-portraits/?smid=pl-share.

[418] Aaron Smith, *U.S. Smartphone Use in 2015*, PEW RESEARCH CENTER (Apr. 1, 2015), http://www.pewinternet.org/2015/04/01/us-smartphone-use-in-2015/.

[419] *Id.*

[420] "Compared with smartphone owners from households earning $75,000 or more per year, those from households earning less than $30,000 annually are nearly twice as likely to use a smartphone to look for information about a job — and more than four times as likely to use their phone to actually submit a job application." *Id.*

d. The Problem of Notice

In the digital world generally, there is lack of notice of what actually happens with one's personal data.[421] However, after Edward Snowden's revelations in 2013 about the bulk electronic information collection, many Americans became aware for the first time that they were being observed by the government.[422] Some of the biggest surprises, such as the fact that the NSA collected text messages, or that there were secret court orders that allowed the NSA to sweep up phone records, were not known—or likely even suspected—by most Americans.[423] Accordingly, Americans have become more concerned about warrantless access of their digital information.[424] Society at large has been much more critical of, or at least vocal about, government infringements of civilian privacy in the wake of Snowden's disclosures.[425]

---

[421] Daniel J. Solove, *"I've Got Nothing to Hide" and Other Misunderstandings of Privacy*, 44 SAN DIEGO L. REV. 745, 757–58 (2007), http://ssrn.com/abstract=998565.

[422] Glenn Greenwald, *NSA Collecting Phone Records of Millions of Verizon Customers Daily*, GUARDIAN (June 6, 2013), http://www.theguardian.com/world/2013/jun/06/nsa-phone-records-verizon-court-order.

[423] Lorenzo Franceschi-Bicchierai, *The 10 Biggest Revelations from Edward Snowden's Leaks*, MASHABLE (Jun. 5, 2014), http://mashable.com/2014/06/05/edward-snowden-revelations/#rqO20Rw7OiqS.

[424] Eighty percent of adults "agree" or "strongly agree" that Americans should be concerned about the government's monitoring of phone calls and internet communications, while only 18 percent "disagree" or "strongly disagree" with that notion. Mary Madden, *Public Perceptions of Privacy and Security in the Post-Snowden Era*, PEW RESEARCH CENTER (Nov. 12, 2014), http://www.pewinternet.org/2014/11/12/public-privacy-perceptions/. *See also*, Nicole A. Ozer, *Get a Warrant! Senate Committee Approves E-Privacy Bill*, ACLU OF S. CAL. (Mar. 24, 2015), https://www.aclusocal.org/senate-calecpa/; Colleen Kriel, *California Senate Says Cops Need Warrant to Search Smartphones, Tablets* SILICONANGLE (Jun. 4, 2015), http://siliconangle.com/blog/2015/06/04/california-senate- says-cops-need-warrant-to-search-smartphones-tablets/.

[425] *Chapter Four: Considering Police Body Cameras*, 128 HARV. L. REV 1794, 1810–11 and n.102 (2015). In response to newly passed law, the NSA will stop its wide-ranging surveillance program and replace it with a scaled-back system, *NSA Ends Bulk Collection of U.S. Phone Records*, AL JAZEERA AM. (Nov. 28, 2015), http://www.aljazeera.com/news/2015/11/nsa-ends-bulk-collection-phone-records-151128172222095.html. *See also*, Ozer, *supra* note 426.

e. The Time is Ripe for Change

The CalECPA has arrived at a particularly critical juncture in history. In the past five years, Google has seen a 250 percent jump in government demands for consumer data.[426] In 2014, AT&T received 64,000 demands from law enforcement – a 70 percent increase from the previous year.[427] Verizon reports that only one-third of its requests had a warrant. Twitter and Tumblr stated that in 2014 they received more demands from California than any other state. [428]

Contemporaneously with the passing of CalECPA, Nancy O'Malley, the District Attorney of Alameda County, was in the process of purchasing a StingRay, a cell site simulator.[429] The

---

[426]   S.B. 178 *(Leno and Anderson) Fact Sheet*, ELEC. FRONTIER FOUND. (Version Feb. 2, 2015), https://www.eff.org/files/2015/02/09/calecpa_fact_sheet.2.9.15.pdf.

[427]   Nicole A. Ozer, *Victory for Privacy Rights in California*, THE PEOPLE'S VANGUARD OF DAVIS, (Sept. 13, 2015), http://www.davisvanguard.org/2015/09/victory-for-privacy-rights-in-california/.

[428]   S.B. 178 *(Leno and Anderson) Fact Sheet*, ELEC. FRONTIER FOUND. (Version Mar. 18, 2015), https://www.eff.org/files/2015/03/18/sb_178_calecpa_fact_sheet_3_18_15.pdf.

[429]   Cell site simulators are devices that act like a cellphone tower. They trick devices in the area into connecting with them which enables law enforcement to get a person's ISMI information or also possibly access communications. A "StingRay" is the brand name for a cell site simulator made by Harris Corp. Even though the device has not been in the public eye for a long time, it appears already to be suffering from "genericide," or brand tarnishment. Devices made by other manufacturers are often referred to as "StingRays." *See Stingray Tracking Devices: Who's Got Them?*, ACLU, https://www.aclu.org/map/stingray-tracking-devices-whos-got-them; Kim Zetter, *Turns Out Police Stingray Spy Tools Can Indeed Record Calls*, WIRED.COM (Oct. 28, 2015), http://www.wired.com/2015/10/stingray-government-spy-tools-can-record-calls-new-documents-confirm.

The device is also known by a number of other names, including an IMSI-catcher, Triggerfish, Kingfish, Amberjack, Hailstorm, Wolfpack, Gossamer, and swamp box. Kim Zetter, *Turns Out Police Stingray Spy Tools Can Indeed Record Calls*, WIRED.COM (Oct. 28, 2015), http://www.wired.com/2015/10/stingray-government-spy-tools-can-record-calls-new-documents-confirm/; *Cell Site Simulators Primer*,

Attorney General's office publically supported the purchase.[430] The desire for this type of purchase illustrates tension in California presently between protecting privacy and legitimate law enforcement interest in acquiring more electronic data.[431]

Nevertheless, at the moment, the tide seems to be supporting privacy protections.[432] Governor Jerry Brown also recently signed a bill[433] that made it illegal for companies to target customers with ads based on data gathered through a voice recognition feature, such as those on Smart TVs.[434] Creating legal boundaries for privacy is especially important given that the "Internet of Things", the name given to the network of physical objects able to connect to the Internet, is rapidly expanding.[435]

Technology companies have also begun to pressure the government for reforms, because eroding customer trust can impact

---

National Association of Criminal Defense Lawyers (NACDL), https://www.law.berkel ey.edu/wp-content/uploads/2015/04/2016-4-28_Cell-Site-Simulator-Primer_Final.pdf.

[430] Ali Winston, *East Bay Cellphone Surveillance Plan Gets Attorney General's Support*, REVEAL NEWS (Sept. 30, 2015), https://www.revealnews.org/article/east-bay-cellphone-surveillance-plan-gets-attorney-generals-support/.

[431] In a meaningful collaboration with privacy advocates, the Alameda County Board of Supervisors passed a comprehensive privacy policy on November 17, 2015. The policy requires a warrant before any deployment of the device and periodic audits of use. *Alameda County Passes Groundbreaking Privacy Policy*, EAST BAY (Nov. 24, 2015), https://www.indybay.org/newsitems/2015/11/24/18780325.php.

[432] Galai and Parmar, *supra* note 377.

[433] CAL. BUS. PROF. CODE §§ 22948.20–22948.25 (West 2017).

[434] Keith Wagstaff, *New California Law Bans Smart TV Snooping*, NBC NEWS (Oct. 7, 2015), http://www.nbcnews.com/tech/security/new-california-law-bans-smart-tv-snooping-n440311.

[435] Catherine Crump and Matthew Harwood, *Invasion of the Data Snatchers: Big Data and the Internet of Things Means the Surveillance of Everything*, ACLU (Mar. 25, 2014), https://www.aclu.org/blog/speakeasy/invasion-data-snatchers-big-data-and-intern et-things-means-surveillance-everything. Recently, Bose was sued by plaintiffs who alleged that its headphones were recording users' music choices. Hayley Tsukayama, *Bose Headphones Have Been Spying on Their Customers, Lawsuit Claims*, WASH. POST (Apr. 21, 2017), https://www.washingtonpost.com/news/the-switch/wp/2017/04/19/bose-headphones-have-been-spying-on-their-customers-lawsuit-claims/?utm_term=.fddaa9b7a8d4&wpisrc=nl_tech&wpmm=1.

their bottom line.[436] In the post-Snowden era, companies are intent on demonstrating that they care about protecting customer information.[437]

Finally, it is a good time to reform the law surrounding electronic searches, because the status quo's lack of clarity is challenging not only for individual privacy but also for law enforcement who must then navigate the murky waters of unclear case law.[438]

III. WHAT THE CALECPA COVERS

a. Clear Standards to Obtain Electronic Information

The CalECPA creates straightforward, uniform standards for the acquisition of electronic information across California for state actors.[439] The authors of the bill hoped that with clearly-defined criteria, law enforcement would be "more confident that they followed due process," and this would demonstrate law

---

[436] For example, the Snowden leaks were estimated to cause companies to lose between $22–35 billion in the three years following his disclosures. Daniel Castro, *How Much Will PRISM Cost the U.S. Cloud Computing Industry?*, INFO. TECH. & INNOVATION FOUND. (Aug. 2013), http://www2.itif.org/2013-cloud-computing-costs.pdf?_ga =1.120059528.1612146265.1450036081

[437] Matt Apuzzo, David E. Sanger, and Michael S. Schmidt, Apple and Other Tech Companies Tangle with U.S. Over Data Access, N.Y. TIMES (Sept. 7, 2015), http://www.nytimes.com/2015/09/08/us/politics/apple-and-other-tech-companies-tangle-with-us-over-access-to-data.html.

[438] Federal Magistrate Judge (S.D. Cal.), the Hon. James F. Stiven, writes: "[d]espite strong support for S.B. 178 in existing law, its passage will bring needed clarity for all those affected, including law enforcement. Ca. State. Ass. Comm. on Privacy and Consumer Protection, Mike Gatto, S.B. 178 (Leno) as Amended June 2, 2015 (Jun. 23, 2015) at 8.

[439] CAL. PENAL CODE § 1546(i).

enforcement's "commitment to finding the right balance between civil liberties and public safety."[440]

In order to compel production of or access to "electronic communication information" or "electronic device information," law enforcement must get a warrant, a wiretap order, or an order of electronic reader records.[441]

Using technology to physically interact with, or to electronically communicate with, a device to obtain any of what the law defines as "electronic device information" triggers the warrant or wiretap order requirement.[442] However, the law also provides for emergency access without obtaining a warrant or wiretap order if there is a risk of "death or serious physical injury,"[443] or if the authorized possessor of the device gives specific consent.[444] If a device is lost or stolen, law enforcement can help locate it, with the specific consent of the owner to do so.[445] Furthermore, if a device is found, and the government believes it was lost or stolen, the government may access the device information, but only to the extent necessary to identify or contact the owner.[446] Law enforcement must comply with these bright-line requirements in order to comply with the CalECPA.[447]

b. Particularity and Avoiding General Warrants

The Fourth Amendment requires that a warrant "particularly describe the place to be searched."[448] However, the storage capacity

---

[440] Dave Maass, *Why Law Enforcement Professionals Should Support CalECPA,* ELEC. FRONTIER FOUND. (Sept. 2, 2015), https://www.eff.org/deeplinks/2015/09/why-law-enforcement-professionals-should-support-calecpa.

[441] CAL. PENAL CODE § 1546.1(b)(1–3).

[442] § 1546.1(c)(1) and (2).

[443] § 1546.1(c)(5).

[444] § 1546.1(c)(3).

[445] § 1546.1(c)(4).

[446] § 1546.1(c)(6).

[447] § 1546.1(a).

of electronic devices might undermine the limiting role of the particularity requirement.[449] For searches of electronic devices, the "place" to be searched may not be as significant of a restriction as it is with physical searches.[450] A house may have many devices, cellphones could have lots of content, and even very particularly described evidence could be located anywhere on a device.[451] As Professor Orin Kerr has argued, the facts of digital storage "create the prospect that computer warrants that are specific on their face will resemble general warrants in execution simply because of the new technological environment.□□[452] The law is very settled on this point: general warrants are constitutionally unreasonable under the Fourth Amendment "even if they may be useful to solve crimes."[453]

The CalECPA requires that "[t]he warrant shall describe with particularity the information to be seized by specifying the time periods covered and, as appropriate and reasonable, the target individuals or accounts, the applications or services covered, and the types of information sought."[454] Thus it seems that this specific provision of the law attempts to solve this concern, and it may help California avoided falling into the trap of general warrants for electronic searches.

c. Metadata and Location Data are Covered

---

[448]   U.S. Const. amend. IV.

[449]   *Executing Warrants, supra* note 412, at 2.

[450]   *Id.* at 16.

[451]   *Id.* at 19.

[452]   *Id.* at 34.

[453]   *Id.* at 29

[454]   Cal. Penal Code § 1546.1(d)(1).

Though often ignored by courts and its importance denied, metadata was given unambiguous protection by the CalECPA.[455] The bill makes no distinction between "deliberate and involuntary expression," a distinction that has long precluded metadata from protection by the judiciary.[456]The CalECPA explicitly protects "electronic information."[457] The bill defines this as both "electronic device information" and "electronic communication information."[458]

The CalECPA's definition of "electronic device information" encompasses "any information stored on or generated through the operation of an electronic device, including the current and prior locations of the device."[459] Therefore, the CalECPA protects private electronic communications such as emails, text messages and location data that are stored on devices, as well as information stored in the cloud.[460] Previously, information stored on the cloud might not have been considered to have a reasonable expectation of privacy, since it was hosted by – and thus had been disclosed to – a third party, in accordance with the third party doctrine.[461]

---

[455] § 1546(d).

[456] Samuel D. Warren and Louis D. Brandeis, *The Right to Privacy,* 4 Harv. L. Rev. 193, 206–207 (1890).

[457] CAL. PENAL CODE § 1546(h).

[458] *Id.*

[459] § 1546(g).

[460] Grant P. Fondo and Nathanial J. Moore, *California Enacts CalECPA, Requiring a Search Warrant to Obtain or Access Users' Electronic Information,* GOODWIN PROCTOR (Oct. 14, 2015), http://www.goodwinprocter.com/Publications/Newsletters/Client-Alert/2015/10_14-California-Enacts-CalECPA-Requiring-a-Search-Warrant-to-Obtain-or-Access-Users-Electronic.aspx?article=1.

[461] For a detailed discussion of this issue, *see* Ryan Watzel, Riley's Implications for Fourth Amendment Protection in the Cloud, 124 YALE L.J. F. 73 (2014), http://www.yalelawjournal.org/forum/rileys -implications-in-the-cloud. The author notes that the Supreme Court's ruling in *Riley* protected only data stored in the cloud accessible on a cell phone. He argues that the Supreme Court explicitly sidestepped a broader discussion of how the third-party doctrine applies to cloud storage generally (citing Riley, 134 S. Ct. at 2489 n.1 "Because the United States and California agree that these cases involve searches incident to arrest, these cases do not implicate the question whether the collection or inspection of aggregated digital information amounts to a search under other circumstances.").

The bill defines "electronic communication information" as "information about an electronic communication or the use of an electronic communication service."[462] The illustrative examples include "the contents, sender, recipients, format, or location of the sender or recipients at any point during the communication, the time or date the communication was created, sent, or received, or any information pertaining to any individual or device participating in the communication, including, but not limited to, an IP address." [463] This definition, in conjunction with section 1546(a)(1) which precludes "the production of or access to electronic communication information from a service provider," effectively closes the gap created by *Smith v. Maryland*.[464]

However, "subscriber information," which includes amongst other things, "name, street address, telephone number, email address, or similar contact information" and the account number is not considered "electronic communication information" or "electronic information" and thus is not afforded any protections by the CalECPA.[465] Also, service providers are still permitted to "voluntarily" turn over phone record metadata or other electronic information,[466] and they may not be sued civilly for doing so.[467]

---

[462] CAL. PENAL CODE § 1546(d).

[463] *Id.*

[464] Smith v. Maryland, 442 U.S. 735 (1979).

[465] CAL. PENAL CODE § 1546(l).

[466] § 1546.1 (a)(3), and it is also repeated in § 1546.1 (f).

[467] "A California or foreign corporation, and its officers, employees, and agents, are not subject to any cause of action for providing records, information, facilities, or assistance in accordance with the terms of a warrant, court order, statutory authorization, emergency certification, or wiretap order issued pursuant to this chapter." § 1546.4(d).

d. Notice is Provided

Another success of the bill is its notice requirement.[468] When a government entity executes a warrant, or obtains information in one of the emergency scenarios defined in § 1546.1, the bill clearly delineates how and when that entity must inform the subject of its investigation.[469] The notice can be served by a variety of means "reasonably calculated to be effective," including email.[470] Notice must be given contemporaneously with the execution of the warrant, or in the case of a § 1546.1 emergency situation, within three days after obtaining electronic information.[471]

In addition to timely notification, the bill further provides that the notice not only indicate that information has been "compelled or requested" by the government but also that it "state[] with reasonable specificity the nature of the government investigation under which the information is sought."[472] A copy of the warrant must be included in the notice, or a "written statement setting forth facts giving rise to the emergency."[473]

If a court does permit law enforcement to delay notification,[474] notice must be still be given in accordance with the above requirements, along with a statement containing the court's grounds for allowing the delay.[475] Furthermore, after a period of delay, the notification must also include either a copy of all the electronic data

---

[468]   § 1546.2.

[469]   *Id.*

[470]   § 1546.2 (a) "[A]ny government entity... shall serve upon, or deliver to by registered or first-class mail, electronic mail, or other means reasonably calculated to be effective, the identified targets of the warrant or emergency request."

[471]   § 1546.2 (a).

[472]   *Id.*

[473]   *Id.*

[474]   The option to delay notification is discussed in further detail in Part II.D.

[475]   CAL. PENAL CODE § 1546.2 (b)(3).

taken or a summary of that information.[476] At a minimum, this summary must include the number and types of records and the date and time when the earliest and latest records were created.[477]

e. Law Enforcement Needs are Given Proper Deference

Law enforcement was actively involved in negotiations with the bill's authors, and thus, by the time CalECPA was signed, their legitimate concerns were alleviated.[478] A letter to Senator Leno on behalf of the California State Sheriffs' Association went so far as to say, "Thank you for working with law enforcement to ensure that the correct balance is struck between the need for law enforcement to obtain information regarding criminal activities from electronic communications and the privacy interests of those who use email and other forms of electronic communication."[479] The CalECPA comports with the aspirational goals of the criminal justice system: that the guilty not escape nor the innocent suffer.[480]

---

[476] *Id.*

[477] *Id.*

[478] The California District Attorneys Association, California Police Chiefs Association, California Sheriffs Association, and the California Statewide Law Enforcement Association were also neutral on the bill. *In Landmark Victory for Digital Privacy, Gov. Brown Signs California Electronic Communications Privacy Act into Law,* ACLU OF N. CAL. (Oct. 8, 2015), https://www.aclunc.org/news/landmark-victory-digital-privacy-gov-brown-signs- california-electronic-communications-privacy. One consideration, which was not raised by law enforcement, but is nonetheless ostensibly resolved by the CalECPA, was the matter of cost. The Senate Appropriations Committee noted that there might be significant one-time costs, as well as ongoing expenses associated with providing notice, though the Committee believed that agencies could be reimbursed using the State General Fund. *See* CAL. SEN. COMM. ON APPROPRIATIONS REP., S.B. 178 - PRIVACY, 2015–2016 Reg. Sess., at 1–2 (2015), https://www.eff.org/document/ senate-appropriations-committee-sb-178-analysis.

[479] Letter from Cal. State Sheriffs' Assoc. to Sen. Mark Leno, *supra* note 17.

[480] Berger v. United States, 295 U.S. 78, 88 (1935).

Prior to changes to the bill, there was opposition by a Tennessee-based group called the National Organization to Protect Children, also known as "PROTECT."[481] Marty Vranicar of the California District Attorneys Association also warned that the bill would "undermine efforts to find child exploitation," specifically child pornography.[482]

PROTECT was concerned primarily that notice requirements could lead to destruction of evidence by telling "child pornography suspects [law enforcement is] coming."[483] The final version of the bill, however, provides the ability to delay notification for up to 90 days when a court determines "there is reason to believe that notification may have an adverse result."[484] A court may also grant additional delays of up to 90 days at a time to support the needs of law enforcement investigations.[485]

PROTECT also worried that law enforcement might not be able to demonstrate the risk of "destruction or tampering with evidence requirement" as defined in § 1546(a)(3) in order to delay notifying the subject of the investigation.[486] Notification, however, can be delayed by the threat of an "adverse result," which includes not only the risk of destruction of evidence,[487] but also the

---

[481] Patrick Mcgreevy, *California Requires Warrants to Access Emails*, L.A. TIMES (Oct. 18, 2015), http://www.latimes.com/local/political/la-me-pc-gov-brown-on-warrants-for-emails-20150918-story.html.

[482] Cyrus Farivar, *California bill requires warrant for stingray use*, ARS TECHNICA (Mar. 25, 2015), http://arstechnica.com/tech-policy/2015/03/california-bill-requires-warrant-for-stingray-use/.

[483] *California Electronic Communications Privacy Act – S.B. 178 – Needs Amending*, NAT'L ASSOC. TO PROTECT CHILDREN (Aug. 6, 2015), http://www.protect.org/California-SB178 [hereinafter PROTECT on CalECPA].

[484] CAL. PENAL CODE § 1546.2 (b)(1) (West 2017).

[485] CAL. PENAL CODE § 1546.2 (b)(2) (West 2017); Patrick Mcgreevy, *California Requires Warrants to Access Emails, supra* note 483.

[486] PROTECT on CalECPA, *supra* note 485.

[487] This provision was amended on August 17, 2015 from "[i]mminent destruction" to just "[d]estruction," as well.

possibility of "[d]anger to the life or physical safety of an individual," "[f]light from prosecution," "[i]ntimidation of a witness" or "[s]erious jeopardy to an investigation."[488]

PROTECT raised additional concerns that seemed to stem from a misunderstanding of some of the provisions of the bill. For instance, the organization protested the bill's "data retention limits."[489] However, the data retention limits would not apply to child porn investigations, because data related to those investigations would not be destroyed. The data retention limits apply to non-responsive data unrelated to what was specified in the warrant.[490] Also, there was a specific exception added to the requirement to destroy information "voluntarily" turned over within ninety days, when "the information relates to child pornography and the information is retained as part of a multi-agency database used in the investigation of child pornography and related crime."[491] PROTECT stated that the bill "eliminates most law enforcement subpoena power in child pornography cases."[492] The bill does not alter the use of subpoena power in criminal cases, and in fact confirms the power of subpoena is not limited or affected in non-criminal cases.[493] Lastly, PROTECT was concerned about how the law would affect out-of-state law enforcement issuing a subpoena or warrant in California.[494] The bill,

---

[488] CAL. PENAL CODE § 1546(a)(1–5).

[489] PROTECT on CalECPA, *supra* note 485.

[490] Destruction of data also is not done until "after the termination of the current investigation and any related investigations or proceedings." CAL. PENAL CODE § 1546.1(e)(2).

[491] §1546.1(g)(3).

[492] PROTECT on CalECPA, *supra* note 485.

[493] CAL. PENAL CODE § 1546.1(g)(3) (West 2017).

[494] PROTECT on CalECPA, *supra* note 485.

of course, would not apply, as it only covers state and local agencies of California.[495]

The authors of the bill also amended the definition of "specific consent" in response to critiques of earlier versions, so the CalECPA would not require that the "originator of the communication have actual knowledge that an addressee, intended recipient, or member of the specific audience is a government entity" to ensure that child pornography stings and operations could proceed effectively.

One legitimate concern of PROTECT not directly addressed by the final version of the bill is that the bill's emergency provision[496] only covers situations where there is a danger of "death or serious physical injury." [497] PROTECT raised the important point that most child sexual abuse and child pornography production generally do not cause "death or serious physical injury." However, this may not be problematic, because when the emergency provision applies, agencies will be able to proceed as necessary and delay notification. In other instances, they will be able to proceed and delay notification for as long as is necessary using the adverse result exception.

f. Many Technology-Specific Issues Were Resolved

The CalECPA effectively addresses many of the technology-specific problems that have long plagued legislation concerning electronic searches and seizures. For example, many provisions in the bill cover both the "owner," as well as an "authorized possessor"

---

[495] "This section does not limit the authority of a government entity to use an administrative, grand jury, trial, or civil discovery subpoena . . ." CAL. PENAL CODE § 1546.1(i) (West 2017).

[496] The bill was passed by the California State government, which does not have jurisdiction over the investigations of other states or by the federal government.

[497] CAL. PENAL CODE § 1546(k) (West 2017). However, PROTECT was still not pleased by this change perhaps again due to sort of confusion: "Is this language, based on the 'intent' of child pornography traffickers, enough to stand up to challenge in California courts? The only honest answer is, 'a judge could tell you.' We expect years of court battles if this bill becomes law, with a danger that convictions could be overturned." *PROTECT Analysis of S.B. 178*, NAT'L ASSOC. TO PROTECT CHILDREN (Sept. 9, 2015), http://www.protect.org/178.

of a device. An "authorized possessor" is defined as one who the owner has allowed to possess a device. [498] This inclusion takes into account how many electronic devices are owned and operated today. The definition would cover individuals who are using "their" cell phones as a part of a family plan in someone else's name, as well as people who share a family iPad, for instance. Normally, under Fourth Amendment jurisprudence, authorized possessors might not have the requisite standing to object to a search of a device that is not "owned" by them.[499]

The law also creates an option for limiting the use of non-responsive data revealed in the course of a search. A court may require that extraneous information unrelated to what is sought by the warrant be deleted.[500] This approach has been endorsed by Professor Orin Kerr as the "best way to minimize the unwarranted intrusions upon privacy."[501] By using this method, as opposed to placing an ex ante limit on non-responsive data, law enforcement has the necessary authority it needs to perform electronic searches, while avoiding the problem of creating general warrants since officers are limited to what is described and to what they have probable cause to seize.[502] Thus,

---

[498] *See* CAL. PENAL CODE § 1546.1(c)(5) (West 2017).

[499] *See* Wong Sun v. United States, 371 U.S. 471, 492 (1963) (holding that while the Fourth Amendment barred the use of drugs found on the premises against one defendant, the other had no reasonable expectation in the same search because it was not his apartment, "[t]he seizure of this heroin invaded no right of privacy of person or premises which would entitle Wong Sun to object to its use at his trial").

[500] CAL. PENAL CODE CAL. PENAL CODE § 1546.1(e)(2) (West 2017).

[501] *Executing Warrants*, *supra* note 412, at 19; *See* Orin Kerr, *Warrant to Search Phone Did Not Allow Opening Folder Unlikely to Contain Evidence Sought, Court Rules*, WASH. POST (Oct. 29, 2015), https://www.washingtonpost.com /news/volokh-conspiracy/wp/2015/10/29/warrant-to-search-phone-did-not-allow-opening-folder-unlikely-to-contain-evidence-sought-court-rules/.

[502] *Executing Warrants*, *supra* note 412, at 11.

officers cannot "receive a windfall from the overseizure."[503]

The CalECPA also has clear definitions of what type of data is covered. California's law is much broader than the Federal Electronic Communications Privacy Act ("ECPA").[504] The ECPA provides only "anemic protections" for metadata because metadata is not considered content.[505] Warrants are only required for access to electronic information less than 180 days old. [506] The CalECPA's broad scope is even more significant because Congress is considering making changes to the ECPA.[507]

IV. WHAT THE CalECPA DOES NOT COVER

a. Plain View Exception to the Warrant Requirement for Electronic Devices?

The CalECPA's warrant requirement may not answer all the questions associated with the practical execution of electronic searches.[508] Specifically, it remains unclear whether the traditional plain view exception to the warrant requirement can or should be permitted. Professor Orin Kerr has argued that the plain view exception should not be available in searches of digital data because there is such a danger of a lawful, particularized warrant becoming an unlimited license to search and seize.[509]

Plain view is an exception to the warrant, but not probable cause,

---

[503] *Id.* at 26.

[504] *See* Godwin, *supra* note 406.

[505] Freiwald, *supra* note 375.

[506] Jacob Gershman, *California Adopts New Strict Digital Privacy Law*, WALL ST. J. (BLOGS) (Oct. 9, 2015), http://blogs.wsj.com/law/2015/10/09/california-adopts-new-strict-digital-privacy-law/.

[507] *Id.*

[508] *See* CAL. PENAL CODE § 1546.1(b)(1) (West 2017).

[509] Orin Kerr, *Searches and Seizures in a Digital World*, 119 HARV. L. REV. 531, 582–84 (2005).

requirement.[510] An officer may search and seize an object in plain view if three requirements are met: the incriminating character is immediately apparent (such that it generates probable cause), the officer is lawfully located in a place from which the object can be seen, and the officer has a lawful right of access to the object itself.[511] For instance, an officer cannot see an item inside a house while walking down the street and then enter the house absent exigent circumstances or a warrant. In an electronic search — given the way files are organized and the quantity of information stored — the traditional analysis may become difficult to apply.

The Supreme Court of Colorado grappled with this question last year in *People v. Herrera*.[512] In *Herrera*, the police had a warrant to search a subject's cell phone for text messages and photos.[513] The officer then chose to search a folder of a third-party messenger application, which he knew was outside the scope of the warrant.[514] There the officer found additional incriminating messages.[515] The Colorado Supreme Court's analysis, albeit somewhat convoluted,[516] held that the plain view exception was not

---

[510] Horton v. California, 496 U.S. 128, 144–45 (1990).

[511] *Id.* at 136–37.

[512] People v. Herrera, 357 P.3d 1227, 1228 (Colo. 2015).

[513] *Id.* at 1235.

[514] *Id.* at 1230.

[515] Professor Kerr took issue with the court's reasoning in a recent article, but he agreed with its conclusion. The court had said that opening the folder was not permitted by the warrant itself because doing so would violate the particularity requirement of the Fourth Amendment. *Id.* at 1228. However, as Kerr pointed out in his article, the particularity requirement is about the "facial validity of a warrant", not about how it is executed. *See* Kerr, *supra* note 391.

[516] People v. Herrera, 357 P. 3d at 1229.

met because the government did not have "lawful access" to the folder contained in the third-party messenger application.[517] Additionally, the Court found that the plain view exception did not permit the search of the folder because it was not reasonable for the officer to think the folder contained evidence described in the warrant.[518] The Court also made the point that the plain view exception must be applied "cautiously" to avoid allowing "a limitless search."[519]

Thus, requiring a warrant will not unilaterally alleviate the threat of the plain view exception - the risk that Fourth Amendment-conforming warrants could be turned into general warrants. The CalECPA does somewhat mitigate this problem because its warrant requirement requires a more comprehensive description of what will be searched,[520] and it also permits a magistrate to order the deletion of non-responsive data. Nevertheless, it is critical for courts or the legislature to determine how, or if, the plain view exception will apply in the searches of electronic devices.

b. A Possible Loophole to the Notice Requirement?

As discussed previously in Part II.A, the notice requirement of the bill is triggered when a government entity "executes a warrant or obtains electronic information in an emergency pursuant to Section 1546.1." [521] However, the law expressly permits the government "to compel the production of or access" to electronic information in

---

[517] *Id.* at 1232.

[518] *Id.* at ¶ 23.

[519] *Id.* at ¶ 35 ("If we were to hold that any text message folder could be searched because of the abstract possibility that it might have been deceptively labeled, we would again be faced with a limitless search .... We instead proceed cautiously in applying the plain view doctrine to searches involving digital data. *Cf.* People v. Gall, 30 P.3d 145, 154 (Colo. 2001) (noting privacy concerns with a search that follows the lawful seizure of a computer "container" that could reasonably contain writings identified in a search warrant). Where such a search does not meet the traditional requirements of Fourth Amendment doctrine, it should not be permitted.").

[520] *See* discussion *supra* Part II.b.

[521] CAL. PENAL CODE § 1546.2 (a) (West 2017).

ways other than the use of a warrant.[522] The government may request the information pursuant to a warrant, a wiretap order, an order for electronic reader records (under Section 1798.90 of the Civil Code), or pursuant to a subpoena, as long as the information requested by the subpoena is not sought for the purposes of investigating or prosecuting a criminal offense.[523] Though this would contravene the spirit of the notice requirement, by the language of the bill, whether the government will be required to provide notice when it seeks information pursuant to a wiretap order or an order for electronic reader records is unclear.

c. Are There Other Ways for the Police to Gather the Same Information?

i. The CalECPA Would Not Prevent Police from Collecting Data Themselves

The CalECPA prohibits law enforcement from"[a]ccess[ing] electronic device information by means of physical interaction or electronic communication with the electronic device."[524] The CalECPA does not contain any provisions proscribing policing technologies when they are used on *individuals*. The law only covers those techniques when used with *electronic devices*.[525] Thus, even though the information might be subject to a warrant requirement when contained in an electronic medium, law enforcement may be able to create and store some types of this information independently, such as individual's location data or other personal information without a warrant or giving notice.[526]

---

[522] § 1546.1 (b).

[523] § 1546.1 (b)(1–4).

[524] § 1546.1 (a).

[525] § 1546.1(a)(3).

Indeed, many law enforcement agencies are employing technologies to collect vast quantities of information, in a process that is sometimes referred to as "dataveillance," a method of surveillance that observes "not through the eye or the camera, but by collecting facts and data.[527]

For example, automated license plate readers ("LPRs"), affixed in public places or on police cars, can take thousands of photos of license plates per minute using a high-speed camera and then store those images in a database.[528] LPRs were designed to be used to alert police to the location of a vehicle associated with a crime, however the devices photograph indiscriminately and regularly capture images of innocent civilians going about their lives.[529] A Bay Area journalist once requested all the LPR records collected from the Oakland Police Department ("OPD"); so much data was available that he was able to make an educated guess about where an individual lived or worked, especially when that person had a regular commute.[530] Interestingly, according to OPD, only .16 percent of the 4.6 million LPR records collected were "hits," meaning vehicles associated with a crime.[531] The location data amassed by the use of LPRs would not fall under the protections of the CalECPA because cars are not "electronic device[s]" by the language of the statute,[532] nor could their relative

---

[526] Jack Smith, *The Constitution Can't Defend You From Predictive Policing — Here's Why*, POLICY MIC. (Nov. 10, 2015), http://mic.com/articles/127823/how-pre-crime-law-works#.2bbqJBZlB.

[527] This term has been used to describe surveillance practices that result in the massive collection of personal data. DANIEL J. SOLOVE, THE DIGITAL PERSON: TECHNOLOGY AND PRIVACY IN THE INFORMATION AGE 33–34 (2004).

[528] *You are Being Tracked: How License Plate Readers Are Being Used to Record American's Movements*, ACLU, https://www.aclu.org/feature/you-are-being-tracked.

[529] *Id.*

[530] Cyrus Farivar, *We Know Where You Have Been: Ars Acquires 4.6M License Plate Scans from the Cops*, ARS TECHNICA (Mar. 24, 2015), http://arstechnica.com/tech-policy/2015/03/we-know-where-youve-been-ars-acquires-4-6m-license-plate-scans-from-the-cops/.

[531] Cyrus Farivar, *EFF, ACLU Appeal License Plate Reader Case to California Supreme Court*, ARS TECHNICA (June 16, 2015), http://arstechnica.com/tech-policy/2015/06/eff-aclu-appeal-license-plate-reader-case-to-california- supreme-court/.

position in the world be considered "electronic device information."[533] LPRs could also be attached to drones for even more effective data collection.[534] Governor Brown vetoed a bill this year, A.B. 1327, which would have required law enforcement agencies to obtain a warrant in order to use drones for surveillance.[535]

Additionally, the police could choose to gather data for predictive policing.[536] The National Institute of Justice, the research and development agency of the DOJ, has made millions of dollars in grants available for police departments to develop predictive crime mapping.[537] Predictive policing aggregates huge amounts of data to try to draw connections between past crimes in order to forecast future criminal behavior.[538] Officers may even "friend request"

---

[532] CAL. PENAL CODE § 1546 (f).

[533] § 1546 (h).

[534] One company, Persistent Surveillance Systems, has developed a surveillance camera that can be attached to small aircraft and will record for hours at a time. This will give the police a "time machine" they can simply rewind as they need it. They could be placed at the highest points of a town or city and provide continuous surveillance. Crump & Harwood, *supra* note 437.

[535] *See* Phil Willon and Melanie Mason, *Governor Vetoes Bill That Would Have Limited Police Use of Drones,* L.A. Times (Sept. 28, 2015), http://www.latimes.com/loc al/political/la-me-ln-governor-vetoes-bill-to-limit-police-use-of-drones-20140928-story. html. In fact, Governor Brown vetoed several bills regarding the use of drones this term. Most related to privacy and would have mandated civil or criminal penalties for unauthorized drone use. The Governor stated the reason he vetoed the bills was that he was unwilling to create more crimes. *See also* Lorraine Reich, *Gov. Brown Has Our Back, Or Does He?* (Opinion), THE UNION (Nov. 5, 2015), http://www.theunion.com/ opinion/columns/18905936-113/lorraine-reich-gov-brown-has-our-back-or.

[536] Smith, *supra* note 528

[537] Matt Stroud, *The Minority Report: Chicago's New Police Computer Predicts Crimes, But is it Racist?,* VERGE (Feb. 19, 2014), http://www.theverge.com/2014/2/19/5 419854/the-minority-report-this-computer-predicts-crime -but-is-it-racist.

[538] Smith, *supra* note 528.

individuals on Facebook for the purpose of gathering information.[539] Depending on how this information is obtained, such practices too may fall outside the CalECPA's regulations.

ii. There are No Provisions Precluding or Limiting the Acquisition of Biometric Data.

The collection of biometric data, intrinsic physical characteristics—fingerprints, facial features, iris scans, tattoos, or DNA—to identify people,[540] is another technology that would likely not be encompassed by the CalECPA. Currently there are no federal laws and few state laws controlling the collection of biometric data.[541] Only Illinois and Texas have laws limiting the use of biometric information.[542] Illinois prohibits a person's biometric data from being "collect[ed], capture[d], purchase[d], receive[d] through trade, or otherwise obtain[ed]."[543] Texas's law is more limited, as it only prevents the capture of biometric data for a commercial purpose. Both laws cover biometric data such as retina or iris scans, fingerprints, voiceprints, or scans of hands or face geometry."[544] However, neither law applies to law enforcement.[545]

---

[539] Jack Smith, *Police Are Sweeping Up Tweets and Friending You on Facebook, Whether You Know It or Not,* POLICY MIC (Nov. 11, 2015), http://mic.com/articles/1282 99/how-police-use-twitter-and-facebook-to-predict-crime #.UCcLPqh5B.

[540] Dave Maass, *California Cops Are Using These Biometric Gadgets in the Field,* ELEC. FRONTIER FOUND. (Nov. 4, 2015), https://www.eff.org/deeplinks/2015/11/how-california-cops-use-mobile-biometric-tech-field.

[541] *See* Marvin Heiferman, *Who's Who? The Changing Nature and Uses of Portraits,* N.Y. TIMES (BLOGS) (Nov. 16, 2015), http://lens.blogs.nytimes.com/2015/11/16/whos-who-the-changing-nature-and-uses-of-portraits/?smid= pl-share.

[542] Illinois's law is called the Biometric Information Privacy Act, 740 I.L.C.S. 14, P.A. 95-994, http://www.ilga.gov/legislation/ilcs/ilcs3.asp?ActID=3004&ChapterID=57 [hereinafter "BIPA"] and Texas has Tex. BC. Code Ann. § 503.001: Capture or Use of Biometric Identifier, http://codes.lp.findlaw.com/txstatutes/BC/11/A/503/503.001.

[543] BIPA, at § 20(b).

[544] *Id.* at § 10; § 503.001(a).

[545] *Id.* at § 25(e)("Nothing in this Act shall be construed to apply to a contractor, subcontractor, or agent of a State agency or local unit of government when working for that State agency or local unit of government."); Texas's law exempts disclosures made

Law enforcement agencies are beginning to deploy new technologies that raise many privacy concerns. For example, facial recognition has become a more readily used practice. [546] In 2014 after the Boston Marathon bombing, the Boston police tested out facial recognition software on crowds at a music festival.[547] In the United Arab Emirates, facial recognition scanners have been mounted to police car siren lights.[548] Because these practices are conducted in the public, where citizens do not have a reasonable expectation of privacy, they currently may be conducted without Fourth Amendment protection.

Furthermore, the FBI is developing a national database called the Next Generation Identification ("NGI") system to house over 51 million facial photographs, and that number is expected to continue growing.[549] The database can search faces for identifying scars,

---

to the police. § 503.001(c)(1)(D).

[546] Facial recognition is not only a tool of law enforcement. Face First, a California company, has a system that will enable retailers to know when "high-value customers" as well as "litigious individuals" enter their stores. *See* Hal Hodson, *Face Recognition Row Over Right to Identify You in the Street*, NEW SCIENTIST (Jun. 19, 2015), https://www.newscientist.com/article/dn27754-face-recognition-row-over-right-to-identify-you-in-the-street/#.V.

[547] *See* Peter Moskowitz, *The Future of Policing Is Here, and It's Terrifying*, GQ (Nov. 9, 2015 2:27 PM), http://www.gq.com/story/the-future-of-policing-is-here-and-its-terrifying.

[548] *UAE Mounts Facial Recognition Cam in Police Car Light*, PLANET BIOMETRICS (Nov. 3, 2015), http://www.planetbiometrics.com/article-details/i/3724/desc/uae-mounts-facial-recognition-cam-in-police-car-lights.

[549] Photos are submitted by police agencies, so the photos can be post-arrest booking photos or stills from video feeds. The F.B.I. also will keep the photos it receives when conducting background checks for job candidates. Jose Pagliery, FBI Launches a Face Recognition System, CNN MONEY (Sept. 16, 2014), http://money.cnn.com/2014/09/16/technology/security/fbi-facial-recognition/.

tattoos, and birthmarks. The NGI system will also include ways to search for eyes, voices, palm prints, walking strides, and other biometric data in the future.[550] Police departments all over the country will be able to use the system.[551]

Some agencies, including the San Diego Police Department ("SDPD") and the Los Angeles Sheriff's Department, now employ facial recognition technology, and others, such as the San Jose Police Department are planning to do so.[552] The Los Angeles Sheriff's Department has its own "Digital Mugshot System" that can match a face in less than 30 seconds against its more than 6.5 million photos.[553] The San Diego program began with a grant from the DOJ two years ago,[554] and the number of collection devices has doubled over the last year to over 400. [555] There is even a mobile app for officers to use in the field to compare images against over 400,000 images in their mugshot database.[556] Each time someone is booked, their photo is added to the database, regardless of whether or not the person is ultimately convicted of a crime.[557] SDPD officers are only allowed to use the devices if the stopped person does not present identification or if the officer suspects the identification is false.[558]

Neither the CalECPA nor any other California law has a provision regarding biometrics, which may ultimately create an incongruent legal result. Consider the following example. The

---

[550] *Id.*

[551] *Id.*

[552] *Id.*

[553] Maass, *supra* note 524.

[554] *Id.*

[555] *Local Police Agencies Expand Use of Facial Recognition Devices,* CBS8 (Nov. 24, 2015), http://www.cbs8.com/ story/30573053/local-police-agencies-expand-use-of-facial-recognition-devices.

[556] Maass, *supra* note 524.

[557] *Local Police Agencies Expand Use of Facial Recognition Devices, supra* note 557.

[558] Maass, *supra* note 524.

recently released Windows 10 operating system includes Windows Hello, a biometric authorization program that allows users to log into the computer using advanced facial recognition hardware.[559] If a San Diego police officer wished to access the encrypted file containing the person's biometric data stored on the device, the officer would need to get a warrant, as the file would fall under the protection of the CalECPA. Conversely, the officer would be permitted to scan that same person's face without a warrant.[560]

If police technology continues to develop outside the reach of the CalECPA, measures may need to be taken to ensure an appropriate balance between the government's interest in effective policing and individual privacy rights. For instance, the New York Police Department recently was found to be driving "backscatter vans," which use X-ray to scan around the city.[561] It is not yet clear why or how the vans are being used.[562] The CalECPA would only cover this technique if it were deployed against electronic devices.[563]

Because neither the CalECPA nor any other California law has a provision regarding biometrics, this may ultimately create an incongruent legal result. To illustrate this, consider the following example. The recently released Windows 10 includes Windows Hello,

---

[559] John Patrick Pullen, *How Windows 10 Could Kill Passwords Forever,* TIME (Nov. 30, 2015), http://time.com/ 4128834/windows-10-hello-facial-recognition/.

[560] Note, this practice is permissible if the suspect for identification purposes and only if the suspect has been detained as part of a criminal investigation. *Local Police Agencies Expand Use of Facial Recognition Devices, supra* note 557.

[561] Peter Moskowitz, *The Future of Policing Is Here, and It's Terrifying,* GQ (Nov. 9, 2015 2:27 PM), http://www.gq.com/story/the-future-of-policing-is-here-and-its-terrifying.

[562] *Id.*

[563] CAL. PENAL CODE § 1546.1(a) (West 2017).

a biometric authorization program that allows users to log into the computer using advanced facial recognition hardware.[564] If a San Diego police officer wished to access the encrypted file containing the person's biometric data stored on the device, the officer would need to get a warrant, as the file would fall under the protection of the CalECPA. Conversely, the officer would be permitted to scan that same person's face without a warrant.[565]

V. CONCLUSION

What has been famously referred to as the "right to be let alone"[566] or the "[recognition] of the sovereignty of the individual,",[567] privacy remains an important and necessary part of a democratic society. Privacy is integral to fostering free speech, including dissent.[568] The CalECPA is a meaningful and positive step in amending Fourth Amendment protections for the modern technological environment.[569] Though it does not solve all of the problems associated with the execution of searches in a digital medium, the CalECPA is a model piece of legislation that other states may wish to follow and improve

---

[564] John Patrick Pullen, *How Windows 10 Could Kill Passwords Forever,* TIME (Nov. 30, 2015), http://time.com/ 4128834/windows-10-hello-facial-recognition/.

[565] Note, this practice is only permissible if the suspect for identification purposes and only if the suspect has been detained as part of a criminal investigation. *Local Police Agencies Expand Use of Facial Recognition Devices, supra* note 202.

[566] Samuel D. Warren and Louis D. Brandeis, *supra* note 458, at 195. Justice Brandeis further articulated this point in his dissenting opinion in *Olmstead:* "The protection guaranteed by the amendments is much broader in scope. The makers of our Constitution undertook to secure conditions favorable to the pursuit of happiness. They recognized the significance of man's spiritual nature, of his feelings and of his intellect. They knew that only a part of the pain, pleasure and satisfactions of life are to be found in material things. They sought to protect Americans in their beliefs, their thoughts, their emotions and their sensations. They conferred, as against the government, the right to be let alone - the most comprehensive of rights and the right most valued by civilized men. To protect, that right, every unjustifiable intrusion by the government upon the privacy of the individual, whatever the means employed, must be deemed a violation of the Fourth Amendment." Olmstead, 277 U.S. at 478 (emphasis added).

[567] Smith v. City of Artesia, 772 P.2d 373, 376 (N.M. Ct. App. 1989).

[568] Professor Phillip Rogaway, *Why Most Cryptographers Don't Care About Mass Surveillance* (Andrew W. Mellon Foundation John E. Sawyer Seminar) (Sept. 22, 2015).

[569] *Executing Warrants, supra* note 412, at 11.

upon.

Autonomous Surgery: The Law of Autonomous Surgical Robots

*David Britton**

---

*   JD/MS dual-degree candidate, Duke University School of Law & Pratt School of Engineering. Student researcher, Brain Tool Laboratory, Humans and Autonomy Lab, & Science, Law, and Policy Lab. Thanks to Professors Arti Rai and Barack Richman for the course that inspired this project and for their helpful comments along the way, to Professor Buz Waitzkin for his thoughtful feedback, and to Dr. Patrick Codd, the Brain Tool Lab, and my fellow lab members for introducing me to surgical robots and supporting my interest in robot law.

TABLE OF CONTENTS

I. Introduction

Surgical robotics is a growing, $3 billion per year market.[570] The biggest player in that market is Intuitive Surgical, Inc., which estimates that its *da Vinci* robotic surgery platform was used in about 600,000 procedures worldwide in 2014--more than triple the number from just five years earlier.[571] The *da Vinci* platform is used by surgeons in minimally-invasive surgery to control surgical tools with greater precision than would be capable without robotic assistance, and represents the current paradigm in surgical robotics.

The *da Vinci* system allows robotic tools inside the patient to be controlled by a surgeon at a nearby computer console. Viewing a 3D video feed of the surgical site from an endoscopic camera, the surgeon manipulates handheld controllers like he or she would move real tools. The controller movements are processed by the computer system and translated into the physical movement of the patient-end tools to recreate the surgeon's motions, often with adjustments on the scale of the movements or filters for eliminating human hand jitters. This setup is known to roboticists as a master-slave system, wherein the surgeon directly maneuvers the 'master' controller while the 'slave' tool mimics those motions.

When using a master-slave system for surgery, the surgeon remains in complete control of the movement of the tools and directly carries out each task necessary to complete the procedure. Thus, instead of saving costs or leading to shorter surgeries, robotic surgery often costs more and may take longer than traditional alternatives.[572] In addition to this lack of added efficiency, many studies found that robotic assistance does not improve patient outcomes when compared to non-robotic surgical techniques for a given procedure.[573] Although

---

[570] *Medical Robotics and Computer-Assisted Surgery: The Global Market*, BCC RESEARCH (June 2014) ("The global market for medical robotics and computer-assisted surgical equipment was worth nearly $2.7 billion in 2013. The market is projected to approach $3.3 billion in 2014 and $4.6 billion by 2019.").

[571] Intuitive Surgical, Annual Report 2014, http://phx.corporate-ir.net/External.File?item=UGFyZW50SUQ9Mjc0MjUxfENoaWxkSUQ9LTF8VHlwZT0z&t=1 (last accessed Feb. 23, 2016).

[572] Gabriel I Barbash & Sherry A. Glied, *New Technology and Health Care Costs — The Case of Robot-Assisted Surgery*, NEW ENGLAND JOURNAL OF MEDICINE 363 (8): 701–4. (2010); Shawn Tsuda et al., *SAGES TAVAC Safety and Effectiveness Analysis: Da Vinci® Surgical System (Intuitive Surgical, Sunnyvale, CA)*, SURGICAL ENDOSCOPY 29 (10): 2873–84 (2015).

no large-scale clinical trials comparing robotically-assisted surgery to alternative methods have been conducted, there may be hundreds of comparative studies which fail to find an objective patient-outcome advantage to master-slave robot-assisted surgery: Intuitive Surgical's 2014 annual report states that 400 comparative studies between robot-assisted surgeries and alternative methods were published in 2014, but could only pull one example that said *da Vinci* was clearly better.[574] In essence, healthcare professionals are beginning to realize that existing surgical robots are not as helpful as once imagined.

Some roboticists have noticed these shortfalls as well, and turned their attention to the key aspect of robotics that is revolutionizing other industries: automation and autonomy. Manufacturing robotics led the latest industrial revolution with precise repetitiveness. Autopilot and other computerized control features on planes made air travel by far the safest mode of transportation through unwavering information monitoring and quick reaction times.[575] Self-driving cars are attempting to bring this level

---

[573] *Id.*; Wright et al., "Robotically assisted v. laparoscopic hysterectomy among women with benign gynecologic disease." JAMA 309(7):689-698 ("To date, robotically assisted hysterectomy has not been shown to be more effective than laparoscopy" despite being "substantially more expensive than any other modality of hysterectomy.") (2013); Huang et al., "Systematic review and meta-analysis of robotic versus laparoscopic distal pancreatectomy for benign and malignant pancreatic lesions." SURGICAL ENDOSCOPY 2016 online http://link.springer.com/article/10.1007%2Fs00464-015-4723-7. (finding no difference in rate of complications or outcomes); Wright et al., "Comparative Effectiveness of Robotic Versus Laparoscopic Hysterectomy for Endometrial Cancer." J. CLINICAL ONCOLOGY vol. 30 no. 8 783-791 (March 10, 2012) ("there were no significant differences in the rates of intraoperative complications, . . . surgical site complications, . . . medical complications . . ., or prolonged hospitalization." But "robotic hysterectomy was significantly more costly.")

[574] Intuitive Surgical, Annual Report 2014, http://phx.corporate-ir.net/External. File?item=UGFyZW50SUQ9Mjc0MjUxfENoaWxkSUQ9LTF8VHlwZT0z&t=1 (last accessed Feb. 23, 2016).

[575] Chris Isidore, *What's the safest way to travel* (May 13 2015) http://money.cnn.com/2015/05/13/news/economy/train-plane-car-deaths/.

of safety to our roadways.[576] Amazon uses warehouse robots to fill orders efficiently and accurately, with a system autonomous to the point that no human needs to know where a given item is in the warehouse.[577] Many of these machines carry out tasks autonomously—that is, they take in information from the environment around them, use that information to plan future actions, and carry out those actions to achieve a given goal, all without direct human intervention.[578] In simpler terms, robots sense, think, and act.[579]

Despite early success in other fields, autonomous robots have not yet reached the operating room. In fact, the United States Food and Drug Administration (FDA) carefully refers to current robotic systems as "robotically-assisted surgical devices (RASD)."[580] An FDA discussion paper explains that RASD "are not considered to be surgical robots," because a "robot" by definition moves within its environment to perform tasks with some autonomy.[581] For example, the FDA's definition means *da Vinci* is not a robot because a human surgeon does the system's thinking and directs its action, so that *da Vinci* is not autonomous. Using this definition, the FDA states that "there are no *surgical robots* on the market."[582]

But these surgical robots are coming: several research groups

---

[576] *See, e.g.,* Robert Montenegro, *Google's Self-Driving Cars Are Ridiculously Safe* http://bigthink.com/ideafeed/googles-self-driving-car-is-ridiculously-safe.

[577] Ryan Calo, *Robots in American Law*, We Robot 2016, 13. Available at http://papers.ssrn.com/sol3/papers.cfm?abstract_id=2737598.

[578] Robot law scholars like to quibble about the definition of "robot." *See* Froomkin, *Introduction*, ROBOT LAW (Calo et al., eds. 2016).

[579] *Id.*

[580] FDA, DISCUSSION PAPER: ROBOTICALLY-ASSISTED SURGICAL DEVICES (2015), available   at http://www.fda.gov/downloads/MedicalDevices/NewsEvents/WorkshopsConferences/UCM454811.pdf.

[581] *Id.* (FDA adopted the International Organization for Standardization (ISO) definition of "robot" from ISO 8373:2012(en), where robot is defined as an "actuated mechanism programmable in two or more axes with a degree of autonomy, moving within its environment, to perform intended tasks." For consistency, I try to follow this definition when I use the term "robot" within this article. "Robotic" is used herein to refer to electro-mechanical systems without autonomy.)

[582] *Id.*

have begun taking a stab at automating surgical subtasks with various levels of autonomy. In industry, Google and Johnson & Johnson recently teamed up to form Verb Surgical, a somewhat mysterious research group aimed at creating "the future of surgery" by teaming Google's artificial intelligence and machine learning expertise with J&J's medical device experience.[583] Meanwhile, academic researchers have worked on automating bone drilling for high-precision ear surgeries,[584] the removal of dead scar tissue,[585] suturing within a surgical site by a laparoscopic robot like *da Vinci*,[586] and needle navigation for lung biopsies.[587]

To give a concrete example, the Brain Tool Laboratory here at Duke is developing a robot to autonomously remove brain tumors.[588] In contrast to a master-slave robotic system which relies on a surgeon's visual determinations and direct controller manipulations, this system will provide an example of true autonomous surgical robot. First, with the help of the surgeon, medical imaging (e.g., computed tomography, magnetic resonance imaging, ultrasound, etc.) is used to align the robot to the patient and delineate the unwanted

---

[583] *About Us*, VERBSURGICAL.COM, http://www.verbsurgical.com/about-us/ (last visited May 2, 2016).

[584] Majdani et al., *A Robot-Guided Minimally Invasive Approach for Cochlear Implant Surgery: Preliminary Results of a Temporal Bone Study*, INT'L J. COMPUTER ASSISTED RADIOLOGY AND SURGERY 4 (5): 475–86. (2009).

[585] Kehoe et al., *Autonomous Multilateral Debridement with the Raven Surgical Robot*, IEEE INT'L CONF. ON ROBOTICS & AUTOMATION (2014) Available at http://cal-mr.berkeley.edu/papers/Kehoe-icra-2014-final.pdf .

[586] Leonard, et al., *Smart Tissue Anastomosis Robot (STAR): A Vision-Guided Robotics System for Laparoscopic Suturing*, IEEE TRANSACTIONS ON BIO-MEDICAL ENGINEERING 61 (4): 1305–17. (2014).

[587] Torres et al., *A Motion Planning Approach to Automatic Obstacle Avoidance during Concentric Tube Robot Teleoperation*, http://robotics.cs.unc.edu/ publications/Torres2015_ICRA.pdf (Last accessed May 2, 2016).

[588] The author of this paper is a member of the research group developing this robot. No publications on the robot are available yet.

tissue. Robotic control algorithms then plan a path for a surgical laser to be aimed and fired at the tumor to safely ablate the cancerous tissue. The robot then executes the cutting path. Importantly, the control system receives real-time feedback from the medical imaging sensors, and uses that information to repeatedly update the tool path and monitor the robot's progress in removing the tumor. In other words, the robot's movements are not preplanned, but rather are adjusted automatically during the course of surgery to account for changes detected by the imaging sensors. This "closed loop" feedback will allow the system to adjust for shifting brain tissue and unpredictable laser-tissue ablation efficiency. The surgeon is relieved of direct manipulation of tumor removal tools, and given a supervisory role over the robot and the surgery.[589] Overall, the device senses the environment, computes a course of action, and deploys surgical action without direct human intervention, making it a "surgical robot" within the FDA's definition.

The line between a non-autonomous RASD and an autonomous "robot" will not always be so clear. For example, researchers at Vanderbilt and the University of North Carolina are developing a tentacle-like, curved needle robot designed to safely reach remote sections of the lung for tumor biopsies.[590] The 'tentacle' in the system is formed by extending and rotating curved, concentric tube segments to navigate the tip of the needle to a target location along a curved path. Researchers demonstrated a system which gives a surgeon full control over the location of the tip of the needle, while leaving the complicated dynamics of the curved tube configuration to computer control.[591] Position sensors along the tube help the control software ensure that the curved tubes avoid touching sensitive nerves and blood vessels, while the physician is in control of the surgical action at the point of interest.[592] In practice, the system may appear to

---

[589] Researchers have yet to determine what role the surgeon should have in monitoring the system. *See infra* note 24 and accompanying table.

[590] *Active cannula*, VANDERBILT INSTITUTE IN SURGERY AND ENGINEERING, https://www4.vanderbilt.edu/vise/viseprojects/active-cannula/.

[591] Torres et al., *A Motion Planning Approach to Automatic Obstacle Avoidance during Concentric Tube Robot Teleoperation,* http://robotics.cs.unc.edu/publications/Torres2015_ICRA.pdf (Last accessed May 2, 2016).

[592] *Id.*

use traditional *da Vinci*-style master-slave control of the tip of the needle, but the computer algorithms are making and executing safety-critical control decisions about the rest of the device dynamics. Such borderline systems call into question the helpfulness searching for a bright-line definition of "robot" that makes sense in the context of surgery.

Table 1[593]	
Automation Level	**Automation Description**
1	The computer offers no assistance: human must take all decisions and actions.
2	The computer offers a complete set of decisions/action alternatives, or
3	Narrows the selection down to a few, or
4	Suggests one alternative, and
5	Executes that suggestion if the human approves, or
6	Allows the human a restricted time to veto before automatic execution, or
7	Executes automatically, then necessarily informs the human, or
8	Informs the human only if asked, or
9	Informs the human only if it, the computer, decides to.
10	The computer decides everything and acts autonomously, ignoring the human.

---

[593] Raja Parasuraman, Thomas B. Sheridan, & Christopher D. Wickens, *A Model for Types and Levels of Human Interaction with Automation*, IEEE TRANSACTIONS ON SYSTEMS, MAN, AND CYBERNETICS—PART A: SYSTEMS AND HUMANS, vol. 30, no. 3 (May 2000); Mary Cummings, *Man versus Machine or Man + Machine*, IEEE INTELLIGENT SYSTEMS (2014) (available at http://hal.pratt.duke.edu/sites/hal.pratt.duke.edu/files/u10/IS-29-05-Expert%20Opinion%5B1%5D_0.pdf).

In fact, designers of surgical robots—guided by policymakers, regulators, and other stakeholders—will need to make more nuanced decisions about the remaining human role in these systems. Experts in human-robot interaction have laid out "levels of automation", shown in Table 1, which describe the spectrum between human-only decision-making and full robot autonomy.[594] At each step above level 1, the computer takes on more and more of the burden of decision making, leaving less for the human. The levels of automation are not intended to make a normative argument about proper robot design, but instead describe how supervisory control of robots can be designed. The levels of automation emphasize that issues surrounding new surgical robots are not limited to just hardware or software, but instead closely involve the evolving role of humans who collaborate with robots.

As robots move higher and higher up the levels of autonomy, legal scholars have begun to realize that robots pose a disruptive threat to existing legal doctrines and regulatory regimes, recognizing how law and policy will shape, and be shaped by, technological innovation.[595] In order to fit into this broader dialogue surrounding robots and the law, this paper follows a framework developed by Professor Ryan Calo in an early work in the nascent field of Robot Law, which identified aspects of robotics that will be disruptive to current standards in American law.[596]

The three key legally-disruptive traits of robotics identified by Professor Calo therefore guide this discussion of medical device law.[597] First, robots transform digital information into physical changes in the real world.[598] This "embodiment" of software redirects the focus of

---

[594] Raja Parasuraman, Thomas B. Sheridan, & Christopher D. Wickens, *A Model for Types and Levels of Human Interaction with Automation*, IEEE TRANSACTIONS ON SYSTEMS, MAN, AND CYBERNETICS—PART A: SYSTEMS AND HUMANS, vol. 30, no. 3 (May 2000); Mary Cummings, *Man versus Machine or Man + Machine*, IEEE INTELLIGENT SYSTEMS (2014) (available at http://hal.pratt.duke.edu/sites/ hal.pratt.duke.edu/files/u10/IS-29-05-Expert%20Opinion%5B1%5D_0.pdf).

[595] *See, e.g.,* ROBOT LAW (Calo, Froomkin, Kerr, eds. 2016); *See also* We Robot Conferences (2012-2016) at robots.law.miami/2016.

[596] Ryan Calo, *Robotics and the Lessons of Cyberlaw*, CAL. L.R. Vol. 103:513-564 (2015).

[597] *Id.*

[598] *Id.* at 532.

medical device safety regulation towards computer code and dynamic movements, adding new questions about device safety and effectiveness that may lead the FDA to conduct a more thorough review of the new wave of surgical robots. Second, autonomous robots may behave in ways not dictated nor expected by their programmers or operators.[599] This "emergence" creates evidentiary challenges to proving safety and effectiveness, but the FDA is well equipped to deal with these challenges. One facet of FDA evaluation, human factors testing, will be critical for ensuring robot safety while pushing the FDA to investigate and attempt to limit the users of a device. Third, people tend to project human social traits onto robots, blurring the line between person and instrument.[600] This "social valence" of robots implicates the limits of federal jurisdiction in regulating the practice of medicine when actions previously carried out by human doctors or nurses licensed by state medical associations are taken over by regulated robots.

Relying on Calo's level of abstraction to gain a better perspective on the legally-interesting characteristics of robots, this paper discusses how federal regulation of medical devices and the underlying issues of federalism will be impacted by increasingly autonomous surgical robots. This approach leads to the conclusion that most challenges presented by robots are not entirely new to the FDA, suggesting that the agency is capable of regulating automated surgical robots without federal-level, outside policy interventions like the creation of a Federal Robotics Commission—something once recommended by Calo.[601] Meanwhile, robots may disrupt existing

---

[599] *Id.*

[600] *Id.*

[601] Ryan Calo once made the case for the creation of a new Federal Robotics Commission, which would offer technical support, guidance, and resources to other agencies encountering new robot-related problems. Ryan Calo, *The Case for a Federal Robotics Commission*, BROOKINGS (2014) (available at http://www.brookings.edu/research/reports2/2014/09/case-for-federal-robotics-

regimes by pulling federal device evaluation and regulation into more direct contact with the practice of medicine itself, infringing on legal territory previously reserved to the Several States.

II. EMBODIMENT: FDA REGULATORY OPTIONS FOR SOFTWARE-CONTROLLED SURGICAL ROBOTS

Robots take sensor inputs, stored data, and computational processing algorithms and turn it into physical action. In the context of medical devices, this embodiment of the cyber-world means that control software becomes an integral part of device safety and effectiveness. The following section discusses the FDA's existing regulatory pathways and an important preemption clause that limits the effect of state law on some devices. Examining which pathway will be applied, I conclude that rigorous premarket approval will likely be preferred for surgical robots, and the extra costs of that process on device companies are offset by the preemption of tort law that it provides.

a. Background on FDA Regulation and Preemption

Medical device regulation attempts to both protect the public health and to advance it through innovation.[602] The balancing act between ensuring safety and facilitating the development of new products is reflected in the FDA's mission statement:

> FDA is responsible for protecting the public health by assuring the safety, efficacy and security of human and veterinary drugs, biological products, medical devices, our nation's food supply, cosmetics, and products that emit radiation. FDA is also responsible for advancing the public health by helping to speed innovations that make medicines more effective, safer, and more affordable and by helping the public get the accurate, science-based information they need to use medicines and foods to maintain and improve their health.[603]

---

commission).

[602] *See, e.g.*, James Flaherty, Jr., *Defending Substantial Equivalence: An Argument for the Continuing Validity of the 510(k) Premarket Notification Process*, 63 FOOD DRUG L.J. 901.

[603] *FDA Mission Statement*, http://www.fda.gov/downloads/aboutfda/reportsmanuals forms/reports/budgetreports/ucm298331.pdf . (last accessed March 22, 2016).

In the context of surgical robots, the FDA's regulatory programs should be tailored to ensure the safety and effectiveness of robots in treating patients without placing overwhelming regulatory obstacles in the way of device developers.[604]

Trying to strike this balance, the FDA currently has two main regulatory pathways for bringing a new medical device to market: premarket approval (PMA) and 510(k) clearances. PMA is the more stringent of the two, and is applied to devices that are "represented to be for a use in supporting or sustaining human life" or that present a "potential unreasonable risk of illness or injury."[605] PMA requires the FDA to determine that sufficient, valid scientific evidence assures that the device is safe and effective for its intended use.[606] Thus, a PMA applicant generally must provide results from clinical investigations involving human subjects showing safety and effectiveness data, adverse reactions and complications, patient complaints, device failures, and other relevant scientific information.[607] The application is often reviewed by an advisory committee made up of outside experts.[608]

---

[604] As stated by William Maisel, FDA's acting director of the Office of Device Evaluation, at a public workshop on Robotic Assisted Surgical Devices (July 27, 2015), "[T] he first prong of our vision is that patients in the U.S. have access to high quality, safe and effective medical devices of public health importance first in the world. ...if we set our evidentiary bars to high, then a lot of really great ideas will never make it. And so, we have to appropriately balance the availability of these technologies, getting these technologies to market and also make sure that they remain safe and effective. ...[W] e also need to think about what is the cost of the development of the technology... [I]f studies, the cost of developing a technology is too high, then many of those technologies will never make it to patients. And so, striking the right balance   important."   (transcript   available   at http://www.fda.gov/MedicalDevices/NewsEvents/WorkshopsConferences/ ucm435255.htm).

[605] 21 U.S.C. § 360c(a)(1)(C)

[606] 21 C.F.R. 814

[607] 21 C.F.R. 814.20(6)(ii)

[608] CRS report, page 12-13.

The FDA expends significant resources reviewing a PMA application, estimating in 2005 that reviewing one PMA application costs the agency an average of $870,000.[609] One survey of medical device companies found that it took an average of 54 months to reach approval from their first communication with the FDA regarding an innovation.[610] The same survey found that the average total costs for a medical device company from the time of product conception to approval was $94 million.[611] Fifty-two new devices received PMA approval in 2015.[612]

The 510(k) pathway is more popular, with 3,006 clearances in 2015.[613] 510(k) applies to moderately risky devices, and clears a device for marketing if it is "substantially equivalent" to a "predicate" device already on the market. A predicate device is a device that was available on the market before 1976, or any device cleared since then via 510(k). The FDA will clear a device as substantially equivalent to an earlier device if:

(1) The device has the same intended use as the predicate device; and

(2) The device:

(i) Has the same technological characteristics as the predicate device; or

(ii) (A) Has different technological characteristics, such as a significant change in the materials, design, energy source, or other features of

---

[609] Gov't Accountability Off., *SHORTCOMINGS IN FDA's PREMARKET REVIEW, POSTMARKET SURVEILLANCE, AND INSPECTIONS OF DEVICE MANUFACTURING ESTABLISHMENTS*, TESTIMONY BEFORE THE SUBCOMMITTEE ON HEALTH, COMMITTEE ON ENERGY AND COMMERCE, HOUSE OF REPRESENTATIVES, 5 (2009) http://www.gao.gov/new.items/d09370t.pdf .

[610] Josh Makower, Aabed Meer, & Lyn Denend, FDA, IMPACT ON U.S. MEDICAL TECHNOLOGY INNOVATION: A SURVEY OF OVER 200 MEDICAL TECHNOLOGY COMPANIES, 23 (Nov. 2010), http://advamed.org/res.download/30.

[611] *Id.* at 28. (Notably, not all of those costs are directly attributable to regulatory compliance activities).

[612] DEVICES APPROVED IN 2015, http://www.fda.gov/MedicalDevices/ProductsandMedicalProcedures/DeviceApprovals andClearances/PMAApprovals/ucm439065.htm.

[613] *Id.*

the device from those of the predicate device;

(B) The data submitted establishes that the device is substantially equivalent to the predicate device and contains information, including clinical data if deemed necessary by the Commissioner, that demonstrates that the device is as safe and as effective as a legally marketed device; and

(C) Does not raise different questions of safety and effectiveness than the predicate device.[614]

A 510(k) applicant must therefore submit information about the device's design, characteristics, and relationship to a predicate device, and any data backing up those claims.[615] In contrast to PMA, human-subject clinical trials for safety and effectiveness are typically not required.[616] However, the FDA can respond to a 510(k) application by requesting additional information it deems relevant,[617] which may lead to frustration over the unpredictability of the clearance process.[618]

A 510(k) application is significantly cheaper for the FDA to review, at an estimated average cost of $18,200 per application.[619] A

[614] 21 CFR 807.100(b)

[615] Congressional Research Service, FDA REGULATION OF MEDICAL DEVICES, 9 (2012).

[616] *Id.*

[617] 21 CFR § 807.100(a)(3)

[618] Josh Makower, Aabed Meer, & Lyn Denend, FDA, IMPACT ON U.S. MEDICAL TECHNOLOGY INNOVATION: A SURVEY OF OVER 200 MEDICAL TECHNOLOGY COMPANIES, 26 (Nov. 2010), 23 (available at http://advamed.org/res.download/30)., (A Stanford-based survey of 200 U.S. medical device companies found that over half ranked FDA regulatory performance as "mostly unpredictable" or "very unpredictable", as compared to less than 5% of respondents ranking European Union device regulation in the same category.).

[619] Gov't Accountability Off., *SHORTCOMINGS IN FDA's PREMARKET REVIEW,*

company's total costs from product concept to clearance is around $31 million on average.[620] Although FDA hopes to reach a final decision on each application within three months, U.S. companies reported an average time of 10 months from first submission of an application to clearance.[621] This faster timeline and the lower evidentiary requirements make 510(k) appealing to device companies over PMA.

A newer, third pathway, known as *de novo 510(k)* review, attempts to fill the gap between 510(k) and PMA. *De novo* review applies to innovative devices which fail the substantial equivalency test outlined above yet are not high enough risk to warrant full PMA inspection.[622] The applicant must present data and information demonstrating that controls similar to those applied to 510(k) devices are sufficient to ensure the safety and effectiveness of the device.[623] Once *de novo* review clears a device, that device becomes a predicate device just like any other 510(k) cleared device and opens up the door for similar devices to be cleared through the regular 510(k) process.[624] *De novo* review has not been widely used thus far.[625]

FDA also has the ability to monitor devices after they are put on the market. Many PMA approvals require postmarket surveillance studies to gather further safety and efficacy data. Postmarket study

---

POSTMARKET SURVEILLANCE, AND INSPECTIONS OF DEVICE MANUFACTURING ESTABLISHMENTS, TESTIMONY BEFORE THE SUBCOMMITTEE ON HEALTH, COMMITTEE ON ENERGY AND COMMERCE, HOUSE OF REPRESENTATIVES, 5 (2009) http://www.gao.gov/new.items/d09370t.pdf .

[620] Josh Makower, Aabed Meer, & Lyn Denend, FDA, IMPACT ON U.S. MEDICAL TECHNOLOGY INNOVATION: A SURVEY OF OVER 200 MEDICAL TECHNOLOGY COMPANIES, 7 (Nov. 2010), (available at http://advamed.org/res.download/30).

[621] *Id* at 26.

[622] *De Novo* Classification Process (Evaluation of Automatic Class III Designation): Draft Guidance for Industry and FDA Staff (Aug. 14, 2014).

[623] *Id.*

[624] NEW SECTION 513(F)(2) – EVALUATION OF AUTOMATIC CLASS III DESIGNATION, GUIDANCE FOR INDUSTRY AND CDRH STAFF, http://www.fda.gov/RegulatoryInformation/Guidances/ucm080195.htm (last accessed May 2, 2015).

[625] Only 10 *de novo* device reclassification decisions were made in 2015. *Device Classifications under Section 513(a)(1)(de novo)*, database at http://www.accessdata.fda.gov/scripts/cdrh/cfdocs/cfPMN/denovo.cfm (last accessed May 3, 2016).

may also be required by 510(k) clearances.[626] FDA regulations also mandate reporting of device-related adverse events by device manufacturers and health care facilities, and allow reporting of such events by patients.[627] Lastly, FDA may issue recall orders for marketed devices which are found to pose health hazards.[628]

Outside of the FDA, tort liability offers another avenue for post-market device regulation. Lawsuits following injuries allegedly caused by defective products are typically governed by state law in the relevant jurisdiction. However, reacting to the patchwork of state-level device regulations that arose in the wake of deaths caused by an IUD,[629] Congress included an express preemption provision in the Medical Device Amendments of 1976:

> [N]o State or political subdivision of a State may establish or continue in effect with respect to a device intended for human use any requirement--
>
> (1) which is different from, or in addition to, any requirement applicable under this Act [21 USCS §§ 301 et seq.] to the device, and
>
> (2) which relates to the safety or effectiveness of the device or to any other matter included in a requirement applicable to the device under this Act [21 USCS §§ 301 et seq.].[630]

Although the U.S. Supreme Court previously found that 510(k) clearance did not invoke this preemption clause,[631] Justice

---

[626] 21 U.S.C. § 360c(a)(1)(B).

[627] Congressional Research Service, FDA REGULATION OF MEDICAL DEVICES, 9, 15-16 (2012).

[628] 21 CFR § 810.

[629] *Riegel v. Medtronic, Inc.*, 552 U.S. 312, 315–16 (2006).

[630] 21 U.S.C. § 360(k)

[631] *Medtronic, Inc. v. Lohr*, 518 U.S. 470 (1996).

Scalia's majority opinion in *Riegel v. Medtronic, Inc.*, 552 U.S. 312 (2008) held that PMA did create requirements for a device which overrule state laws under the explicit preemption clause.[632] Further, the court held that state common law tort claims are among the laws preempted.[633] As a result, Medtronic could not be held liable after a Medtronic catheter ruptured in Riegel's right coronary artery.[634] For autonomous robots, this means software errors—embodied by a robot physically injuring a patient—will not lead to tort liability if the device and its software went through the rigorous PMA review process, at least so long as the manufacturer complies with applicable federal regulations.[635]

Thus, a choice between 510(k) and PMA changes not only the regulatory process and applicable federal law, but also decides how state law will apply to the robot. Because no realistic process exists for a third party challenge to a 510(k) or *de novo* clearance,[636] FDA has significant discretion in deciding what to do with a new technology. Additionally, device companies will certainly shape this territory through the paths they choose to pursue first based on their competitive regulatory strategies. The following section discusses which pathways could apply to surgical robots and considers what regulatory strategy may be best for robotics companies.

b. Regulatory Pathway Decisions for Surgical Robots

The first RASD, *da Vinci*, was approved via the 510(k) pathway as being substantially equivalent to the non-robotic laparoscopic tools and holders that it aimed to replace.[637] FDA

---

[632] *Riegel*, 552 U.S. 312 at 322-3.

[633] *Id.* at 323-326.

[634] *Id.* at 320.

[635] *See Hughes v. Boston Scientific Corp.*, 631 F.3d 762 (5th Cir. 2011) (holding that plaintiff's state law failure to warn claim was not preempted where it was based on Boston Scientific's failure to report serious injuries or malfunctions related to the device as required by FDA regulations); *See also Bausch v. Stryker Corp.*, 630 F.3d 546 (7th Cir. 2010) (preemption protection "does not apply where the patient can prove that she was hurt by the manufacturer's *violation* of federal law.").

[636] *See, e.g., Ivy Sports Medicine v. Burwell*, 767 F.3d 81 (D.C. Cir. 2014) (holding that revocation of a 510(k) clearance requires notice-and-comment rulemaking to reclassify the device as a higher-risk Class III device).

[637] Maisel, *supra* note 35 at 27-28 (July 27, 2015)

reviewers apparently deemed that the leap from hands-on mechanical control of tools to master-slave computer-mediated control did not raise significant new questions about the safety and effectiveness different than those asked of existing devices.[638] Following this precedent, RASD have been approved via the 510(k) process for the last 15 years.[639]

Recall, however, that the FDA maintains that RASD "are technically not robots, since they are guided by direct user control."[640] At least as of July 2015, FDA's acting Deputy Director of the Division of Surgical Devices believed that "to date, FDA has not seen any . . . surgical devices that have autonomous features in them."[641] Although perhaps repeating this language merely to clarify the state of the art, FDA's definition of RASD may be signaling how autonomous systems will be regulated.

In particular, FDA's statement that RASD are not robots implies that any device the FDA recognizes as meeting their definition of an autonomous robot will fail the 510(k) substantial equivalency test.[642] First, because no existing surgical systems are "robots", no available predicate devices have autonomous features. Second, by implying that FDA knows to look for autonomy in a robotic device, the definition indicates that autonomous capability would be a "different technical characteristic" than anything present in a predicate device under 21 CFR § 807.100(b)(ii)(A).[643] The

---

[638] There is no public record of the application or FDA reasoning behind clearing the da Vinci. That is, the FDA database shows no 'summary' for the first da Vinci clearance, unlike for many other devices at http://www.accessdata.fda.gov/scripts/cdrh/cfdocs/cfpmn/pmn.cfm?ID=K002489).

[639] Maisel, *supra* note 35 at 28,

[640] Maisel, *supra* note 35 at 27

[641] *Id.*

[642] 21 CFR 807.100(b).

device must therefore fulfill the two additional requirements found in (ii)(B) and (C), which require both the submission of data to establish safety and effectiveness equivalent to the predicate device and a finding that the "device does not raise different questions of safety and effectiveness than the predicate device."[644]

Although an applicant could plausibly satisfy (B) with convincing-enough testing, a fully autonomous surgical robot certainly raises a different question of safety and effectiveness than a master-slave RASD. In particular, errors in actively completing the surgical task targeted by the tool—which could previously be blamed on surgeon misuse or mistake—now enter the immediate attention of device evaluators. Because of this new question, cautious regulators would likely not allow 510(k) clearance for an autonomous surgical robot. For example, the Duke tumor resection robot described above should not receive 510(k) clearance, but instead should be evaluated through PMA, because the closed-loop feedback, tool path planning, and automatic laser steering and firing are new features that ask significant new questions of device safety and effectiveness. These features may pose enough risk that *de novo* reclassification will also be unavailable at first.

However, a case could be made for the curved tube robot example—or other systems lower on the levels of automation in Table 1—to be cleared through 510(k) or at least through *de novo* review. Because the surgeon remains in direct control of the tool at the point of interest, the regulator need not ask whether the robot knows how to effectively complete the surgical tasks. Instead, questions about the autonomous capabilities of the tube obstacle avoidance part of the system may be deemed similar enough to questions about the reliability of existing surgical robotic motors, actuators, arms, and end effectors to make 510(k) clearance plausible. Although intraoperative obstacle avoidance is fundamentally different than those issues from an engineering perspective, the analytical jump is no larger than the leap made to clear the first RASD under 510(k). If such a device is seen as posing about the same level of risk as current RASD, *de novo* clearance may be available. Federal regulators under pressure to keep regulatory costs low and confronted by these borderline systems might be willing to let more and more automation slide into devices

[643] *Id.*

[644] *Id.*

through a series of *de novo* and 510(k) applications.

In terms of what will be preferred by robotics companies, 510(k) clearance is certainly cheaper and may at first appear to be the only way to ensure economic feasibility given the limited size of the surgical robotics market in today's health care reimbursement climate. *De novo* review also can save regulatory compliance costs, but could be problematic from the competitive standpoint that it exposes a new kind of technology to copycats who can then use the first device as a predicate device for future 510(k) applications.[645] In other words, the first company that convinces the FDA to approve an autonomous robot through *de novo* rather than PMA will lower regulatory hurdles—and thus economic barriers to entry—for all other players in the competitive market who can now use that robot as a predicate device for 510(k) submissions.[646] A PMA approved device, still considered high risk, does not create a new predicate device and therefore sustains a high regulatory barrier to competitor entry.[647]

In addition, PMA's preemption of state-law tort claims against the device manufacturer is particularly advantageous for autonomous robots. A tortious device-related medical injury can result from two broad categories: a device mechanism fails and injures the patient, or a doctor misuses the tool in a way that injures the patient. Typically, device companies only need to worry about the first category, focused on physical design failures and manufacturing defects. However, when autonomy is introduced into a device, it encroaches on the second category: the software may misuse the physical tools in a way that injures the patient. For device companies considering autonomy, this is the essence of the "embodiment" problem: the code they write may physically injure real people and

---

[645] Michael Drues, *Secrets of the De Novo Pathway, Part 2: Is De Novo Right For Your Device?*, MED DEVICE ONLINE (2014) http://www.meddeviceonline.com/doc/secrets-of-the-de-novo-pathway-part-is-de-novo-right-for-your-device-0001 (last accessed May 2, 2016).

[646] *Id.*

[647] *Id.*

open the companies up to tort liability for actions formerly carried out only by healthcare professionals.

One might question whether medical malpractice tort reforms, like caps on noneconomic damages, intended to protect physicians and hospitals would now apply to autonomous surgical robots. Regardless, because robots create new ways for a product to hurt someone, developers will likely find that it would make good economic sense to pay extra up front for *ex ante* PMA than to be caught dealing with uncertain, potentially massive tort damages *ex post*. The estimated difference in cost to developers of $60 million from concept to market between 510(k) and PMA approval[648] could be eaten up quickly by a handful of tort cases and the accompanying bad publicity. With the additional consideration that more good data is good for marketing, these considerations suggest that a strategic company may be wise to choose PMA despite its higher price tag and longer timeline.

Patients injured by PMA robots will not be huge fans of this system. Thus far, most RASD-related injuries could be blamed on surgeons.[649] However, autonomous robots might injure a patient even though human medical staff did everything right. Despite a human urge to blame the closest human operator of automated technology for catastrophic system failures,[650] robot malfunction may be the only legal cause of the patient's injury in many cases. If the robot went through PMA, Congress's choice of *ex ante* regulation means the individual patient may go uncompensated.[651] State courts and legislatures trying to be fair to injured plaintiffs are not likely to be happy with that result. If these injuries become widespread, patients and state courts may hunt for ways around the Medical Device Act's preemption clause, or pressure Congress to modify it.

---

[648] Josh Makower, Aabed Meer, & Lyn Denend, FDA, IMPACT ON U.S. MEDICAL TECHNOLOGY INNOVATION: A SURVEY OF OVER 200 MEDICAL TECHNOLOGY COMPANIES, 41, 45 (Nov. 2010), (available at http://advamed.org/res.download/30), (and accompanying text.)

[649] *See, e.g., Taylor v. Intuitive Surgical Inc.*, 188 Wn. App. 776 (Wash. Ct. App. 2015) (petition for review by Wash. granted Feb. 10, 2016).

[650] M.C. Elish, *Moral Crumple Zones: Cautionary Tales in Human-Robot Interaction*, WE ROBOT 2016, http://robots.law.miami.edu/2016/wp-content/uploads/2015/07/ELISH_WEROBOT_cautionary-tales_03212016.pdf.

[651] *Riegel v. Medtronic, Inc.*, 552 U.S. 312, 315–16 (2006).

In sum, 510(k) clearance is the faster, cheaper path to market for medical devices and is exploited by current robotically-assisted surgical devices. Some statements by the FDA and its officers seem to suggest that 510(k) clearance will not be available for true surgical "robots" with autonomous capabilities, but the real-world evolution of such clearance will be shaped by the capabilities of early technologies and the competitive regulatory strategy of device companies. Because PMA maintains more initial barriers for competitors and preempts state tort claims, PMA may actually be preferable to 510(k) or *de novo* review for device companies. PMA thereby offers incentives to develop novel robots, but does so at the cost of quick innovation and robust competition and to the detriment of individual plaintiffs injured by robots. These costs may be justified if the FDA is capable of testing and evaluating robots to ensure a high-level safety and effectiveness to fulfill the "protect the patients" half of their mission statement. The following section argues that the FDA is capable of understanding and evaluating robots' novel technical traits like emergent behavior, and how investigation of crucial engineering design principles will lead FDA even deeper into interference with regulation of the practice of medicine.

III. EMERGENCE: UNDERSTANDING AND TESTING ROBOTS IN THE FACE OF UNCERTAINTY.

Autonomous robots, making their own decisions based on sensor inputs, stored data, deterministic algorithms or probabilistic machine learning may take actions not understood by their users and sometimes not predicted by their designers. Figuring out how to successfully test these "emergent" behaviors would contribute immensely to a world which will soon be teeming with safety-critical autonomous robots. Fortunately, FDA may be the best equipped of any federal agency to develop and execute sufficient testing programs for new autonomous technologies. At the very least, FDA is capable of understanding these systems significantly better than state trial courts. The following attempts to explain why "emergence" makes a system difficult to test and points out the advantages the FDA has in addressing the problem.

Computers and robots are best at highly structured tasks.[652] A simple calculator, for instance, is excellent at executing the axiomatic rules of arithmetic. Computer programs solving structured problems rely on a limited set of inputs and determine outputs based on deterministic algorithms.[653] Manufacturing robotics take advantage of automation by repeating precisely the same motion to create assembly lines full of identical products.

However, most human problems are not so structured: we often deal with uncertainty.[654] In surgery, for example, patients vary based on height, weight, physical fitness, and gender, and the presentation of a pathology or injury may change significantly from case to case in terms of anatomical structure. A manufacturing robotics system moving in exactly the same way repeatedly cannot account for this kind of diversity. Instead, humans cope with the uncertainty of each new circumstance by following experience-based intuition to judge how to proceed.[655]

Robots and computer systems can be designed to deal with this sort of uncertainty in several ways.[656] The first is to redesign the task to limit automation to a structured task.[657] For example, the task of mail-ordering a book, perhaps done in the past through long-hand letter, was replaced by the Amazon "buy-with-one-click" button.[658] Computers can process these standardized button clicks much easier than they could interpret handwritten letters.[659] For surgical robotics,

---

[652] *See, e.g.,* Dana Remus & Frank Levy, *Can robots be lawyers? Computers, Lawyers, and the Practice of Law* (2016), http://papers.ssrn.com /sol3/papers.cfm?abstract_id=2701092.

[653] *Id.*

[654] Mary Cummings, *Man versus Machine or Man + Machine*, IEEE INTELLIGENT SYSTEMS (2014), http://hal.pratt.duke.edu/sites/hal.pratt.duke.edu/files/u10/IS-29-05-Expert%20Opinion%5B1%5D_0.pdf.

[655] *Id.*

[656] Dana Remus & Frank Levy, *Can robots be lawyers? Computers, Lawyers, and the Practice of Law,* 10-12 (2016), http://papers.ssrn.com/sol3/papers.cfm?abstract _id=2701092.

[657] *Id.* at 11.

[658] *Id.*

this example urges roboticists to reimagine the delivery of surgical action rather than attempt to replicate current human surgical practice with a robot.

Second, the scope of issues dealt with by the system can be bounded. As one example, consider an airport self-check-in kiosk.[660] A self-check-in kiosk operates automatically through structured steps when it finds no problems with any of your information, but stops helping and directs you to a human agent when an issue outside its ability arises.[661] By knowing its limits, the kiosk avoids dealing with unusual problems.[662] For surgical robotics applications, the FDA can accomplish this sort of limitation through definition of the device's "indication"—the disease the device is approved to treat.[663] By approving a robot only for use on a certain pathology, for use on a limited group of patients, or perhaps even for a limited set of presentations of a given disease, some uncertainty in the robot's operation can be mitigated. Any limitation on the indication for use, however, reduces the pool of potential patients for a device company marketing to hospitals. Additionally, the FDA cannot keep a physician from using a device for off-label use.[664]

Lastly, the system can be designed to guess a best solution when faced with uncertainty.[665] Guessing—more accurately

---

[659] *Id.*

[660] *Id.*

[661] *Id.*

[662] *Id.*

[663] Emphasizing the importance of the indication choice, the scope of indications for RASD was the topic of an FDA public workshop in July 2015. http://www.fda.gov/MedicalDevices/NewsEvents/WorkshopsConferences/ucm435255. htm.

[664] 21 U.S.C. § 396.

[665] Dana Remus & Frank Levy, *Can robots be lawyers? Computers, Lawyers, and the Practice of Law,* 12 (2016), http://papers.ssrn.com/sol3/papers.cfm?abstract

described as choosing the most likely answer from a group of probability distributions—sounds undesirable, but will be necessary when the other two options are not available.[666] For instance, a self-driving car company cannot afford to redesign all road infrastructure to simplify driving, nor will it be safe to hand off control to humans in all unusual situations. Thus, the self-driving car will need to deal with the uncertainty inherent in the human task of driving and stemming from the limitations of its sensors. Is that object detected by the sensors a person or a tree? How likely is it that the pedestrian will cross the road? Who will move first at a four-way-stop?[667] To deal with such questions, autonomous decision making begins to rely on choosing the most likely solution based on probability distributions instead of finding deterministic solutions.

Rather than trying to explicitly write out all of the rules needed to navigate situations like this, software engineers use a technique known as "machine learning." In essence, the robot is 'trained' to do something. Perhaps the best example of machine learning for lawyers to understand is e-discovery document review, which allows a computer program to assist attorneys in sorting through gigabytes of digital document files during discovery.[668] To operate this software, an attorney starts by working through a training set of documents, indicating which are relevant to the case and which are not.[669] Based on the attorney's labelling, the computer 'learns' what words, patterns of words, and other traits are present in the 'relevant' set of documents.[670] The program then sorts the rest of the documents based on these learned standards.[671] These systems are

---

_id=2701092.

[666] *Id.*

[667] *See* Harry Surden & Mary-Anne Williams, *Self-Driving Cars, Predictability, and Law*, WE ROBOT (2016), http://papers.ssrn.com/sol3/papers.cfm?abstract_id=2747491.

[668] Dana Remus & Frank Levy, *Can robots be lawyers? Computers, Lawyers, and the Practice of Law,* 16-18 (2016), http://papers.ssrn.com/sol3/papers.cfm?abstract_id=2701092.

[669] *Id.*

[670] *Id.*

[671] *Id.*

much more effective than simple term searching. Importantly, because neither the user nor the original software designer knows exactly what the computer has decided to look for in the documents, neither person will be able to explain exactly why the system returned a particular document as relevant. In some cases, the system may flag a document for reasons no one would have predicted. For more complicated algorithms and problems, unpredictability increases and the robot's thinking becomes a black box. The main takeaway of this explanation is the phenomena Ryan Calo calls "emergence": a robot trained to deal with uncertainty may exhibit behavior not foreseen by the designer.[672]

Unpredictability is problematic for a regulatory system which seeks to ensure safety.[673] When a robot is acting based on probabilistic guesses or sensors with error rates, a chance of mistake is always present and that mistake may not be foreseeable to designers or users.[674] At present, the proper way to test autonomous systems which operate in environments with high uncertainty is an open question of extraordinary importance. Real-world testing would require an unreasonable number of test trials to reach acceptable levels of certainty.[675] To return to the self-driving car example, a tested car could drive hundreds of millions of miles along every street in the country and still fail to test obscure combinations of weather, traffic, pedestrians, construction workers, and road conditions that the car cannot safely handle.[676] Computer models of a system can more

---

[672] Ryan Calo, *Robotics and the Lessons of Cyberlaw*, CAL. L.R. Vol. 103:513-564 (2015).

[673] *See* Harry Surden & Mary-Anne Williams, *Self-Driving Cars, Predictability, and Law*, WE ROBOT (2016), http://papers.ssrn.com/sol3/papers.cfm?abstract_id=2747491.

[674] *Id.*

[675] *See, e.g.,* Miles S. Thompson, *Evaluating Intelligent Systems with Performance Uncertainty in Large Test Spaces*, PROCEEDINGS OF THE 10TH PERFORMANCE METRICS FOR INTELLIGENT SYSTEMS WORKSHOP (2010), http://dl.acm.org/citation.cfm?id=2377602.

quickly test across all random combinations of modelled variables, but any results are limited by the fact that a model is inherently a simplified version of the real world system.[677]

Unlike other regulatory bodies dealing with these emergent robot behavior (e.g., the National Highway Traffic Safety Administration), FDA has experience determining safety in the face of unpredictability. In pharmaceutical evaluation, FDA's highest-profile job, the true effect in the human body is always uncertain. Even after millions of dollars in pre-clinical research, only about one in ten drugs that start Phase I safety clinical trials make it through to approval.[678] The drugs that are approved often have side effects that frequently cannot be mitigated or predicted, and are more effective for some people for unknown reasons. Despite all the unknowns surrounding pharmacological action in diverse people's bodies, FDA manages to certify drugs for market.

Drugs are a significantly different technology than stochastic robots, and the gold standard of clinical drug trials may not be feasible for robots nor get at all of the relevant risks.[679] As mentioned earlier, proper methodologies for testing autonomous systems in any context are still important research goals. Despite the differences between drugs and robots, the comparison at least makes clear that robot control unpredictability and "emergence" is not scarier than

---

[676] Nidhi Kalra & Susan M. Paddock, *Driving to Safety: How Many Miles of Driving Would It Take to Demonstrate Autonomous Vehicle Reliability*, RAND CORPORATION (2016), http://www.rand.org/pubs/research_reports/RR1478.html (finding that "fully autonomous vehicles would have to be driven hundreds of millions of miles and sometimes hundreds of billions of miles to demonstrate their safety in terms of fatalities and injuries").

[677] Patrick J. Hayes, *The Frame Problem and Related Problems in Artificial Intelligence*, STANFORD UNIV. DEPT. OF COMPUTER SCIENCE (1971).

[678] Bill Berkrot, *Success rates for experimental drugs falls: study*, REUTERS (2011), http://www.reuters.com/article/us-pharmaceuticals-success-idUSTRE71D2U920110214.

[679] Although beyond the scope of this project, one could imagine designing a testing protocol for robots based on the staged approval process for drugs, building from lab testing, simulations, and animal models into multiphase safety and effectiveness human-subject studies. Differences would of course arise: for example, it makes no sense to replicate Phase I safety trials by testing a brain tumor removal robot on a healthy patient by having it carve out part of his brain. Failure modes are also different: a robot might have problems with power outages or earthquakes or other events that might not occur at all—or could not ethically be inflicted—during a clinical trial.

what the FDA regularly analyzes.

Even in the device space, FDA has experience dealing with cyber-physical systems which nearly fit their definition of robot. A pacemaker, for example, has sensors that read electrical signals from a patient's heart, a computer which deterministically processes those signals and looks for irregularities, and the ability to send electric pulses when necessary to correct arrhythmias. The only piece missing from the FDA's definition of "robot" is the ability to move in physical space. Pacemakers go through PMA, and FDA is apparently successful at certifying these deterministic systems.

As a specific example of automated device regulation, FDA recently approved Johnson & Johnson's Sedasys sedation system, which automates anesthesiology.[680] The device monitors a patient's breathing, heart rate, and blood oxygen levels calculates an appropriate dosage of a sedation drug; and applies the drug through an intravenous line drip.[681] FDA approved the device via PMA, limiting the device's indication of use to colonoscopies and endoscopies in healthy patients where an anesthesia professional is "immediately available for assistance or consultation."[682] Even for that limited indication, Sedasys is poised to capture significant value from the one billion dollar per year market for colonoscopy-related anesthesia services.[683] While FDA has recent experience in reviewing and

---

[680] FDA, *SEDASYS Computer-Assisted Personalized Sedation System*, http://www.fda.gov/MedicalDevices/ProductsandMedicalProcedures/DeviceApprovals andClearances/Recently-ApprovedDevices/ucm353950.htm (2015).

[681] Todd C. Frankel, *New machine could one day replace anesthesiologists*, WASH. POST (May 11, 2015), http://www.washingtonpost.com/business/economy/new-machinecould-one-day-replace-anesthesiologists/2015/05/11/92e8a42c-f424-11e4-b2f3- af5479e6bbdd_story.html.

[682] FDA, *SEDASYS Computer-Assisted Personalized Sedation System*, http://www.fda.gov/MedicalDevices/ProductsandMedicalProcedures/DeviceApprovals andClearances/Recently-ApprovedDevices/ucm353950.htm (2015); (Use of the automated system without an anesthesiologist available would merely be an off-label use, which the FDA has no power to restrict.); 21 U.S.C. § 396.

[683] Todd C. Frankel, *New machine could one day replace anesthesiologists*, WASH.

approving an autonomous medical device which may replace a medical specialty,[684] Sedasys has not been used enough yet in practice to know whether FDA's testing was really effective or not.

Beyond past experience, FDA is committed to staying ahead of the curve on technical development.[685] The Center for Devices at the FDA has an Office of Science and Engineering Laboratories with several hundred employees who work on regulatory science, and some of these researchers are beginning to study how to evaluate autonomous systems.[686] The Office of Device Evaluation has also been increasing its software expertise, as exhibited in a recent guidance document about cybersecurity.[687] In general, FDA review is interdisciplinary and draws on expertise from across engineering and statistical specialties, and now will include computer scientists and roboticists.[688] Like everyone else trying to test autonomous systems, FDA does not yet know how to evaluate stochastic robots and should be actively working to figure it out.[689] But, as put by one expert on government bureaucracies, "the FDA has the resources to keep its people up to date on technology, hire people with new skills, and, when needed, bring in outside expertise through advisory panels."[690]

POST (May 11, 2015), http://www.washingtonpost.com/business/economy/new-machinecould-one-day-replace-anesthesiologists/2015/05/11/92e8a42c-f424-11e4-b2f3- af5479e6bbdd_story.html.

[684] *Id.*

[685] Aaron Mannes, *Institutional Options for Robot Governance*, WE ROBOT 2016, 16. http://robots.law.miami.edu/2016/wp-content/uploads/2015/07/Mannes_ RobotGovernanceFinal.pdf.

[686] *Id.*

[687] *Id.*; *see e.g.* FDA, POSTMARKET MANAGEMENT OF CYBERSECURITY IN MEDICAL DEVICES: DRAFT GUIDANCE FOR INDUSTRY AND FOOD AND DRUG ADMINISTRATION STAFF (2016) http://www.fda.gov/downloads/medicaldevices/deviceregulationand guidance/guidancedocuments/ucm482022.pdf.

[688] Aaron Mannes, *Institutional Options for Robot Governance*, WE ROBOT 2016, 16. http://robots.law.miami.edu/2016/wp-content/uploads/2015/07/Mannes_ RobotGovernanceFinal.pdf.

[689] *See, e.g.,* Testimony of Miss Cummings, *Hands Off: The Future of Self-Driving Cars*, SENATE COMMITTEE ON COMMERCE, SCIENCE, AND TRANSPORTATION (March 15, 2016).

[690] *Id.*

FDA is thus relatively well situated to eventually handle new challenges posed by robotics.

One field of expertise that will be critical for ensuring safety in autonomous systems is human factors engineering, which focuses on the ways humans interact with technology. Human factors engineering—and its subfield, human-robot interaction—applies knowledge of human sensory, cognitive, and physiological capabilities and limitations to guide product design with the goal of making products safe and easy to use.[691] For the FDA—which does not have the authority to directly dictate physician practice or punish misuse of a device[692]—human factors principles can be used to reach across that line by requiring a device to be designed and sold in a way that minimizes the risk of operator errors. In simpler terms, a medical device is neither dangerous nor effective until someone tries to use it, so FDA has an interest in studying how the human uses the tool.

Recently, FDA released a guidance document reemphasizing the importance of human factors testing for medical devices.[693] This document outlines requirements for usability testing, which assesses "user interactions with a device user interface to identify use errors that would or could result in serious harm to the patient or user."[694] A

---

[691] *Human Factors: The Journal of the Human Factors and Ergonomics Society,* http://www.hfes.org/publications/ProductDetail.aspx?ProductId=1 ("Papers published in *Human Factors* leverage fundamental knowledge of human capabilities and limitations – and the basic understanding of cognitive, physical, behavioral, physiological, social, developmental, affective, and motivational aspects of human performance – to yield design principles; enhance training, selection, and communication; and ultimately improve human-system interfaces and sociotechnical systems that lead to safer and more effective outcomes.").

[692] 21 U.S.C. § 396 ("Nothing in this chapter shall be construed to limit or interfere with the authority of a healthcare practitioner to prescribe or administer any legally marketed device to a patient for any condition or disease within a legitimate health care practitioner-patient relationship.")

[693] FDA, APPLYING HUMAN FACTORS AND USABILITY ENGINEERING TO MEDICAL DEVICES: GUIDANCE FOR INDUSTRY AND FOOD AND DRUG ADMINISTRATIVE STAFF (Feb. 6, 2016) http://www.fda.gov/downloads/MedicalDevices/.../UCM259760.pdf..

related proposed guidance offers a list of technology types that will require human factors testing and includes surgical robotics.[695]

With increasing automation, careful analysis of human-robot interaction principles becomes even more critical to system safety. The highest profile failures of automated systems—from the Three Mile Island partial meltdown to the 2009 Air France flight 447 crash—cannot be fairly characterized as only a user failure or only an automation failure, but instead resulted from a breakdown in the interaction between humans and automated systems.[696] In response, experts in human-robot interaction have identified several key problems that must be addressed when designing or regulating safety critical systems. First, "mode confusion" refers to situations where the human user does not understand what the system is doing or why it is doing it.[697] Caused by system complexity or insufficient information communication—and especially problematic for "emergent" system behaviors—mode confusion can lead humans into dangerous decisions made with poor situational awareness. Second, automation may reduce a person's mental workload, leading to boredom and an immediate degradation in performance, while the skills needed to carry out the task without the robot erode over time.[698] Third, an appropriate level of trust in the robot is hard to instill, given human over-reliance on generally successful automation and human

---

[694] *Id.* at 3 (Def. 3.7).

[695] FDA, LIST OF HIGHEST PRIORITY DEVICES FOR HUMAN FACTORS REVIEW: DRAFT GUIDANCE FOR INDUSTRY AND FOOD AND DRUG ADMINISTRATIVE STAFF (Feb. 3, 2016) http://www.fda.gov/downloads/MedicalDevices/DeviceRegulationandGuidance/Guida nceDocuments/UCM484097.pdf.

[696] *See, e.g.*, M.C. Elish, *Moral Crumple Zones: Cautionary Tales in Human-Robot Interaction*, WE ROBOT 2016, http://robots.law.miami.edu/2016/wp-content/uploads/ 2015/07/ELISH_WEROBOT_cautionary-tales_03212016.pdf..

[697] See, e.g., Butler et al., *A Formal Methods Approach to the Analysis of Mode Confusion*, DIGITAL AVIONICS SYSTEMS CONFERENCE, PROCEEDINGS 17TH.

[698] E.g., Reuters & Andy Echkart, *Controller in Deadly German Train Crash Was Playing Game on Phone*, NBC NEWS (Apr. 12, 2016) http://www.nbcnews.com/news/world/controller-deadly-german-train-crash-was-playing-game-phone-prosecutors-n555121 (train operator was playing cellphone game during crash: journalists and train company say this isn't a "technical problem," but human factors engineers would argue that automated system design that makes the human so bored that he decides to play a game instead of monitor the train is absolutely an engineering design flaw).

annoyance with frequent false alarms.[699]

To create a safe automated system, all of these factors must be considered when designing or testing a surgical robot. Testing for these factors requires observations of real systems in use by real users while monitoring workload, performance, error rates, and other human behavior to locate potential for mistakes. These tests necessarily involve inspection of users in their natural environment: which for the FDA is medical professionals in hospitals and clinics. FDA's update to its human factors engineering guidance document and the related proposed guidance requiring human factors submissions for robotic surgery devices indicate that the agency has begun to orient itself to these problems.

In practice, FDA's approval letter for the automated anesthesiology system Sedasys, required a post-market study of how users respond to system alarms to see if real users would listen to what the system was trying to tell them, and an evaluation of whether the availability of a professional anesthesiologist for emergency intervention is necessary.[700] Through these tests and associated limitations on device use, FDA is using human factors engineering tests and principles to influence physician and hospital practice as much as possible without directly regulating the practice of medicine.

In sum, FDA is charged with evaluating device safety and effectiveness, and is certainly capable of doing so even for robots with emergent behavior. Through human factors testing, which will only become more critical with the introduction of autonomy, FDA can examine and somewhat constrain the actions of healthcare professionals in an effort to maximize device safety. FDA is generally regarded as lacking the authority to regulate "the practice of medicine." Human factors tests and related policies blur the line

---

[699] *See, e.g.*, Raja Parasuraman & Christopher D. Wickens, *Humans: Still Vital After All These Years of Automation*, HUMAN FACTORS (June 2008), 512–20 http://peres.rihmlab.org/Classes/PSYC6419seminar/ParasuramanWickens08.pdf.

[700] Christy Foreman, Office Director, *Clearance Letter: SEDASYS Computer-Assisted Personalized Sedation System* (May 3, 2013), http://www.accessdata.fda.gov/cdrh _docs/pdf8/p080009a.pdf.

between device regulation and physician practice, particularly as robots demand more thorough user testing and training. Therefore, in order to sufficiently test and effectively monitor the use of surgical robots, FDA will necessarily expand its influence over the practice of surgery.

Moving forward, as described in the next section, the robot itself might be a social actor practicing medicine. Regulation of such robots leads the federal government undeniably into territory previously reserved to the States.

III. SOCIAL VALENCE: SURGICAL ROBOTS AS ANTHROPOMORPHIZED MEMBERS OF THE SURGICAL TEAM

After robots get past the FDA's *ex ante* regulation by demonstrating safety, effectiveness, and usability, the next question becomes how the new technology fits into the social structure of the operating room.[701] Human-robot interaction research has found that robots evoke different human responses than traditional tools.[702] For example, a Roomba autonomous vacuum cleaner robot "has no social skills whatsoever, but just the fact that it moves around on its own prompts people to name it, talk to it, and feel bad for it when it gets stuck under the couch."[703] More dramatically, soldiers using robotic units to deal with improvised explosive devices in Iraq and Afghanistan began to name their robotic tools, award them medals, and even hold funerals for them.[704] Empirical robotics research backs up this anecdotal notion that humans tend to anthropomorphize robots and attribute social value to them.[705] In other words, as a robot begins

---

[701] The scope of this paper leaves out discussion of the "payer" side of the health care system: that is, will Medicare/Medicaid and private insurers agree to pay for robot surgery?

[702] Kate Darling, *Extending legal protection to social robots: The effects of anthropomorphism, empathy, and violent behavior towards robotic objects*, ROBOT LAW, 217 (2016).

[703] *Id.*

[704] Nidhi Subbaraman, *Soldiers <3 robots: Military bots get awards, nicknames ... funerals*, NBC NEWS, HTTP://WWW.NBCNEWS.COM/TECHNOLOGY/SOLDIERS-3-ROBOTS-MILITARY-BOTS-GET-AWARDS-NICKNAMES-FUNERALS-4B11215746__(2013); Further, a rumor in the HRI and robot law community tells of soldiers trying to sacrifice themselves to save robots, but a reliable source with that story cannot be located.

[705] *See, e.g.,* Kate Darling, *Extending legal protection to social robots: The effects of anthropomorphism, empathy, and violent behavior towards robotic objects*, ROBOT

to move in the physical world apparently under its own volition, people come to value the robot less like a toaster and more like a pet.[706] Embracing this human psychological response, Ryan Calo's last disruptive trait of robotics is "social valence," the idea that people tend to ascribe anthropomorphic social traits to autonomous robots.[707] For the law, social valence raises questions about allowing robots to hold legal rights and responsibilities.[708]

In the surgical setting, this human-robot interaction research implies that autonomous surgical robots will feel less like another tool and more like a member of the surgical team. An operating room is already a dynamic team environment—an attending surgeon oversees several nurses and residents while working with an anesthesiologist to coordinate complicated preparatory, sterilization, and surgical tasks.[709] For the surgeon, deploying a surgical robot to complete certain tasks will likely feel more like delegating a task to a resident than using a scalpel, especially if the robot is designed with social behaviors like voice recognition or facial expressions.[710] If the robot acquires anthropomorphic social value similar to that of its human coworkers, people might feel like the robots should be treated more like the

---

LAW, 217 (Calo et al., eds. 2016).; Kate Darling, *"Who's Johnny?" Anthropomorphic framing in human-robot interaction, integration, and policy*, WE ROBOT, (2015) http://www.werobot2015.org/wp-content/uploads/2015/04/Darling_Whos_Johnny_ WeRobot_2015.pdf.

[706] Kate Darling, *Extending legal protection to social robots: The effects of anthropomorphism, empathy, and violent behavior towards robotic objects*, ROBOT LAW, 217.

[707] Ryan Calo, *Robotics and the Lessons of Cyberlaw*, CAL. L.R. Vol. 103:513-564 (2015).

[708] *Id.*

[709] Personal observations at Duke University Hospital, 4/7/2014

[710] Kate Darling, *Extending legal protection to social robots: The effects of anthropomorphism, empathy, and violent behavior towards robotic objects*, ROBOT LAW, 217, 218 (2016).

humans under the law. Like the human members of the surgical team, robots might be seen as social actors engaged in the practice of medicine.

Then, FDA review, regulation, and control of a robot's medical practice would be directly infringing on each state's traditional control over the actors it allows to practice medicine in its jurisdiction. When the federal government is encroaching on state power, the broadest legal question becomes whether the Constitution allows—that is, whether it authorizes and does not prohibit—the federal government to directly regulate the practice of medicine.

First, the federal government is constitutionally authorized to regulate the practice of medicine, especially by robots. Under the Commerce Clause, regulations related to surgical robots or other medical devices are authorized as being directed at items traded in interstate commerce.[711] Additionally, because health care costs are a significant portion of the nation's economy, services provided by medical professionals are commercial in nature, and managed care networks and hospital chains are increasingly multi-state operations, Congress is authorized to regulate the practice of medicine because it has a substantial relation to interstate commerce.[712] The spending power could also be leveraged, given that the federal government spends the majority of the money in the healthcare sector.[713]

Second, nothing prohibits the federal government from regulating the practice of medicine. In an earlier era in federalism jurisprudence, the Supreme Court wrote that "[o]bviously, direct control of medical practice in the states is beyond the power of the federal government."[714] The Court, however, upheld the federal controlled substances statute at issue in that case, and the very next

---

[711] U.S. Const. Art. 1 § 1 clause 3; See, e.g., *United States. v. Lopez*, 514 U.S. 549, 558 ("Congress is empowered to regulate and protect the instrumentalities of interstate commerce, or persons or things in interstate commerce, even though the threat may come only from intrastate activities.") Robots will be sold, tested, potentially even operated across state lines.

[712] See, e.g., *U.S. v. Lopez,* 514 U.S. at 548–49 ("Congress' commerce authority includes the power to regulate those activities having a substantial relation to interstate commerce.").

[713] U.S. Const. Art. 1 § 1 cl. 1; Lars Noah, *Ambivalent Commitments to Federalism in Controlling the Practice of Medicine*, 53 U. KAN. L. R. 149, 169 (2004).

[714] *Linder v. U.S.* 268 U.S. 5, 22-23 (1925).

year upheld a Prohibition-era medicinal liquor prescribing law against the objections of four dissenters who argued that states held "the exclusive power . . . of controlling medical practice."[715] Forecasting a doctrine more akin to what is accepted today, Justice Brandeis wrote for the majority in the latter case that "[w]hen the United States exerts any of the powers conferred upon it by the Constitution, no valid objection can be based upon the fact that such exercise may be attended by some or all of the incidents which attend the exercise by a State of its police power."[716] Since then, "the full Court has discarded the notion that the Tenth Amendment allocates exclusive authority over certain domains to the states,"[717] opening the door for federal government to regulate medical practice. Robots may very well push the FDA through that door. Thus, the regulation of the practice of medicine, especially by robots, is within the power of the federal government.

A state's response to robots practicing medicine may be to attempt to license them similar to physicians or pharmacists. Under current law, a state licensing requirement for a PMA robot would be preempted by the Medical Device Act because it adds an additional requirement to those imposed by federal law with respect to the device itself.[718] In fact, Justice Scalia's account of the history of the MDA in *Riegel* suggests state regulation of this type was the target of the preemption provision, and robot licensure would fit cleanly into the language of the preemption clause.[719] State licensure would not be preempted for a 510(k) device,[720] creating another reason for

---

[715] *Lambert v. Yellowley*, 272 U.S. 581, 604 (1926) (J. Sutherland dissenting).

[716] *Id.* at 596.

[717] Lars Noah, *Ambivalent Commitments to Federalism in Controlling the Practice of Medicine*, 53 U. KAN. L. R. 149, 161 (2004).

[718] § 360k(a)(1); *See, Riegel v. Medtronic, Inc.*, 552 U.S. 312, 315–16 (2006) at 906.

[719] *Riegel v. Medtronic, Inc.*, 552 U.S. 312, 315–16 (2006) at 315–316,

[720] *Lohr.*

device developers to pursue PMA.

A related question is whether preemption provisions would apply to state robot-related rules not acting directly on the robots. For instance, state medical boards, led by physicians afraid of losing their jobs to robots, might try to restrict who is allowed to operate a surgical robot. For instance, a state could decide that nurse practitioner is in violation of scope of practice laws if he or she uses a surgical robot on a patient without a physician present.[721] When FDA approvals include a requirement on the personnel needed to operate a device—like the requirement of availability of an anesthesiology professional in the Sedasys indication[722]—such scope of practice laws may be at odds with federal regulation.

Currently, the FDA regulation on the preemption clause claims the clause does "not preempt State or local permits, licensing . . . or other requirements relating to the approval or sanction of the practice of medicine or . . . related professions that administer, dispense, or sell devices."[723] However, the majority opinion in *Riegel* was not impressed by FDA's interpretation of the preemption clause, stating that the agency's interpretation "can add nothing to our analysis but confusion."[724] Following the Supreme Court's indifference to FDA's interpretation, a court might find that state scope of practice laws about robots—even when not directly regulating the robots—relate to the safety or effectiveness of the medical devices, are different from federal requirements applicable to the devices, and are therefore preempted.

With robots also coming to other phases of health care—for

---

[721] State medical boards have attempted to limit the practice of Advance Practice Registered Nurses in other contexts, and a medical board rule about nurses not using robots might be an antitrust violation. Federal Trade Commission, *Policy Perspectives: Competition and the Regulation of Advanced Practice Nurses* (March 2014).

[722] FDA, *SEDASYS Computer-Assisted Personalized Sedation System*, http://www.fda.gov/MedicalDevices/ProductsandMedicalProcedures/DeviceApprovals andClearances/Recently-ApprovedDevices/ucm353950.htm (2015).; Christy Foreman, Office Director, *Clearance Letter: SEDASYS Computer-Assisted Personalized Sedation System* (May 3, 2013) http://www.accessdata.fda.gov/cdrh_docs/pdf8 /p080009a.pdf.

[723] 21 CFR §808.1(d)(3).

[724] *Riegel v. Medtronic, Inc.*, 552 U.S. 312, 330 (2006).

example, elder care robots are of particular interest to many researchers[725]—these issues will not be confined to the surgical arena. Across the healthcare sector, regardless of how particular futuristic cases will play out, surgical robots will take on social value and disrupt the existing federalist framework for regulating the practice of medicine.

IV. CONCLUSION

Autonomous surgical robots are coming. Robots will use sensors to measure patients' physiology and pathologies, use that information to plan how to complete the necessary surgical operations, and execute those plans by physically moving surgical instruments, all without direct, immediate human control. Device manufacturers are likely to submit these robots for FDA approval via the PMA pathway which, although slower and costlier than its alternatives, provides the competitive barrier to entry of a more thorough safety review and the advantage of preemption of state tort and licensure laws. FDA has experience evaluating unpredictable new technologies, and is well-equipped to evaluate this incoming wave of surgical robot applications. In particular, human factors testing will help FDA assure that robots are designed to minimize mistakes on the part of their human supervisors. As FDA-approved surgical robots assume social status within operating room staffs, federal and state law is likely to clash over control of the practice of medicine.

This paper discussed a specific application for robots. Alongside surgical robots, other robots and cyber-physical systems will emerge for other healthcare applications as well as in other industries. The hope is that this discussion contributes to a broader discourse on robots and law in several ways. First, it demonstrates the value of discussing the legal issues in some particularity, with reference to particular industries, regulatory regimes, engineering

---

[725] Broekens et al., *Assistive social robots in elderly care: a review*, GERONTECHNOLOGY (2009) (available at http://gerontechnology.info/index.php/journal/article/view/gt.2009.08.02.002.00/997).

principles, and examples of at least a few real robots. Second, it explores how at least one federal agency will be capable of evaluating new robots, albeit slowly and expensively. Third, it illustrates how questions in robot law will often involve new interactions between state and federal law.

Studying surgical robot law is a deeply interdisciplinary endeavor. This paper's goal is to distill some related concepts into language that is understandable across disciplines. Guiding and stimulating early discussions between patients, physicians, nurses, healthcare administrators, insurance companies, regulators, lawyers, device companies, and roboticists—or at least the academics who study those things—could have a lasting, positive impact on the safe and effective development of incredible new technologies.

From Immunity To Regulation: Turning Point Of Internet Intermediary Regulatory Agenda

*Kai Jia**

* Fulbright Scholar, California International Law Center, University of California, Davis; Ph.D. candidate, the School of Public Policy and Management, Tsinghua University, Beijing, China. This article is based on a working paper on American Society of Comparative Law Younger Comparativists Committee Second Workshop on Comparative Business and Financial Law at the Law School of UC Davis. I am grateful for Professor Anupam Chander for the valuable discussion and direction. I'm indebted to Professor John Hunt for comprehensive modification and revision. I thank Professor Frank Gevurtz for the newest materials offered to me from the Comparative Law Congress. I also thank Professor Afra Afsharipour, Professor Virginia Harper Ho, Uyen P. Le and Cathy Hwang for the valuable comments and encouragements. All errors are solely mine.

TABLE OF CONTENTS

I. Introduction

In the early days of the Internet, it was widely accepted that Internet intermediaries should be protected from sovereign power and left self-governed. However, the recent accusation against Facebook about its systemic political bias underscores a critical question concerning the growing impact of Internet intermediaries on society.[726] As Internet service providers ("ISPs") increasingly become the so-called chokepoint of online communication, to what extent should they be regulated?

In recent years, there has been a series of cases in which Internet intermediaries were held liable for content uploaded by third-parties, a trend that is surprising those who have long advocated intermediary immunity around the world. The Communications Decency Act (CDA) and the Digital Millennium Copyright Act (DMCA), enacted in 1996 and 1998 respectively, followed closely by the E.U.'s E-Commerce Directive (ECD), established a legal framework that offered broad immunity or "safe harbor" to Internet intermediaries from illegal third-party content. However, recent cases indicate changes are making way. In *Doe v. Internet Brands, Inc.*[727] and *Delfi v. Estonia*,[728] both websites were refused the privilege based

---

[726] Michael Nunez, "Former Facebook Workers: We Routinely Suppressed Conservative News", Gizmodo (May 09, 2016), *available at* http://gizmodo.com/former-facebook-workers-we-routinely-suppressed-conser-1775461006 (Gizmodo, the technology news site, cited two former Facebook news curators as saying that Facebook routinely suppressed conservative content on the social network's influential "trending" news. This report later aroused heavy critics against Facebook about whether we should continue to trust the neutral position of Internet intermediary and what liability should be imposed on them).

[727] Doe v. Internet Brands, Inc., *767 F.3d 894 (9th Cir. 2014)*. The plaintiff Jane Doe sued Internet Brands, Inc., the owner of Model Mayhem which was a networking website allowing third-parties to provide job information for models, alleging that they should be liable for the unlawful acts of others as they failed to warn her the potential risk on the website. Jane was lured to a house and then assaulted by two unrelated individuals through the website. The district court dismissed the plaintiff's claim on the grounds that Internet Brands was immune from prosecution under CDA, 47 U.S.C. Section 230(c) (2012). However, the Ninth Circuit overthrew the judge, ruling that a tort based on duty that would require such a warning fell outside of section 230(c) and thus the website should be liable. The Court concluded that, "the CDA does not declare 'a general immunity from liability deriving from third party content'" and "Congress has not provided an all-purpose-get-out-of-jail-free card for Internet intermediaries."

[728] *Delfi AS v. Estonia, (Application no. 64569/09) (2013)*. The case concerns the

on CDA and ECD, respectively, as a defense to negligence claims. In *Fair Housing v. Roommates.com LLC*, the majority in the 9th Circuit aptly reflected this new direction:

> The Internet is no longer a fragile new means of communication that could easily be smothered in the cradle by overzealous enforcement of laws and regulations applicable to brick-and-mortar business. Rather it has become a dominant means through which commerce is conducted. And its vast reach into the lives of millions is exactly why we must be careful not to exceed the scope of the immunity provided by Congress and thus give online businesses an unfair advantage over their real-world counterparts, which must comply with the laws of general applicability.[729]

---

liability of an online news portal for the offensive comments posted by its readers below one of its online news articles. In Jun. 2015, the Grand Chamber of the European Court of Human Rights supported the Estonian courts' decision and ruled that Delfi, the largest internet news portals in Estonia, was liable for the insult comments against plaintiff posted by readers, although Delfi had expeditiously removed them as soon as it had been informed. According to the court, as a professionally managed news platform who had an economic interest advertising income by inviting readers to post comments, Delfi was considered to be a provider of content services, rather than of technical services. As a publisher, Delfi was expected to take special care in assessing the potential risk of a specific article and effectively prevented clearly unlawful comments from being published.

[729] *Fair Hous. Council of San Fernando Valley v. Roommates.com, LLC, 521 F.3d 1157 (9th Cir. 2008)*. Roommates.com is a website that operates to match individuals renting rooms with those who need rooms. In this case, the Ninth Circuit held that Roommates.com could not claim immunity under CDA § 230 where as a condition of use, as it required users to choose among set answers to questions, such as sexual orientation, family status of a future roommate, which violated the anti-discrimination laws. The court reasoned, by requiring subscribers to provide the information as a condition of accessing its service, and by providing a limited set of pre-populated answers, Roommate becomes much more than a passive transmitter of information provided by others. Therefore, it at least in part developed the content which exempted itself from the protection of section 230.

Given these new developments in Section 230 jurisprudence, several important questions naturally arise: After nearly twenty years since Section 230's enactment, have ISPs found themselves at a turning point? That is, will judicial interpretation of Section 230 eventually shift from broad immunity to more regulation? If so, what are the causes behind such a transformation and why might increasing regulation be necessary?

Early critics and their accompanying propositions for reform of the current legal framework tended to focus on the congressional intent and the broad interpretation by the courts. Most commentators criticized the court's conclusion in *Zeran v. America Online, Inc.*,[730] which they thought could not reflect congressional intent because it foreclosed adequate legal remedies for private individuals harmed by defamation or infringements.[731] However, as the principles outlined in *Zeran* became widely accepted, the original critics shifted their focus on the greater implications of offering such broad immunity to

---

[730] *Zeran v. America Online, Inc., 129 F.3d 327 (4th Cir. 1997)*. In this case, the plaintiff, Ken Zeran, was defamed by an unknown AOL subscriber who made several posting on AOL advertising that Zeran had for sale certain tasteless t-shirts regarding the bombing of the Alfred P. Murrah Building in Oklahoma City. Zeran was then inundated with telephone complaints and death threats. Although AOL removed the postings and cancelled the account of the unknown poster, Zeran still sued AOL for defamation. Zeran claimed that § 230 immunity eliminates only publisher liability, leaving distributor liability intact. According to Zeran, interactive computer service providers like AOL were normally considered instead to be distributors, like traditional news vendors or book sellers. However, the Court refused his claim, stating that "distributor liability is merely a subset, or a species, of publisher liability, and is therefore also foreclosed by § 230".

[731] Most commentators strongly criticized the Zeran court's conclusion, stating that could not be what Congress intended. *See, e.g.,* Emily K. Fritts, Note, *Internet Libel and the Communications Decency Act: How the Courts Erroneously Interpreted Congressional Intent with Regard to Liability of Internet Service Providers,* Ky. LJ, 2004, 93:765. (arguing that "the First Amendment has never garnered an absolute right for the people to say whatever they want wherever they want", therefore, "Congress should step in with a clearer mandate for the courts to keep in line with the traditional common law of defamation"); Robert T. Langdon, Note, *The Communications Decency Act § 230: Make Sense? Or Nonsense? -A Private Person's Inability to Recover if Defamed in Cyberspace,* John's L. Rev. 73 (1999): 829. (explaining "the elements that a person must prove to recover in a defamation action" and arguing that "[T]he Communications Decency Act impedes a private person's ability to recover if defamed on the Internet by foreclosing adequate legal remedies."); Sewali K. Patel, Note, *Immunizing Internet Service Providers from Third-Party Internet Defamation Claims: How Far Should Courts Go?* Vand. L. Rev. 55 (2002): 647. (concerning "[the]CDA immunity become an absolute bar to a plaintiff's recovery" and arguing that "distributor liability is consistent with § 230(c) and therefore should be imposed on ISP".

Internet intermediaries, suggesting amendments intended to effectuate policies of efficiency and cost allocation.[732] Thus, reforms such as "censorship by proxy" or "chokepoints of control" were proposed; these reforms involved calling ISPs into the "service of the law" by imposing vicarious liability.[733]

Despite the evident merit and insight underlying these critics' comments about Section 230 interpretation, most of the proffered arguments are problematically one-sided. That is, they were mainly based on analyses from given premises or goals to a specific solution, e.g., efficiency of law enforcement or absolute right of free speech, which usually failed to balance competing values because of ignorance of the contexts of the legal framework. Those who criticized the inadequate legal remedies for the victims did not see the positive aspects to promote innovation. Likewise, those who advocated "censorship by proxy" reform overlooked the serious threat to free speech of such a reform. Put simply, most of the Section 230 reforms that have been offered so far are largely skewed against the compelling public interest that sits on the opposite side of the balance

---

[732] *See* Doug Lichtman and Eric Posner, *Holding Internet Service Providers Accountable*, SUP. CT. ECON. REV. 221-59 (2006) (challenging "the trend of in the courts and Congress away from liability and toward complete immunity for Internet service providers" and arguing "service providers should bear some responsibility not only for stopping malicious code, but also for helping to identify individuals who originate it."). *See also* Ronald J. Mann and Seth R. Belzley, *The Promise of Internet Intermediary Liability*, WM. & MARY L. REV. 47, 239 (2005) (arguing that "[T]he Internet's rise has brought about three changes that make intermediaries more likely to be least cost avoiders in the Internet context than they previously have been in offline contexts.").

[733] *See* Neal Kumar Katyal, *Criminal Law in Cyberspace*, U. PA. L. REV. 149.4, 1003-114 (2001) (arguing that "Internet service providers will often be essential in preventing cybercrime."). *See also* Joel R. Reidenberg, *States and Internet Enforcement*, U. OTTAWA L. & TECH. J. 1-18 (2004) (commending that "intermediaries offer the most efficient and attractive means to reach rule violators," thus "states must find ways to transpose the powers of enforcement to the internet."). *See also* Uta Kohl, *The Rise and Rise of Online Intermediaries in the Governance of the Internet and Beyond–Connectivity Intermediaries*, INT'L REV. OF L. COMPUTERS & TECH. 26.2-3, 185-210 (2012) (arguing that "intermediaries acting as transactional and communicative chokepoints have become popular regulatory targets.").

beam. Ergo, in this article, I will argue that a comprehensive and context-based analysis is essential to understanding the benefits and struggles of current legal framework for Internet intermediary immunity. By closely tracing the Internet industry's rapid progress and its increasing impact on society, I will suggest that the Internet intermediary immunity legal framework is losing the factual basis that was once its supporting rationales. This factual and foundation shift suggests a future reform in the regulatory agenda.

This article proceeds as follows. Part I traces the history behind the development of intermediary liability regulation and the surrounding legal framework as well as introduces its main contents. Part II outlines and assesses the three primary rationales that support the current legal arrangements, which, at present, offer immunity or "safe harbor" for Internet intermediaries from tortious liability from unlawful third-party content. Part III articulates the three big changes, brought about by the rapid progress of Internet, that pose significant challenges to the former rationales after twenty years' development.

II. The Problem of Intermediary Liability

a. Definition of Intermediary and Its Liability in the Internet Era

Generally speaking, an intermediary is "any entity that enables the communication of information from one party to another."[734] Based on this definition, any tangible artifact—a writing, a painting, or a sound recording—is by itself an intermediary that facilitates the communication of ideas or expression from one person to another.[735] Newspapers, bookstores, libraries, as well as the recent digitalized information service providers including telephone companies, cable companies and Internet service providers are all intermediaries too.

Intermediaries function as a mediator between parties. However, as intermediaries become increasingly pervasive in daily life, a growing concern for policymakers is whether and to what extent these entities should be liable when others use their services to

---

[734] In this article, we mainly focus on speech intermediaries instead of other mediators like banks in money markets and brokers in real estate markets. For a detailed definition, see Thomas F. Cotter, *Some Observations on the Law and Economics of Intermediaries*, Mich. St. L. Rev. 67 (2006).

[735] *See* Thomas F. Cotter, *Memes and Copyright*, Tul. L. Rev. 80, 331 (2005).

engage in unlawful conducts.[736] Traditionally, we refer to common law to answer (at least in part) this question.

According to the defamation law, speech intermediaries are divided into three categories: publishers, distributors, and conduits. Based on their variant impacts, these speech intermediaries are associated with tailored sets of liabilities. To illustrate, a party that, by analogy, most resembles a newspaper, which acts as a publisher that edits and controls the communication, is held legally responsible regardless of whether it was specifically aware of the materials at issue.[737] Factors that indicate publisher liability include evidence of exercising editorial control and judgment over the choice of the materials published. At the other end of the spectrum, entities that are mere conduits of third-party content are not liable for the content they carry, even if they have, in a particular instance, actual knowledge of the content and its implications.[738] One justification for such immunity is that the conduits, like a telephone company, can either not exercise editorial control over the contents they carry, or are

---

[736] A more comprehensive analysis related to Internet intermediaries refer to the report of the OECD's Committee for Information, Computer and Communications Policy (ICCP). In the OECD meeting at Ministerial level in Seoul in 2008, *[T]he Declaration on The Future of the Internet Economy* invited the OECD to examine "the role of various actors, including intermediaries, in meeting policy goals for the Internet economy in areas such as combating threats to the security and stability of the internet, enabling cross-border exchange, and broadening access to information". In response, ICCP conducted the report, *The Role of Internet Intermediaries in Advancing Public Policy Objectives*, in which the legal liabilities problems of Internet intermediaries were proposed, *available* *at* http://www.oecd.org/sti/ieconomy/theroleofinternetintermediariesinadvancingpublicpol icyobjectives.htm.

[737] When it comes to matters of public figures, the plaintiff must also show some form of fault on the part of the defendant. *See* New York Times Co. v. Sullivan, 376 U.S. 254 (1964).

[738] *See* Anderson v. New York Tel. Co., 35 N.Y.2d 746, 320 N.E.2d 647 (1974). (Judge Gabrielli, J. concurring that "if there was no publication by defendant, then there is no need even to consider the further privilege and constitutional points also relied upon by the dissent.").

restricted to refusing services to specific customers. Between publishers and conduits lie the distributors who exercise a certain control over the contents, such as refusing to distribute specific materials. With respect to distributors, which are most like bookstores and libraries, it is widely accepted that they are subject to liability "if, but only if, he knows or has reason to know of its defamatory character."[739] The rationale for imposing a lesser standard of liability for distributors is supported by *Smith v. California*,[740] a case in which the court clearly stated the policy concerns over "the bookseller's self-censorship" and "the impediment for the distribution of all books."[741]

Although the categorization of the differing intermediaries into the three strains (each with its own requirements for finding legal liability) appears clear-cut, it is somewhat difficult to apply practically. For example, actual or constructive knowledge of the illegal third-party content, while certainly a prerequisite for distributor liability, may not be sufficient. Additionally, if knowledge of falsity is required, then the liability of distributors is arguably hard to distinguish from that of conduits.[742] Thus, the questions remain as to whether an intermediary should be considered a distributor or a conduit and what kind of liability should be imposed in this scenario. That being said, problem was not a critical one in the pre-Internet era, when publishers, like newspapers, controlled most mass-produced contents and thus took reasonable responsibility for those contents.[743] However, when it comes to contents of the Internet era, the problem becomes a challenging one.

---

[739] Restatement (Second) of Torts § 581 (1977).

[740] Smith v. California, 361 U.S. 147 (1959). Smith, a bookstore proprietor, was convicted of violating a Los Angeles City ordinance for having an obscene book in his inventory. Judicial interpretations of the ordinance made simple possession of obscene books unlawful even if the person possessing them had no knowledge of their contents. However, the Supreme Court reversed the state court and concluded that Mr. Smith was protected under the Due Process clause of the Fourteenth Amendment.

[741] *Id.* at 153-54.

[742] Knowledge of falsity is a kind of actual malice, which is a standard notoriously difficult to meet.

[743] *See* Yonchai Benkler, *The Wealth of Networks: How Social Production Transforms Markets and Freedom* (2006).

According to the Organization for Economic Cooperation and Development ("OECD"), Internet intermediaries can be classified into three categories: Internet service providers, search engines, and participative networked platforms.[744] ISPs offer access to the internet, connecting different parties to form a given online communication. Search engines link related websites in connection with search inquiries, while participative networked platforms mainly host or cache contents uploaded by users. It is unclear whether an ISP can be considered as a conduit if it refuses to follow the network neutrality principle and discriminates against traffic and applications. It is also unclear whether a search engine can be deemed as a distributor if search results are biased by advertisements. As for participative networked platforms, it is still difficult to clarify their roles, especially as they induce users to upload contents. To summarize, the categorical boundaries among publishers, distributors and conduits are increasingly blurring as the number of Internet intermediaries rises, resulting in an inconsistent understanding among courts in the early cases, which we discuss in the following section.

b.   Development of Internet Intermediary Liability Legal Framework

Confronted with the problem of liability, courts, in cases concerning Internet intermediaries, doctrinally diverged, as reflected in the *Cubby, Inc. v. CompuServe, Inc.*[745] and *Stratton Oakmont, Inc.*

---

[744] *See* Karine Perset, *The Economic and Social Role of Internet Intermediaries* (2010).

[745] Cubby Inc. v. CompuServe Inc., 776 F. Supp. 135 (S.D.N.Y. 1991). CompuServe was an Internet service provider hosting an online news forum where third-parties could upload contents for subscribers. Cubby Inc. sued CompuServe for defamatory contents in its forum. The court rejected the plaintiff's claim and ruled that CompuServe was merely a distributor, rather than a publisher. As a distributor, CompuServe could only be held liable for defamation if it knew, or had reason to know, of the defamatory nature of the content. The case established a precedent for Internet service provider liability by applying defamation law, which was originally intended for hard copies of written works, to Internet intermediaries.

v. Prodigy Services Co. cases.[746]

The court in *Cubby* ruled that CompuServe was a "distributor" and could not be held liable for defamatory material if it had no knowledge of the illegal contents uploaded by its users. However in *Stratton*, the intermediary was ruled a "publisher" and thus was held liable, regardless of whether it had knowledge of the contents.[747] Beyond *Cubby* and *Stratton,* which centered on defamatory contents, cases involving copyright infringements issues faced similar conflicts. *Religious Technology Center v. Netcom*[748] and *Playboy Enterprises v. Frena*[749] are two examples of such cases. In *Netcom,* the court ruled

---

[746] Stratton Oakmont Inc. v. Prodigy Services Co., 1995 WL 323710 (N.Y. Sup. Ct. 1995). Prodigy was an online service provider running a bulletin board on which users could upload contents. Stratton Oakmont, Inc. sued Prodigy for the defamatory contents in the bulletin board from an unidentified user. The court held that Prodigy was liable as the publisher of the content created by its users because it exercised editorial control over the messages on their bulletin boards. The court found that Prodigy's decision to implement a screening program and to allow its Board Leaders to remove content evidenced sufficient editorial control to deem Prodigy a publisher.

[747] Although the *Stratton Oakmont* court distinguished itself from *Cubby* by two points, it may not be sufficient to support an exactly opposite judgment. The *Stratton* stated that, "First, Prodigy held itself out to the public and its members as controlling the content of its computer bulletin boards. Second, Prodigy implemented the control through its automatic software screening program." In this way Prodigy was considered to be publisher rather than distributor. Despite differences in business strategy, Prodigy and CompuServe's roles as Internet intermediaries were the same. The *Cubby* and *Stratton* decisions meant that an ISP that attempted to monitor content on its network would most likely be subject to publisher liability, while an ISP that followed a completely "hands-off" approach would only be subject to distributor liability. *See also* Freiwald, Susan. *"Comparative Institutional Analysis in Cyberspace: The Case of Intermediary Liability for Defamation."* Harv. JL & Tech. 14 (2000): 569.

[748] Religious Technology Center v. Netcom Online Communication Services, Inc., 907 F.Supp. 1361 (N.D. Cal. 1995). In this case the plaintiff, Religious Technology Center ("RTC"), argued that defendant Netcom, the operator of a computer bulletin board service ("BBS"), was directly, contributorily, and vicariously liable for copyright infringement. The court ruled that Netcom could not be held directly liable for any infringing material posted by its clients since Netcom itself did not upload the material. As RTC could prove that Netcom had knowledge of the infringing activities, the contributory infringement claim of the plaintiff was also refused. The court finally concluded that RTC's claims of direct and vicarious infringement failed. This case set an important precedent stating that any interceding service that did not upload infringing content directly should not be held directly responsible for the illegal and/or infringing actions of its customers.

[749] *Playboy Enterprises Inc. v Frena*, 839 F. Supp. 1552 (M.D. Fla. 1993). In this case, the plaintiff, Playboy Entertainment, charged the defendant, George Frena, who operated a subscription computer bulletin board service (BBS) for copyright

that Netcom could not be held liable for infringing materials posted by its clients. However in *Frena*, George Frena, the operator of a subscription computer bulletin board service, was held liable for the infringing photos uploaded by subscribers.[750]

Although there are slight variations in different cases, the basic questions are the same: Should Internet intermediaries be held liable for unlawful contents that originate from third parties? If so, what kind of liability should be imposed? The conflicts between these cases have caused serious confusion about how to solve these problems. As the Internet developed, intermediaries such as search engines and social networks emerged and functioned in an even more complex way than outdated computer bulletin boards. These conflicts had to be settled in order to boost the burgeoning industry. However, it was not until the turn of the millennium that the legal framework offering Internet intermediaries limited liability or even immunity was established. In the United States, the Communications Decency Act ("CDA") was enacted in 1996.[751] Section 230(c)(1) of the CDA states that "No provider or user of an interactive computer service shall be treated as publisher or speaker of any information provided by another information content provider."[752] The CDA does not extend its coverage to copyright infringements.[753] Instead this was addressed

---

infringement. The defendant claimed to have never uploaded Playboy's copyrighted photographs which were posted by subscribers and as soon as he was acknowledged about the infringements, he removed the photographs. However, the court held that it did not matter that Frena was not the originator of the authorized copies, because as long as he supplied a product containing unauthorized copies, he violated the plaintiff's exclusive rights. Additionally, it didn't matter that the defendant might have been unaware of the copyright infringement; intent or knowledge are not an elements of infringement, and thus even an innocent infringer can be liable for infringement. *See Sega Enterprises Ltd. v. MAPHIA*, 948 F. Supp. 923 (N.D. Cal 1996).

[750] *Id.* at 1562.

[751] Common Decency Act, 47 U.S.C. § 230(e)(1) (1996).

[752] 47 U.S.C. § 230(c)(1).

[753] 47 U.S.C. § 230(e) (2).

by the enactment of the Digital Millennium Copyright Act ("DMCA")[754] in 1998.[755] Specifically, Section 512 of the DMCA provides "conditional safe harbor from liability" as long as intermediaries do not have "actual knowledge" of infringement, do not directly benefit from the infringement, and do have a notice-and-takedown policy in order to be granted for the legal immunity.[756] The EU legal frameworks followed the footsteps of the U.S. regimes. The Electronic Commerce Directive ("ECD")[757] adopted the basic idea of Section 512 of DMCA, offering safe harbors from liability for specific intermediary activities.[758] However, the EU differs from the U.S. in its so-called *horizontal* approach, applying safe harbor to cover *any* kind of unlawful contents, including copyright infringements or defamations.[759]

To reinforce the legal frame, the courts chose to interpret the CDA broadly. In *Zeran*, the 4th Circuit ruled that knowledge-based distributor liability was a subset of publisher liability and therefore was also foreclosed by Section 230. Although subsequent commentators pointed out some factors that made *Zeran* controversial, that controversy was not reflected in the trend of judicial decisions, which overwhelmingly followed *Zeran*'s holdings.

According to legal scholars, the broad immunity that the legal

---

[754] Digital Millennium Copyright Act, 17 U.S.C. § 512 (1998).

[755] The reason why copyright was given different treatment from other infringements lies in the systematic bias within the legislative process. Copyright scholarship argued that the well-organized group of copyright owners had used their political power to affect the legislation while the public was unable to effectively advocate for themselves. Therefore, the protection of copyright infringements is better than protection of defamation. See also Lev-Aretz, Yafit. "Copyright Lawmaking and Public Choice: From Legislative Battles to Private Ordering." Harv. 27. JL & Tech. 203 (2013).

[756] 17 U.S.C. § 512.

[757] Council Directive 2000/31/2000 O.J. (L 178) 1 (EC).

[758] *See* Kohl U. *The rise and fall of online intermediaries in the governance of the Internet and beyond–connectivity intermediaries.* International Review of Law, Computers & Technology, 2012, 26(2-3): 185-210.

[759] *See* Miguel Peguera, *The DMCA Safe Harbors and Their European Counterparts: A Comparative Analysis of Some Common Problems*, 32 Colum. J.L. & Arts 481 (2009).

frameworks (i.e., the CDA and the DMCA) offered to Internet intermediaries was a "policy choice," one which bypassed the chance to strike a balance between different values and instead merely chose to protect Internet intermediaries.[760] Given the irreparable loss to the copyright holders from infringements and the irremediable harm to persons defamed, strong rationales supporting the intent of the congress and courts were needed.

III. THE RATIONALES TO SUPPORT INTERNET INTERMEDIARY IMMUNITY

By offering immunity or safe harbor for unlawful contents originating in third parties, Internet intermediaries were given the privileges against Internet users who became victims in such cases. Given their vital roles in encouraging the development of Internet as a commercial and political resource, the current legal frameworks were championed as the "cornerstone of Internet freedom."[761] However, every coin has two sides. The protection for Internet intermediaries had has also proven to be ripe for exploitation; this is best seen in cases that involve revenge porn[762], child pornography[763], and defamation. While attempts at legislative reform have been minimal

---

[760] *See* James Grimmelmann,. "Internet Law: Cases and Problems 4.0." 177-189 (2014).

[761]. Berin Szoka, "*Section 230: The Cornerstone of Internet Freedom*, TECHnology LIBERATION FRONT, (Aug. 18, 2009), https://techliberation.com/2009/08/18/section-230-the-cornerstone-of-internet-freedom.

[762] Abby Ohlhelser, *Revenge porn purveyor Hunter Moore is sentenced to prison*," The Washinton Post: The Intersect, (Dec. 3, 2015), https://www.washingtonpost.com/news/the-intersect/wp/2015/12/03/revenge-porn-purveyor-hunter-moore-is-sentenced-to-prison.

[763] Suzanne Choney, "*Classified ad site Backpage in crosshairs over child sex ads*," NBC NEWS: TECH NEWS, (July 29, 2013), http://www.nbcnews.com/tech/tech-news/classified-ad-site-backpage-crosshairs-over-child-sex-ads-f6C10789250.

at best,[764] and "legislative debates in the US seemed pretty much settled for around two decades now,"[765] we can still argue confidently that "cyber-tort law is not settled until it is settled right."[766] Given the massive criticism and proposals for reform, it is critical to review the rationales supporting the current legal frameworks. Through understanding these rationales, we can clearly see congressional intent when the laws were enacted twenty years. The rationales can be understood in three categories: free speech, innovation and neutrality. However, as will be explained below, whether their validity remains today is in doubt.

a. Free Speech

Although it has been widely accepted that the rise of Internet promotes free speech,[767] the positive impacts of the Internet cannot be gained without prerequisites. The immunity granted to Internet intermediaries is such a prerequisite because of the concern for "collateral censorship."[768]

Collateral censorship occurs when an intermediary suppresses the speech of others in order to avoid the imposition of liability on it due to that speech.[769] Imposing liability on an intermediary could result not only in the suppression of unlawful speech, but also in overreach to the lawful contents, causing a "chilling effect."[770]

---

[764] Joel R. Reidenberg, et al., Legal Research Paper, *Section 230 of the Communications Decency Act: A Survey of the Legal Literature and Reform Proposals*, FORDHAM L. SCH.—CTR. ON L. & INFO. POL'Y 23-24, 46 (2012) (also noting that "the majority of scholarly literature identified is critical of section 230").

[765] Marcelo Thompson, *Beyond Gatekeeping: The Normative Responsibility of Internet Intermediaries*, VAND. J. ENT. & TECH. L. 4 (2015).

[766] Michael L. Rustad & Thomas H. Koenig, *Rebooting Cybertort Law*, 80 WASH. L. REV. 335, 376 (2005).

[767] The relationship between Internet and free speech is bidirectional. On one hand, Internet promotes free speech. On the other hand, the notion that free speech is a fundamental right also supports the development of Internet. Anupam Chander & Uyen P. Le, *Free Speech*, 100 IOWA L. REV. (2014) 501, 504. In this section, I mainly focus on the positive impacts of Internet on free speech and its prerequisite to be realized.

[768] Jack M. Balkin, *Free Speech and Hostile Environments*, COLUM. L. REV., 2295-2320 (1999).

[769] *Id.* at 2298.

Speakers can rarely capture the full social value of their speech, causing the externality problem. This is more serious for intermediaries than for original speakers. The latter, speak for all kinds of reasons, from monetary rewards to reputation aggregation, none of which accrue to the benefit of intermediaries. Thus, if the threat of liability casts on intermediaries, it is rational to expect them to steer clear from the unlawful zone as they have "a peculiarly fragile commitment to the speech that they facilitate."[771] Additionally, although intermediaries obtain benefits in other ways such as advertising with user-generated content, they are insensitive to the value of any specific piece of content, meaning that they lose little for deleting such content.

The collateral censorship problem applies to traditional intermediaries such as newspapers and book publishers, not only to Internet Intermediaries. However, immunity is only granted to Internet Intermediaries. The editorial control traditional intermediaries had over the contents partly explain the difference between the intermediaries. However, focusing on the communication environment might be more impactive. According to scholars, who hailed the Internet in its early days, Internet intermediaries dissolved the restrictions on speech and even provided "cheap speech" for the marginalized who would never have had the chance to be heard via newspapers.[772] The rise of Internet intermediaries enabled individuals to speak directly to the masses without having to rely on traditional intermediaries, who had long determined the substance of media content. Thus, Internet intermediaries were claimed to have perfectly realized the promise of the First Amendment. The Supreme Court's decision in *Reno v. ACLU*,[773] echoed similar themes, stating that

---

[770] Frederick Schauer, *Fear, Risk and the First Amendment: Unraveling the Chilling Effect*, 58 B.U. L. REV. 685, (1978).

[771] Seth F. Kreimer, *Censorship by Proxy: The First Amendment, Internet Intermediaries, and the Problem of the Weakest Link*, 155 PENN ST. L. REV. 11, (2006).

[772] Eugene Volokh, *Cheap Speech and What It Will Do*, 104.7 YALE L.J. 1805, (1995).

"through the use of chat rooms, any person with a phone line can become a town crier with a voice that resonates farther than it could from any soapbox. Through the use of web pages, mail exploders, and newsgroups, the same individual can become a pamphleteer."[774]

Given the dramatic shift, collateral censorship is much more severe for Internet intermediaries than their traditional counterparts. When Internet intermediaries are liable for online contents, they are likely to build new barriers and cripple ordinary people's ability to speak online. In contrast with the traditional intermediaries, Internet intermediaries promote more freedom, which supports the rationale to offer privileges of immunity or safe harbor.

While collateral censorship is not the only rationale, it is considered to be the core factor undergird the limited liability legal framework for Internet intermediaries, both in theoretical literature[775], and in case law.[776]

b. Innovation and the Industry Development

In *Configuring the Networked Self*, Julie Cohen argues that "gaps and inconsistencies within the system of legal rights, institutional arrangements and associated technical controls…protect the play of everyday practice[,]"[777] which "create[s] opportunities for

---

[773] Reno v. ACLU, 521 U.S. 844 (1997). (In this case, Supreme Court struck down the anti-indecency provisions of the Communications Decency Act (CDA), stating that they violated the First Amendment's guarantee of freedom of speech. The Supreme Court explained that the Government may not "reduc[e] the adult population…to…only what is fit for children". This was the first major Supreme Court ruling on the regulation of materials distributed via the Internet. Although the anti-indecency portions of the CDA were ruled unconstitutional, section 230 survived and became "the most important piece of law" in cyberspace); *See* James Grimmelmann, INTERNET LAW: CASES AND PROBLEMS 4.0, 200 (2014), http://internetcasebook.com/.

[774] *Id.*

[775] *See* Seth F. Kreimer, *Censorship by proxy: the First Amendment, Internet Intermediaries, and the Problem of the Weakest Link.* U. Pa. L. Rev. 11-101. (2006) (explaining more comprehensively about the collateral damage of proxy censorship).

[776] *Zeran v. America Online, Inc.*, 129 F.3d 327 (4th Cir. 1997). *See* Flex T. Wu, *Collateral Censorship and the Limits of Intermediary Immunity*, 87.1 Notre Dame L. Rev. 293, (2011).

[777] Julie E. Cohen, *Configuring the Networked Self: Law, Code, and the Play of Everyday Practice*, 234 (2012).

experimentation by a wide variety of participants where creative practice flourishes."[778] Following Cohen, Balkin comments that "immunities or safe harbor rules for intermediaries create discontinuities in digital enforcement regimes."[779] In their views, the current legal frameworks characterized by limited intermediary liability allow people to play with information and culture, thus fostering innovation in the gaps of the scope and coverage of copyright law.

Besides intentionally providing gaps where Internet intermediaries are free to experiment, the legal framework also reduces the innovation costs, which further promotes the generative nature of the Internet. By criticizing the gatekeeping theory,[780] Zittrain clearly states his concern over the burdens imposed on innovation by holding intermediaries liable for third-party content.[781] He argued that Internet intermediaries, like chat rooms or message boards who were incapable of coping with monitoring costs, could be induced either to "shut down entirely" or "to raise drastically the cost for their services."[782]

Similar ideas were also explicitly expressed by Anupam Chander. By focusing on the legal framework, Anupam proposed a new explanation for the rise of Silicon Valley.

---

[778] *Id.* at 246.

[779] Jack M. Balkin, *Room for Maneuver: Julie Cohen's Theory of Freedom in the Information State*, 6 Jerusalem Review of Legal Studies 92, 79-95 (2012).

[780] Reinier Kraakman laid the legal foundation of gatekeeping theory, describing that how regulators can make use of gatekeepers' privileged positions for law enforcements. *See also* Reinier H. Kraakman, *Gatekeepers: the Anatomy of a Third-party Enforcement Strategy*, 2 J.L. Econ. & Org. 53, 104 (1986).

[781] *See* Jonathan L. Zittrain, *The Generative Internet*, 119 Harv. L. Rev. 1974, 2040 (2006). *See also* Jonathan L. Zittrain, *The Future of the Internet and How to Stop It* (2008).

[782] *See* Jonathan L. Zittrain, *The Future of the Internet and How to Stop It* 261 (2008).

U.S. authorities…acted with deliberation to encourage new Internet enterprises by both reducing the legal risks they faced and largely refraining from regulating the new risks they introduced.[783]

It is not only the political concern for free speech and economic rationale for innovation that determine the current legal framework, but also a longstanding utopian culture propagated by cyber libertarians.

c. Internet Exceptionalism and Self-governance

The argument for the current legal framework provided for the Internet intermediaries has a close relationship with the long-lasting belief of Internet exceptionalism.[784] Since the Internet began to reach the masses in the early 1990s, Internet exceptionalism emerged as a popular alternative for Internet governance proposed by so-called "cyber-libertarians".[785] According to these cyber-libertarians, the particular architecture of Internet distinguished cyberspace from the real world. This distinction has laid the foundation for Internet exceptionalism.[786]

Because of a series of basic communication protocols,

---

[783] *See* Anupam Chander, *How Law Made Silicon Valley*, 63 Emory L.J. 645, 639-694 (2013).

[784] Internet exceptionalism was an influential theory in the early days of Internet, stating that the online world was naturally independent of sovereignty power in the real world. It refused regulation extended from physical world, arguing that cyberspace would develop its own effective legal institutions. Leading scholars proposing Internet exceptionalism including David R. Johnson, David Post and John Perry Barlow. *See* Johnson, David R., and David Post. *Law and borders: The rise of law in cyberspace.* Stanford Law Review (1996): 1367-1402. *See also* Barlow, John Perry. *A Declaration of the Independence of Cyberspace.* (1996), *available at* http://wac.colostate.edu/rhetnet/barlow/barlow_declaration.html.

[785] *See* Radin, Margaret Jane, and R. Polk Wagner. *The myth of private ordering: rediscovering legal realism in cyberspace.* *available at* http://papers.ssrn.com/sol3/papers.cfm?abstract_id=162488, (proposing the word "cyber-liberatarians").

[786] The Internet architecture was called "end-to-end", which contemplates networks designed so that intelligence rests in the ends, and the network itself remains simple. *See* Lawrence Lessig, *The Architecture of Innovation*, 51 DUKE L.J. 1783, 1789 (2002).

including TCP/IP and WWW, the architecture of Internet was characterized by open structure and non-discriminatory data transfer. As David Isenberg stated, the network was simple, or "stupid", whose fundamental feature was neutrality among data packets, resulting in the inability to discriminate lawful data from unlawful data transferred on the network.[787] Because of the particular architecture, Internet was conceived to be decentralized, borderless, and nearly unlimited in data capacity, all of which conflicted with the territorially-based sovereigns of power in the real world to regulate online activities. In their views, self-governance was not only the preferable and effective way in creating a cyberspace sought to be preserved, but also the legitimate process in cyberspace where traditional sovereign authority and external control were invalid.

Following the idea of Internet exceptionalism, the broad immunity or limited liability for Internet intermediaries were established, creating a legal environment where the norms and regulatory mechanism in the real world were effectively inapplicable. To govern the online relationship and approach intermediary liability for wrongdoing, a "Good Samaritan" defense was built into the CDA. Through this defense Internet intermediaries were welcomed for self-regulation but not duty-bound to stop illegal online content. The proposition of self-governance is also supported by arguing that civil liability is fault-based, therefore it was unfair to impose liability to intermediaries for illegal content when they have very limited awareness of the substance of users' communications or transactions.

The three factors mentioned above supported the legal framework providing immunity or safe harbor to Internet intermediaries for the illegal content originated with third-parties. Additionally, these three factors are interconnected and cannot be analyzed separately. Free speech concern restrained government intervention, which promoted innovation and neutrality. Innovation

---

[787] *See* Isenberg, David. "Rise of the stupid network." Computer Telephony 5.8 (1997): 16-26. (arguing that the value of network is based on intelligent end users which must be supported by a stupid network).

boosted the prosperity of Internet which was helpful for free speech. The neutral position of Internet intermediaries stimulated end-user innovation and avoided collateral censorship.

Given the relative small and weak position of the Internet industry twenty years ago, it was reasonable to adopt these policies to promote its development. However, when the information environment has greatly changed and Internet intermediaries have risen to be the chokepoints of communication, it's time to reexamine whether the rationales are still valid and the current legal framework is sufficient to realize those goals.

IV. ARE THEY STILL VALID?

In *Fair Housing Council of San Fernando Valley v. Roommates.com*,[788] the majority of Ninth Circuit decided Roommates.com "materially contributed" to the online contents by requiring users to answer questions, which made it claim no immunity from Section 230 of CDA. In the EU, the Court of Justice of European Union ruled in *L'Oreal v. eBay*,[789] that eBay had played an "active role" in producing online contents which failed it to be exempted from liability. The two cases revealed the complex role of Internet intermediaries play when they are producing and displaying the online content. In contrast to the fragile means of communication that they used to be, Internet intermediaries have grown to be the chokepoints of communication.

Actually, this is only one of the big changes to Internet intermediaries. As the Internet pervades and Internet intermediaries' business models evolve, they gradually become centralized platforms.

---

[788] 521 F.3d 1157 (9th Cir. 2008).

[789] L'Oreal SA & Ors v. EBay International AG & Ors [2009] EWHC 1094. The case concerned eBay's liability for the sale of counterfeit L'Oréal products on its UK Web site. One of Oreal's important claims was eBay should be primarily liable for the use of keywords in the Link Mark and sponsored links on third party search engines, both of which attracted customers and directed them to those infringing goods. The court ruled that, the use of keywords by eBay was not only to promote its own services as an online marketplace, but also to promote its users' postings which helped attract customers. When eBay provided assistance like optimizing the presentation of online offers for sale or promoting those offers, it played an "active role" which gave it knowledge of or control over the data relating to the offers for sale. Although E-Commerce Directive restricted the intermediary liability, it only applied where that operator had not played an active role allowing it to have knowledge or control of the data stored. Therefore, eBay was held liable by the court.

They not only passively mediate information between parties, but also actively intervene the information environment where people live with. Given these changes, it is important to ask the question: are the rationales supporting the current legal framework which provided broad Internet intermediaries immunity or "safe harbor" still valid?

a. Internet Intermediary Becomes the Potential Threat to Free Speech

Existing rationale supporting the Internet intermediary immunity or "safe harbor" concerned the collateral censorship problem. Unlike traditional intermediaries, the communication model of Internet intermediaries shifted from a centralized "one-to-many" structure to a decentralized "many-to-many" structure. It even seemed as if the communication was conducted without intermediaries.[790] However, as the role of Internet intermediaries grew, the rationale gradually became invalid.

According to Own Fiss, "the purpose of the First Amendment was to broaden the scope of public discussion to make people understand different opinions, which empower them to pursue their goals freely."[791] Similar ideas were also clearly expressed in Jerome Barron's classic article. He strongly stated that "what matters is providing citizens greater access to conflicting viewpoints, not because speakers with disruptive ideas have rights to be heard, but because we as a society have an interest in hearing them."[792] Barron's concern focused on the power of private censorship, especially the traditional intermediaries who controlled the access to mass media, which permitted only millionaires to speak while repressing

---

[790] *See* Sullivan, Kathleen M. *First Amendment Intermediaries in the Age of Cyberspace.* 45 UCLA L. Rev. 1653, (1997) (arguing that "the decentralization of speaking and listening over the Internet eliminates a host of familiar middleman").

[791] *See* Fiss, Owen. *The Irony of Free Speech.* Harvard University Press (2009).

[792] *See* Barron, Jerome A. *Access to The Press. A New First Amendment Right.* Harv. L. Rev. 1641-1678, (1967).

competing ideas from others. In contrast to their traditional counterparts, like newspapers and broadcasters, Internet intermediaries offered a ubiquitous and comprehensive information environment where "not only everyone is capable to be heard, but also everything worth saying shall be said."[793] It was for this reason that Internet intermediaries were offered the privileges.

With the rapid development of technology and business model, however, the modern Internet is no longer merely an intermediary for "many-to-many" communication, but a dominant platform controlling the bottleneck of mass communication. Internet service providers were found to discriminate data and favor certain content or applications either by giving them different levels of priority or charging them differently.[794] Search engines were frequently criticized for skewing search results to tip their own services.[795] Participative network platforms such as YouTube and Facebook were also accused of manipulating online contents to benefit advertisers and investors.[796] All of these comments showed growing concern for the power of the Internet intermediaries' effect on the information environment. As Berman & Weitzner stated, "decentralized open access and user control over content are two key features to best serve First Amendment values relating to the freedom of expression."[797] First Amendment values were impeded when the

---

[793] *See* Meiklejohn, Alexander. *Political Freedom* (1965).

[794] *See Formal Complaint of Free Press and Public Knowledge against Comcast Corporation for Secretly Degrading Peer-to-Peer Applications,* Memorandum Opinion and Order, WC Docket No. 07-52 (2010).

[795] *See* Oren Bracha & Frank Pasquale, *Federal Search Commission? Access, Fairness, and Accountability in the Law of Search,* 93 CORNELL L. REV. 1149, 1161–79 (2008). (arguing that "search engines are capable to manipulate and structure the search results...and neither market discipline nor technological advance is likely to stop it"). *See also* Jennifer A. Chandler, *A Right to Reach an Audience: An Approach to Intermediary Bias on the Internet,* 35 HOFSTRA L. REV. 1095 (2007). (arguing that "despite the positive stories, there are also numerous stories of how intermediaries like search engines undermine the flow of information from speaker to listener.")

[796] *See* Rebecca Tushnet, *Power Without Responsibility: Intermediaries and the First Amendment,* 76 GEO. WASH. L. REV. 986, 996–1002 (2008). (arguing that "Facebook and Youtube are likely to sacrifice individual users for a better image for advertisers and investors").

[797] *See* Jerry Berman & Daniel J. Weitzner, *Abundance and User Control: Renewing the Democratic Heart of the First Amendment in the Age of Interactive Media,* 104

Internet intermediaries became more closed, which held the communication bottleneck, and users could not control the content in cyberspace. . Therefore, if the Internet intermediaries become similar to their traditional counterparts who are likely to determine what the audience will hear and in what manner they will be able to respond, why should we treat them differently and offer Internet intermediaries extra privileges to be immune from liability?

Besides the broad immunity or "safe harbor" offered to Internet intermediaries, the current legal framework further restrained government intervention, encouraging self-regulation by intermediaries themselves. For example, the EU forced governments to require Internet intermediaries "to monitor the information which they transmit or store, not a general obligation actively to seek facts or circumstances indicating illegal activity."[798] However, the lack of government intervention doesn't necessarily mean that there won't be censorship any more. On the contrary, surveillance on online data is a ubiquitous business model which has already been adopted by nearly every Internet intermediary. For example, by tracking individuals' searching history, search engines are able to push targeted advertisements, which are their main revenue sources. As Balkin stated, Internet intermediaries, who once claimed to be the democratized digital infrastructure of speech, also become "the infrastructure of surveillance and speech regulation."[799]

Despite the best efforts of great scholars to expand the scope of the First Amendment, the Supreme Court squarely foreclosed the possibility. Under current law, it is the government's' attempt to restrict freedom of speech that would be constitutionally problematic.[800]

YALE L.J.1619, 1628–29, 1636–37 (1995)

[798] Guadamuz, Andrés. "Developments in Intermediary Liability." *Research Handbook On EU Internet Law, Andrej Savin and Jan Trzaskowski (eds)*, Edward Elgar (2014) (2013).

[799] *See* Balkin, Jack M. "Old school/new school speech regulation." Harvard Law Review, Forthcoming (2014).

Private power over free speech is still out of the reach of the First Amendment which cannot be invoked to require governmental intervention. However, as the impacts of Internet intermediaries on the information environment grow, it is still an open question whether more regulation should be imposed on them, especially when they have already moved away from the initial expectations of cyber-libertarians.

b. Innovation is Impeded: Collusion Among Oligarch

In the comments on Julie Cohen's book *Configuring the Networked Self*, Balkin stated that "gaps in legal and technological enforcement might benefit the powerful far more than the powerless."[801] This also applies to the legal framework offering immunity and "safe harbor" for Internet Intermediaries. Although § 230 of CDA and § 512 of DMCA and other statutes grant the same privileges for all kinds of Internet intermediaries, it is the big player who benefits most. Worse still, when they gain power they will collude with other oligarchs to restrain latecomers and to impede innovation.

One example is the conflict between competition law and the privileges offered to Internet intermediaries by CDA and DMCA. In *Search King v. Google,*[802] Google was sued for lowering the ranking of plaintiff's websites on Google's search results.[803] The court denied the plaintiff's application as it considered that Google's search result

---

[800] There are still some objections arguing that the First Amendment does not prohibit government regulation on Internet intermediaries. *See,* e.g., Oren Bracha & Frank Pasquale, *Federal Search Commission? Access, Fairness, and Accountability in the Law of Search*, 93 CORNELL L. REV. 1149, 1161–79 (2008).

[801] Balkin, Jack M. "Room for maneuver: Julie Cohen's theory of freedom in the information state." Jerusalem Review of Legal Studies 6.1 (2012): 79-95.

[802] Search King v. Google, No Civ-02-1457-M, 11-12 (WD Okla 13 January 2003). The plaintiff sued Google for intentionally lowered the ranking of the plaintiff's websites on Google's search engine. The court rejected the plaintiff's claim and upheld Google's argument, stating that "[a] page rank is an opinion protected by the First Amendment, and any act aimed at knowingly and intentionally modifying the ranking of websites is legitimate expression of the freedom of speech." Similar opinion can refer to *Langdon v Google, Yahoo! and Microsoft Corp.*, 474 F Supp 2d 622 (D Del 2007).

[803] In Europe, Google was involved into a series of anti-trust litigations for lowering search results of its competitors, which was claimed to impede competition. *See e.g.,* Analyzing Google's Public Response to the EC's Statement of Objections, available at http://www.foundem.co.uk/fmedia/Foundem_Jun_2015_Analysis/.

was an *opinion* and thus entitled *full* protection of the First Amendment. According to the rule, Google was recognized to legitimately exercise an *editorial decision* and had a constitutionally protected right to choose what information to display in search results and what to exclude. However, when considering issues related to intermediary liability, like in *Google France, Google Inc. v. Louis Vuitton Malletier*[804] and *Obado v. Magedson, et al.,*[805] both courts concluded that Google would be immunized from liability as it was sufficiently neutral "in the sense that its conduct is merely technical, automatic and passive."[806] Thus, paradoxically, the defense that immunized Google in a competition case would eventually make it liable in an infringement case, basically concerning the same behavior. If we treat the search results as *opinions* of Google, it is weird to say that they are merely generated by an algorithm which is not based on *purposeful* action of Google.

YouTube Content ID system is another example to show how these Internet oligarchs affect the market and innovation. Content ID system is a suite of content management tools to give rights holders control of their content.[807] When a video is uploaded, the system will search for a match in the Content ID database. In this way, rights

---

[804] Google France, Google Inc. v Louis Vuitton Malletier, C-236/08 CJEU,Grand Chamber (23March 2010). The plaintiff sued Google for trademark violations. According to the plaintiff, the search results of Google, under the heading "sponsored links", linked to imitation versions of plaintiff's products. The court rejected the plaintiff's claim, stating that the search results were "natural results" and Google's role is "neutral" which arguably put them beyond the liability.

[805] Obado v. Magedson, et al, 2014 WL 3778261 (D. N.J. July 31, 2014). The plaintiff sued several Internet intermediaries including Google for displaying allegedly defamatory information. The court rejected the plaintiff's claim, stating that search results were determined by algorithm based on the content produced by third-part sites, and not by some purposeful act of search engines to create the content. Therefore, the defendants including Google were immune from liability.

[806] Google France (CJEU), ibid, para 114.

[807] For a brief introduction to Content ID systems refer to http://itlaw.wikia.com/wiki /Content_ID (Last accessed June 26, 2016).

holders can identify user-uploaded videos comprised entirely or partially of their content. Once a match is found, rights holders can choose, in advance, how to deal with them: license the materials to make money or block the content from YouTube altogether. Content ID system was fiercely criticized for failing to protect fair use and automatically blocking contents without transparency and due process.[808]

Besides the YouTube Content ID system, we are seeing more similar cases about the collusion between Internet intermediaries and content industry. For example, Google and book publishers signed agreement for sharing online revenues related to the display of scanned books.[809] Additionally, the *Memorandum of Understanding (MOU)* between several ISPs and copyright holders stated clearly their cooperation to take measures against infringing users.[810] By collusion with right holders, Internet intermediaries might not only generate large profits by revenue sharing,[811] but also squeezed out latecomers who might be a potential threat to the incumbents. After growing and becoming oligarchs, the Internet intermediaries cynically started to advocate to strengthen infringement liability for that which they were used to be relieved. This was similar to the theory of Ha-Joon Chang on the economic history, who argued that the developed countries would always "kick away the ladder" after they climbed up the hill and became rich while the developing countries were still struggling for growth.[812]

---

[808] *See* Gotham, Elizabeth, *Lessons from Content ID: Searching for a Balance between Editorial Discretion and Free Expression on Application Platforms, available at* SSRN 2258861 (2012).

[809] *See* Publishers and Google Reach Settlement, *available at* http://publishers.org/news/publishers-and-google-reach-settlement (Last accessed June 26, 2016).

[810] *See* Memorandum of Understanding, Center for Copyright Understanding (July 6, 2011), *available at* www.copyrightinformation.org/wp-content/uploads/2013/02/Memorandum-of-Understanding.pdf (Last accessed June 26, 2016).

[811] *See* Op-Ed: When your YouTube video becomes a corporate profit center, *available at* http://www.latimes.com/opinion/op-ed/la-oe-0628-witt-youtube-copyright-20150628-story.html (Last accessed June 26, 2016).

[812] Ha-Joon Chang observed that the developing countries were forced by the developed countries to adopt a set of "good policies", such as liberalization of trade and strong patent law, to foster their economic development. However, before the developed countries became rich, they usually preferred trade protectionism and poor patent protection. Ha-Joon Chang thus argued, the developed countries "kicked away

Once promoted as a stimulus for innovation, the immunity regime for Internet intermediaries might turn in the opposite direction. It is not saying that legal framework is disadvantageous to small players, but rather a laissez-faire regulation system will finally lead to oligopoly and impede innovation.

c. Internet Intermediary is Not the Exception

As noted above, Internet exceptionalism was based on the belief that Internet architecture was *naturally* neutral and decentralized. However, as Lessig convincingly argued, architecture itself was remarkably fluid and thus configurable.[813] As he clearly noted:

> Cyberspace...has different architectures...An extraordinary amount of control can be built into the environment...What data can be collected, what anonymity is possible, what access is granted, what speech will be heard—all these are choices, not "facts". All these are designed, not found.[814]

Building on the observation, Lessig warned that the greatest threat to the exceptional characteristics of cyberspace came from the perfect control embedded in the market forces.[815] The "invisible hand", he argued, had no motivation to protect the fundamental values

---

the ladder" after they succeed and taught the developing country a contrary way. *See* Chang, Ha-Joon. "Kicking away the ladder." (2002).

[813] *See* Lessig, Lawrence. *Code and other laws of cyberspace.* Vol. 3. New York: Basic books, 1999.

[814] *Id.* at 217.

[815] *Id.* at 6, (arguing that "the invisible hand, through commerce, is constructing an architecture that perfects control—an architecture that makes possible highly efficient regulation).

promoted by cyber-libertarians, for which political and collective action was needed to counteract the influences of concentrated private power.[816]

Lessig's concern is not a theoretical hypothesis, but rather what is actually, currently happening. After twenty years since the current legal framework was enacted, several important changes have happened to Internet intermediaries and there was an increasing trend of converging control over access, content and users.

First, technological advancement and the greatly reduced cost of computing and storing data made it possible for Internet intermediaries to monitor all the content uploaded by users. The expert reports on *Scarlet v. SABAM*[817] stated thirteen feasible filtering systems, seven of which were considered possible to be deployed to filter P2P transmissions. The YouTube Content ID system is another example. Once considered to be impractical, it is common to see the surveillance system embedded in all kinds of Internet intermediaries.[818]

Second, Internet intermediaries' business model heavily relies on exploiting data on their platforms to make profits. Different from the *cheap* conduits they were used to be, Internet intermediaries have complicated their neutral role by getting involved into the process of content production and distribution. This was especially explicit in the *L'Oreal v. eBay* case when eBay profited from advertising the infringing trademarks.

Third, more communication controlling systems are installed by Internet intermediaries, voluntarily or pushed by governments. Websites blocking and generated response are becoming popular mechanisms to fight against online infringements,[819] which proposed

---

[816] *Id.* at 225-30 (discussing the need for greater and better democracy as a response to a changing cyberspace).

[817] Case C-70/10, Scarlet Extended SA v. Société belge des auteurs, compositeurs et éditeurs SCRL (SABAM), 2011 E.C.R. I-11959.

[818] Christina Angelopoulos, *Filtering the Internet for Copyrighted Content in Europe*, Amsterdam Law School Research Paper No. 2012-04, 9 (2012).

[819] *See* Twentieth Century Fox Film Corp & Ors v British Telecommunications Plc., 2011 EWHC 1981 (the plaintiff, several Hollywood film studios, sought to order British Telecommunications (BT), an Internet service provider, to filter content from Newzbin, a popular file-sharing site which was found copyright infringement in a former case. The High Court agreed with the plaintiff and issued an order to force BT technically block access from its subscribers to the Newzbin website.); Corynne Mcsherry, *Graduated Response Program: Let's Press the Reset* Button (2012),

serious problems of fundamental rights emphasizing equal and free access to the Internet.[820]

As Internet intermediaries are more proactive in accumulating and distributing online content, the utopian expectations of cyber-libertarian fail, as well as the rationale supporting Internet intermediary immunity or "safe harbor".

V. CONCLUSION

During the past twenty years, the immunity and "safe harbor" protection provided for Internet intermediaries against liability for online content that originated from third-parties had greatly promoted free speech and innovation. §230 of CDA, §512 of DMCA as well as the articles in the E-commerce Directive were considered to be the fundamental legal frameworks to facilitate a prosperous and robust Internet. After twenty years' development, Internet intermediaries are no longer the fragile means of communication, but rather a dominant platform holding the bottleneck. Therefore, whether the existing legal frameworks are still valid may be questionable.

Three factors that supported the rationales of providing immunity or "safe harbor" to Internet intermediaries are examined while three corresponding critics are argued. Internet intermediaries themselves might harm free speech when they purposefully modified the information environment for commercial reasons. Collusion among monopolistic Internet intermediaries and powerful content

https://www.eff.org/zh-hans/deeplinks/2012/04/graduate-response-program-lets-press-reset-button-backroom-deal.

[820] *See* Scarlet v. SABAM. (a conflict between the E-Commerce Directive (ECD) and the European Convention on Human Rights (ECHR) was explored by the European Court of Justice (ECJ). The plaintiff, the Belgian Society of Authors, Composers and Publishers (SABAM) sued against Scarlet, an Internet service provider for its users' illegal downloading behavior. SABAM wanted Scarlet to install filtering software and curb further infringement. The court considered that there were fundamental rights concerning Internet access of users that would be affected by the filtering system proposed by SABAM. Therefore, the court rejected the plaintiff's proposition. However, the court further stated that specific injunctions are still allowed).

industry might impede innovation and squeeze out late-comers. The centralized and non-neutral position Internet intermediaries held might not meet the expectation of Internet exceptionalism.

Despite these transformations, I am not arguing here for direct government intervention and imposing strict liability on Internet intermediaries. On the contrary, this would merely replace one "big brother" for another and in turn deteriorate the current information environment we are living with. What is really needed is a balance between strict liability and complete immunity. We cannot afford another policy choice going to the other extremity, especially when Internet has pervaded the whole society. Further detailed policy suggestions go beyond this article. However, before we adopt any reform, a clear understanding of the rationales of the current legal framework and the reasons why they need modification is very important, which is exactly what this paper wants to achieve.

www.ingramcontent.com/pod-product-compliance
Lightning Source LLC
Chambersburg PA
CBHW031840170526
45157CB00001B/372